Groovy 2 Cookbook

Over 90 recipes that provide solutions to everyday
programming challenges using the powerful features
of Groovy 2

Andrey Adamovich

Luciano Fiandesio

BIRMINGHAM - MUMBAI

Groovy 2 Cookbook

First published: October 2013

Production Reference: 1151013

Published by Packt Publishing Ltd.
Livery Place
35 Livery Street
Birmingham B3 2PB, UK.

ISBN 978-1-84951-936-6

www.packtpub.com

Cover Image by Jarek Blaminsky (milak6@wp.pl)

Credits

Authors
Andrey Adamovich

Luciano Fiandesio

Reviewers
Kunal Dabir

Ayan Dave

Fergal Dearle

Eric Kelm

Guillaume Laforge

Acquisition Editors
Kartikey Pandey

Rebecca Youe

Lead Technical Editor
Ankita Shashi

Technical Editors
Pragnesh Bilimoria

Jinesh Kampani

Sandeep Madnaik

Chandni Maishery

Ankita Thakur

Project Coordinator
Apeksha Chitnis

Proofreaders
Ameesha Green

Katherine Tarr

Indexer
Hemangini Bari

Graphics
Ronak Dhruv

Yuvraj Mannari

Production Coordinator
Shantanu Zagade

Cover Work
Shantanu Zagade

About the Authors

Andrey Adamovich is a software craftsman with many years of experience in different lifecycle phases of software creation. He is passionate about defining good development practices, documenting and presenting architecture, the reuse of code and design patterns, the profiling and analysis of application performance, as well as extreme automation of development and operations activities.

He is a longtime Groovy user and has a deep knowledge of the language internals. He uses Groovy in his day-to-day development job for simplifying the development process, which includes: code generation, super cool DSLs, and rapid prototyping.

He has Master's degree in Computer Science from the Latvian State University.

I would like to thank my wife Lena for her patience and understanding that gave me enough time and energy to focus on the book. Many thanks to my friends, Sergey and Dmitry, who attentively reviewed book chapters and shared their insightful comments. And, of course, I'm very grateful to Luciano for the exciting experience we had together while working on this book.

Luciano Fiandesio is a programmer, technology enthusiast, and entrepreneur living in Zurich, Switzerland. Luciano has been working for the last 18 years in 12 different countries as an architect and developer for large corporations and small start-ups: Nokia, European Central Bank, BNP Paribas, and Ericsson are among his clients. He loves coding and designing solutions that are both elegant and rock solid. When not busy learning the next big thing, he likes playing with his analog cameras and cooking Italian food. Two years ago, he started a consulting company focused on software factory automation, Aestas IT, where Groovy plays a big role. He holds a Master's degree in Literature and Philosophy from Rome University.

I'd like to thank Andrey, my business partner, friend, and co-author on this book; Laura, my life partner for her patience; Matteo, my brother, for his help; and Pierluigi for reviewing the book.

About the Reviewers

Ayan Dave is a software engineer that takes pride in building and delivering high quality applications using languages and components in the JVM ecosystem. He is passionate about software development and enjoys exploring open source projects. He is enthusiastic about Agile and Extreme Programming, and frequently advocates for them. Over the years, he has provided a consulting service to several organizations and has played many different roles. Most recently, he is the "Architectus Oryzus" for a project team with big ideas, and he subscribes to the idea that running code is the system of truth.

He has a Master's degree in Computer Engineering from the University of Houston-Clear Lake and holds PMP, PSM-1, and OCMJEA certifications. He is also a speaker on various technical topics at local user groups and community events. He currently lives in Columbus, Ohio, where he works with Quick Solutions Inc. In the digital world, he can be found at `http://daveayan.com`.

Fergal Dearle has been writing code since he started writing BASIC as a bellbottom-wearing teenager in the 70s. The jeans aren't bellbottoms anymore and the code is in Groovy, not BASIC but he's still wearing jeans and he's still coding. Recently, he can be found mostly working on web-based projects in Groovy on Grails as his framework of choice. He is the author of Groovy for Domain Specific Languages and is a passionate advocate of Agile methods.

Eric Kelm is senior software developer with over nine years of experience as a developer, senior developer, and technical lead, delivering top-notch solutions to customers. His current focus is developing Java web applications, particularly with the Groovy-based Grails framework.

He holds a Bachelor's degree in Computer Science from the Sam Houston State University. Along with his day-to-day work, he also shares his insights into some of his technical solutions with a broader audience through his blog `http://asoftwareguy.com`.

Guillaume Laforge is the project lead of the Groovy language. He works for Pivotal, formerly the SpringSource division of VMware. Guillaume co-authored the Groovy in Action best-seller, and speaks regularly about Groovy, Domain-Specific Languages, and various Groovy related topics at conferences worldwide.

www.PacktPub.com

Support files, eBooks, discount offers and more

You might want to visit www.PacktPub.com for support files and downloads related to your book.

Did you know that Packt offers eBook versions of every book published, with PDF and ePub files available? You can upgrade to the eBook version at www.PacktPub.com and as a print book customer, you are entitled to a discount on the eBook copy. Get in touch with us at service@packtpub.com for more details.

At www.PacktPub.com, you can also read a collection of free technical articles, sign up for a range of free newsletters and receive exclusive discounts and offers on Packt books and eBooks.

http://PacktLib.PacktPub.com

Do you need instant solutions to your IT questions? PacktLib is Packt's online digital book library. Here, you can access, read and search across Packt's entire library of books.

Why Subscribe?

- ▶ Fully searchable across every book published by Packt
- ▶ Copy and paste, print and bookmark content
- ▶ On demand and accessible via web browser

Free Access for Packt account holders

If you have an account with Packt at www.PacktPub.com, you can use this to access PacktLib today and view nine entirely free books. Simply use your login credentials for immediate access.

Table of Contents

Preface

Groovy 2 Cookbook consists of problem-solving recipes for Groovy, one of the most flexible programming languages we have ever used. This book contains solutions to more than 100 common problems, shown with more than 500 Groovy code snippets.

There are a few unique things about this book:

▶ As a cookbook, it's intended to save your time by providing solutions to the most common problems you'll encounter.

▶ Most of the examples can be run as Groovy scripts or directly in the GroovyConsole. As a result, whether you're sitting by a computer or in a plane, you get the benefit of seeing their exact output.

▶ The book covers not only the Groovy language, but also has several recipes on Groovy libraries and tools, including Gradle, concurrent programming, and functional testing.

This book covers Groovy 2.0 and 2.1.

The Groovy language

Groovy arises from the self-imposed limitations of the Java language. Java is an "old" language, originally conceived in 1990 and released at the beginning of 1996 (Java 1.0). We are looking at a 20 year life span that, in our field, is equivalent to an ice age. Java was portable (remember the motto "write once, run anywhere"?), sported a truly object-oriented core, and provided an automatic management of memory. The Java platform evolved in two directions: **Java Virtual Machine** (**JVM**), an outstanding piece of software engineering, which has become increasingly powerful and more performant over the years, and the actual Java language. The latter unquestionably matured and changed since its origin, but it did so in an unnerving slow-motion pace. The reason for this pondered evolution lies in the strong ties that the Java language historically had with the enterprise world. This bond acted as a double-edged weapon. It gave the language the massive adoption and popularity that it enjoys today, but it tampered the ability to quickly adapt to an ever-changing IT landscape.

In order to counteract the lethargic adoption of new features in Java, new languages based on the JVM started to see the light. Groovy is one of these languages, along with Scala, Clojure, JRuby, Jython, and many others. So what is Groovy? Groovy is an optionally typed, dynamic language for the JVM with many features influenced by languages such as Python, Ruby, and Smalltalk, making them available to Java developers using a Java-such as syntax. Groovy is designed to work seamlessly with Java at every level, from syntax alignment to bytecode generation (although it creates different bytecode). The language evolved from being a limited scripting language to a fully-fledged programming language that can be used in very different contexts, such as web applications and services, backend servers, background jobs, and desktop applications.

The dynamic nature of the language allows a degree of flexibility hardly achievable with Java. Thanks to the language's metaprogramming features, it is possible to modify or augment the code and behavior at runtime, or even at compile time (using AST) and create **Domain-Specific Languages** (**DSL**) in a breeze. Furthermore, Groovy adds a huge number of convenience methods and approaches that simplify your code and make it more powerful.

We, the authors, have been programming in Groovy for many years now. We hope that through this book, we will be able to convey the great fun and productivity boost that we enjoyed by using this language.

What this book covers

Chapter 1, Getting Started with Groovy, covers the installation process on different operating systems and the basic tools that come with the language distribution.

Chapter 2, Using Groovy Ecosystem, introduces the Groovy ecosystem—a set of tools for compiling, embedding, building, documenting, and running code analysis with Groovy.

Chapter 3, Using Groovy Language Features, shows the different facets of the Groovy language that allows you to write a terser, readable, and less ceremonious code in comparison to Java.

Chapter 4, Working with Files in Groovy, covers I/O with Groovy, from simple cases such as reading a file to more complex endeavors such as mining data from a PDF file or an Excel spreadsheet.

Chapter 5, Working with XML in Groovy, introduces you to the recipes that discuss how to consume and produce XML, as well as more advanced topics such as serialization.

Chapter 6, Working with JSON in Groovy, covers Groovy's native support for reading and producing JSON documents.

Chapter 7, Working with Databases in Groovy, presents recipes related to data persistence, either through a relational SQL database or a NoSQL data store.

Chapter 8, Working with Web Services in Groovy, explains how to use Groovy to interact with SOAP and REST-based web services.

Chapter 9, Metaprogramming and DSLs in Groovy, covers advanced metaprogramming concepts such as dynamically extending classes with new methods, creating DSLs, and using AST transformation to modify the code at compilation time.

Chapter 10, Concurrent Programming in Groovy, introduces you to the GPars framework and several approaches to execute tasks concurrently.

Chapter 11, Testing with Groovy, covers how to use Groovy for testing not only code using unit tests, but also databases, web services, and the performance of your application. This chapter is available online at: `http://www.packtpub.com/sites/default/files/downloads/Testingwithgroovy.pdf`.

What you need for this book

In order to be able to run the examples in the book, you will need the Java Development Kit 1.6 or newer, and v2.0 (or higher) of Groovy.

Who this book is for

This book is for Java and Groovy developers who have an interest in discovering new ways to quickly get the job done using the Groovy language, which shares many similarities with Java. The book's recipes start simple, therefore no extensive Groovy experience is required to understand and use the code and the explanations accompanying the examples. Some advanced recipes assume that the reader already has the necessary background to understand the topic at hand (for example, general knowledge of computer science, data structures, complexity, and concurrent programming). Moreover, the recipes are often just skeletons that aim to provide essential information for getting started, but which require the reader to do more research to fill in the details. As such, it is assumed that the reader knows how to use search engines and how to access Groovy's online documentation.

Conventions

In this book, you will find a number of styles of text that distinguish between different kinds of information. Here are some examples of these styles, and an explanation of their meaning.

Code words in text, database table names, folder names, filenames, file extensions, pathnames, dummy URLs, user input, and Twitter handles are shown as follows: "It also ensures that the `reader` object gets closed after the method returns."

A block of code is set as follows:

```
class Person {
   String name
   String lastName
}

p = new Person()
```

Any command-line input or output is written as follows:

```
groovy -e "throw new Exception()"
Caught: java.lang.Exception
java.lang.Exception
        at script_from_command_line.run(script_from_command_line:1)
```

New terms and **important words** are shown in bold. Words that you see on the screen, in menus or dialog boxes for example, appear in the text like this: "Click on the **Advanced system settings** to open the **System Properties** window".

 Warnings or important notes appear in a box like this.

Tips and tricks appear like this.

Reader feedback

Feedback from our readers is always welcome. Let us know what you think about this book—what you liked or may have disliked. Reader feedback is important for us to develop titles that you really get the most out of.

To send us general feedback, simply send an e-mail to feedback@packtpub.com, and mention the book title via the subject of your message.

If there is a topic that you have expertise in and you are interested in either writing or contributing to a book, see our author guide on www.packtpub.com/authors.

Customer support

Now that you are the proud owner of a Packt book, we have a number of things to help you to get the most from your purchase.

Downloading the example code

You can download the example code files for all Packt books you have purchased from your account at http://www.packtpub.com. If you purchased this book elsewhere, you can visit http://www.packtpub.com/support and register to have the files e-mailed directly to you.

Errata

Although we have taken every care to ensure the accuracy of our content, mistakes do happen. If you find a mistake in one of our books—maybe a mistake in the text or the code—we would be grateful if you would report this to us. By doing so, you can save other readers from frustration and help us improve subsequent versions of this book. If you find any errata, please report them by visiting http://www.packtpub.com/submit-errata, selecting your book, clicking on the **errata submission form** link, and entering the details of your errata. Once your errata are verified, your submission will be accepted and the errata will be uploaded on our website, or added to any list of existing errata, under the Errata section of that title. Any existing errata can be viewed by selecting your title from http://www.packtpub.com/support.

Piracy

Piracy of copyright material on the Internet is an ongoing problem across all media. At Packt, we take the protection of our copyright and licenses very seriously. If you come across any illegal copies of our works, in any form, on the Internet, please provide us with the location address or website name immediately so that we can pursue a remedy.

Please contact us at copyright@packtpub.com with a link to the suspected pirated material.

We appreciate your help in protecting our authors, and our ability to bring you valuable content.

Questions

You can contact us at questions@packtpub.com if you are having a problem with any aspect of the book, and we will do our best to address it.

1
Getting Started with Groovy

In this chapter, we will cover:

- ▶ Installing Groovy on Windows
- ▶ Installing Groovy on Linux and OS X
- ▶ Executing Groovy code from the command line
- ▶ Using Groovy as a command-line text file editor
- ▶ Using Groovy to start a server on the command line
- ▶ Running Groovy with invokedynamic support
- ▶ Building Groovy from source
- ▶ Managing multiple Groovy installations on Linux
- ▶ Using groovysh to try out Groovy commands
- ▶ Starting groovyConsole to execute Groovy snippets
- ▶ Configuring Groovy in Eclipse
- ▶ Configuring Groovy in IntelliJ IDEA

Introduction

The first chapter focuses on the basics of getting started with Groovy. We begin by showing how to install Groovy on the most popular operating systems and we move to some command-line tools available with the language distribution. The remaining recipes offer an overview of how the language easily integrates with the most popular Java IDEs.

Installing Groovy on Windows

In this recipe, we will provide instructions on installing the Groovy distribution on the Windows operating system.

Getting ready

The requirement for installing Groovy 2.0 is JDK 1.5 and higher. We assume that you have JDK installed and know how to use Java. In case you use JDK 7 or later, then you can take advantage of the dynamic language optimization present in that version. For instance, the `invokedynamic` bytecode instruction (see the *Running Groovy with invokedynamic support* recipe).

To install Groovy on Windows, you need to download the ZIP distribution from `http://groovy.codehaus.org/Download`.

The latest major version at the time of writing is 2.1.6. The latest minor version is 2.0.8. Since v2.0, Groovy has changed the release version numbering, so the next major version of Groovy will be 3.0 and the next minor versions will have the second digit increased (2.1, 2.2, 2.3, and so on).

Alternatively, you can build Groovy from the source distribution which is described in the *Building Groovy from source* recipe.

How to do it...

After downloading the zipped distribution, you need to unzip the archive to a directory of your choice and carry out the following steps to install Groovy on Windows:

1. For simplicity, we will assume that the directory is `C:\Applications\groovy-2.0`. The contents of the directory should look as shown in the following screenshot:

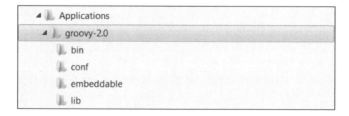

2. In order to have the `groovy` command available on your command line, you need to add it to your system's path by setting the environment variable named `PATH`. We also advise you to create a `GROOVY_HOME` variable for simpler reference.

3. To access the Windows environment variables, you need to press the *Windows + Break* key combination. On Windows Vista, Windows 7, or later, it will open the **Control Panel** page for system settings.

4. Click on **Advanced system settings** to open the **System Properties** window.

5. Then you need to click on the **Environment Variables...** button to finally get to the list of the system variables.

6. Click on the **New...** button and add the GROOVY_HOME variable pointing to your Groovy installation path:

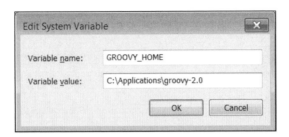

7. Then find the Path variable in the list of system variables and append or insert the %GROOVY_HOME%\bin; string to it:

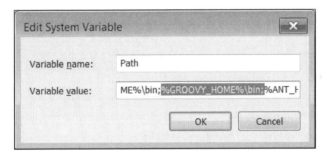

8. You can now fire the Windows command line and verify that Groovy is installed correctly by issuing the groovy --version command:

If you get the output displayed as in the previous screenshot, your Groovy installation is complete.

There's more...

As an alternative to the zipped archive, Windows users can also download a one-click installer (you can find the link on the same download page under the **Download Windows-Installer** link). Execute the installer and follow the instructions to get a fully functional Groovy installation.

Installing Groovy on Linux and OS X

This recipe gives you instructions for installing Groovy on any Linux distribution and Mac OS X.

How to do it...

As a starter, download the Groovy 2.0 binaries as described in the *Installing Groovy on Windows* recipe and perform the following steps to install Groovy on Linux and OS X:

1. Create a new folder for the Groovy distribution:

   ```
   sudo mkdir /usr/share/groovy
   ```

2. Move the unzipped Groovy folder into `/usr/share/groovy` and create a `symlink` to the folder, without using the version number:

   ```
   sudo mv groovy-2.1.6 /usr/share/groovy/
   sudo ln -s /usr/share/groovy/groovy-2.1.6 current
   ```

3. Finally, add Groovy to the path by editing your `~/.profile` (or `~/.bash_profile`) file. You can use vi or an editor of your choice:

   ```
   export GROOVY_HOME=/usr/share/groovy/current
   export PATH=$GROOVY_HOME/bin:$PATH
   ```

4. Your `JAVA_HOME` variable should be set as well. On OS X, the recommended way to set the variable is as follows:

   ```
   export JAVA_HOME=$(/usr/libexec/java_home)
   ```

5. Reload your `~/.profile` file by typing:

   ```
   source `~/.profile`
   ```

6. To test if your installation is successful, type:

   ```
   groovy -version
   ```

The output should display the installed Groovy version and the JDK in use.

Downloading the example code

You can download the example code files for all Packt books you have purchased from your account at http://www.packtpub.com. If you purchased this book elsewhere, you can visit http://www.packtpub.com/support and register to have the files e-mailed directly to you.

How it works...

Using the symbolic link called current, which we created in step 2, makes it very easy to upgrade to a newer version of Groovy by changing the folder to which the symbolic link points to.

There's more...

Most *nix-based operating systems (such as Linux or Mac OS X) have package manager systems that allow you to install Groovy by simply typing a command in the terminal.

In Ubuntu, Groovy can be installed by simply typing:

```
sudo apt-get install groovy
```

The version installed by the Ubuntu package manager is quite old (1.7.10), so you may want to install Groovy manually as described in this recipe.

In OS X, you can use Homebrew as follows:

```
brew install groovy
```

If you are happy with running a stable version of Groovy, but possibly not the most recent one, a package manager is the recommended way to get Groovy quickly and easily. If you want to install a beta version of Groovy or a version that is not yet available on the package manager system used by your OS, install the binaries from the website.

See also

▶ *Managing multiple Groovy installations on Linux*

Executing Groovy code from the command line

Groovy, by definition, is a language with scripting features. Many developers approach Groovy by writing short scripts to automate repetitive tasks. The language provides a set of command-line tools that help you create scripts that are usable within your favorite shell.

In this recipe, we will cover the execution of a simple script with the help of the `groovy` command, which is made available to you after a successful Groovy installation (see the *Installing Groovy on Windows* recipe and *Installing Groovy on Linux and OS X* recipe).

How to do it...

Let's start with the most abused example in programming books, printing **Hello, World!**:

1. The simplest way to execute Groovy code is by using the `-e` option and starting to write Groovy code on the same line:

   ```
   groovy -e "println 'Hello, World!'"
   ```

2. You can also place the `println 'Hello, World!'` statement in a separate file; for example, `hello.groovy`, and execute that script with the following simple command:

   ```
   groovy hello.groovy
   ```

3. In both cases, you'll see the same results:

   ```
   Hello, World!
   ```

How it works...

In step 1, the actual Groovy code resides in the double quotes (`"`) and uses the predefined `println` method to print a `Hello, World!` string. But to explain where the `println` method actually comes from, we need to give a bit more details on Groovy internals.

Every script in Groovy (a command-line parameter or a standalone script file) is compiled on the fly into a class that extends the `groovy.lang.Script` class (Javadoc for this class can be found at `http://groovy.codehaus.org/api/groovy/lang/Script.html`).

Naturally, a `Script` class is eventually inherited from `java.lang.Object`, which is the base class for all classes in both Java and Groovy. But since Groovy adds its own extension methods to many standard JDK classes (see the *Adding a functionality to the existing Java/Groovy classes* recipe in *Chapter 3, Using Groovy Language Features* for Information on Custom Extension Modules), `java.lang.Object` is enriched with many useful methods including `println` (the relevant Java documentation can be found at `http://groovy.codehaus.org/groovy-jdk/java/lang/Object.html#println(java.lang.Object)`).

There's more...

In fact, the `groovy` command has several other useful command-line options. If you type `groovy --help`, you can get a full list of them as shown in the following screenshot:

```
c:\>groovy --help
usage: groovy [options] [args]
options:
 -a,--autosplit <splitPattern>        split lines using splitPattern (default '\s')
                                      using implicit 'split' variable
 -c,--encoding <charset>              specify the encoding of the files
 -classpath <path>                    Specify where to find the class files - must
                                      be first argument
 -cp,--classpath <path>               Aliases for '--classpath'
 -d,--debug                           debug mode will print out full stack traces
 -D,--define <name=value>             define a system property
    --disableopt <optlist>            disables one or all optimization elements.
                                      optlist can be a comma separated list with
                                      the elements: all (disables all
                                      optimizations), int (disable any int based
                                      optimizations)
 -e <script>                          specify a command line script
 -h,--help                            usage information
 -i <extension>                       modify files in place; create backup if
                                      extension is given (e.g. '.bak')
 -l <port>                            listen on a port and process inbound lines
                                      (default: 1960)
 -n                                   process files line by line using implicit
                                      'line' variable
 -p                                   process files line by line and print result
                                      (see also -n)
 -v,--version                         display the Groovy and JVM versions
```

Let's go through some of those options to get a better overview of the possibilities.

First of all, -classpath, --classpath, and -cp options work in a very similar way to the java command. You just specify a list of the *.jar files or list of directories with the *.class files. The only peculiarity is that -classpath must come as the first parameter in the command line; otherwise Groovy will not recognize it.

Another parameter that is common with the java command is -D, which allows to pass the system properties to your script in the following way:

```
groovy -Dmessage=world
       -e "println 'Hello, ' + System.getProperty('message')"
```

One of the strengths of Groovy (as opposed to Java) is its conciseness. This rule is also applied to what Groovy prints out if an exception occurs in your script:

```
groovy -e "throw new Exception()"
```

```
Caught: java.lang.Exception
```

```
java.lang.Exception
  at script_from_command_line.run(script_from_command_line:1)
```

To print the conventional full Java stack trace, you can use the -d or -debug options (some stack trace lines are omitted for brevity):

```
groovy -d -e "throw new Exception()"
```

```
Caught: java.lang.Exception
```

```
java.lang.Exception
    at sun.reflect.Native...
```

```
...
at script_from_command_line.run(script_from_command_line:1)
...
at org.codehaus.groovy.tools.GroovyStarter.main(...)
```

See also

For additional command-line features, please refer to the following recipes:

- ▶ *Using Groovy as a command-line text file editor*
- ▶ *Using Groovy to start a server on the command line*

For more information on the Groovy script structure and Groovy additions, go to:

- ▶ `http://groovy.codehaus.org/api/groovy/lang/Script.html`
- ▶ `http://groovy.codehaus.org/groovy-jdk/java/lang/Object.html`

Using Groovy as a command-line text file editor

The `groovy` command, which we introduced in the *Executing Groovy code from the command line* recipe, can also be used as a stream editor or text file filter. In this recipe, we will cover the `-i`, `-n`, and `-p` parameters that can be used to leverage file editing and processing functionality.

How to do it...

Assume that you have a file, `data.txt`, which contains five lines with numbers from 1 to 5:

1. To multiply each number by 2, you can use the following command:

   ```
   groovy -n -e "println line.toLong() * 2" data.txt
   ```

2. We can even omit the `println` method call if we pass additional the `-p` parameter to the command:

   ```
   groovy -n -p -e "line.toLong() * 2" data.txt
   ```

3. In both cases, Groovy will print the following output:

```
2
4
6
8
10
```

How it works...

Due to the fact that we are using the -n option, the code in double quotes is applied to each line read from the datafile specified as the last parameter in the command line. The line variable is predefined by Groovy, and you can use it to access, filter, or modify the line's content.

There's more...

If you add the -i option to the previous command, then it will actually modify the input file, with output values as follows:

```
groovy -i -n -p -e "line.toLong() * 2" data.txt
```

Adding a suffix .bak to the -i option will save the original input file data.txt under data.txt.bak:

```
groovy -i .bak -n -p -e "line.toLong() * 2" data.txt
```

You can use the -n and -p options to filter the input stream of other operating system commands. For example, if you want to filter the output of a directory listing command (dir) to show only the *.jar files, on Windows you can use the following command:

```
dir | groovy -n -e "if (line.contains('.jar')) println line"
```

Or on *nix-based operating systems, you can use the following command:

```
ls -la | groovy -n -e "if (line.contains('.jar')) println line"
```

Of course, the result of the previous commands can be easily achieved by more efficient operating system instructions. However, these examples are given to demonstrate that you can actually leverage the full power of the Groovy and Java programming languages to implement more complex processing rules.

See also

- ▸ *Executing Groovy code from the command line*

- ▸ *Using Groovy to start a server on the command line*

Using Groovy to start a server on the command line

In this recipe, we continue to explore the `groovy` command's features at one's disposal. This time, we show how to create a process capable of serving client requests through TCP/IP directly from the command line and with one line of code.

How to do it...

The command-line option that we are going to use for this purpose is `-l`:

1. By using the `-l` option, it is trivial to start a simple socket server in Groovy:

   ```
   groovy -l 4444 -e "println new Date()"
   ```

2. The previous line will start a server that listens to port 4444 and returns the date and time string for every line of data it receives from the clients:

   ```
   groovy is listening on port 4444
   ```

3. In order to test whether the server actually works, you can start any telnet-like program (for example, KiTTY, if you are on Windows) to connect to a localhost on port 4444, and type any string (for example, What time is it?), and press *Enter*. The server should reply with a date/time string back as shown in the following screenshot:

In this way, you can quite easily organize communication channels for ad hoc notifications on different hosts.

See also

▶ *Executing Groovy code from the command line*

▶ *Using Groovy as a command-line text file editor*

Running Groovy with invokedynamic support

One of the biggest improvements introduced in Groovy 2.0 is the support for the `invokedynamic` instruction. The `invokedynamic` is a new JVM instruction available in Java 7, which allows easier implementation and promises increased speed and efficiency of dynamic languages (for example, Groovy).

Dynamic languages generate a bytecode that often necessitates a number of JVM method invocations to perform a single operation. Furthermore, reflection and dynamic proxies are used extensively, which comes with a costly performance toll. Also, the **JIT (Just-In-Time)** compiler that helps to improve the runtime performance of a JVM, cannot work its magic by applying optimization to the bytecode because it lacks information and patterns, which are normally possible to optimize. The new bytecode instruction, `invokedynamic`, is able to mitigate partially these issues, including support for better JIT optimization.

In this recipe, we will show how to run Groovy with the `invokedynamic` (also known as `indy`) support and Java 7.

Getting ready

The `invokedynamic` support is a compile-time and runtime feature only. In other words, a developer cannot use it from within the source code. What `invokedynamic` brings to Groovy 2.0 (and even more to 2.1) is basically improved runtime performance.

How to do it...

As explained in the introduction, Java 7 is the required version of the JVM to compile Groovy code that leverages the `invokedynamic` instruction:

1. Make sure that Java 7 is your current JVM. Type `java -version` and confirm that the output mentions Version 7:

   ```
   java version "1.7.0_25"
   ```

2. The following steps will let us fully enable the `indy` support in your Groovy distribution. First of all rename or remove all the JAR files starting with `groovy-` in the `lib` directory of your Groovy 2.x `home` directory.

3. Replace them with the files in the `indy` directory located in the root of the Groovy distribution folder.

4. Remove the `-indy` classifier from the JAR names.

5. Finally, invoke either `groovy` or the `groovyc` compiler with the `--indy` flag to execute your code:

```
groovy --indy my_script.groovy
```

There's more...

It is important to note that if the `--indy` flag is omitted, the code will be compiled without the `invokedynamic` support, even if Java 7 is used and the Groovy JAR files have been replaced.

The performance gain introduced by the new JVM instruction greatly varies depending on a numbers of factors, including the actual JVM version and the type of code that is optimized. JVM support for the `invokedynamic` instruction improves at each version. The upcoming Java 8 will use `invokedynamic` to support lambda functions, so it is very likely that newer JVMs will offer even greater optimization. Given the current state of things, some benchmarks that we have run have shown an improvement of around 20 percent when given the same code compiled with the `invokedynamic` instruction enabled.

See also

▶   The *InvokeDynamic support* documentation at
    `http://groovy.codehaus.org/InvokeDynamic+support`

Building Groovy from source

In this recipe, we introduce a procedure for building Groovy from the source code. The only requirement needed to build Groovy from source is Java JDK 1.7 or higher.

Java 7 is required to leverage the new `invokedynamic` instruction used by Groovy 2. You can read more about the benefits of `invokedynamic` in the *Running Groovy with invokedynamic support* recipe.

Getting ready

Like many of today's open source projects, Groovy source is maintained on GitHub. GitHub is a website that provides a Git hosting service. You have probably heard of Git, the version control system started by the Linux creator, Linus Torvalds.

In order to build Groovy, you need a local copy of the source code that must be fetched from GitHub via Git. If you are running a Linux or OS X operating system, chances are that you already have Git installed on your box.

For Windows, there are several ways to install Git. You may want to use Cygwin (http://www.cygwin.com/) or the officially released version available on the Git website (http://git-scm.com/download/win).

For this recipe, we assume that a recent version of Git is available in your shell. To test that Git is indeed available, open a shell and type the following command:

```
git --version
```

How to do it...

Assuming that `git` is installed and operational, we can proceed with the following steps to build Groovy from source:

1. Open a shell in your operating system and type:

   ```
   git clone https://github.com/groovy/groovy-core.git
   ```

2. Wait for Git to fetch all the source code and proceed to build Groovy. On Windows, open a DOS shell, move to the `groovy-core` folder you just cloned, and type:

   ```
   gradlew.bat clean dist
   ```

   On Linux or Mac OS X, open a shell, move to the `groovy-core` folder, and type:

   ```
   ./gradlew clean dist
   ```

3. If you already have Gradle installed, you can run the following command instead:

   ```
   gradle clean dist
   ```

How it works...

The `git clone` command in the first step fetches the Groovy repository, around 125 MB, so be patient if you are on a slow connection. Groovy has switched to the Gradle build tool from Ant. The `gradlew` command is a convenient wrapper for Gradle that takes care of downloading all the required dependencies and triggering the build. *Chapter 2, Using Groovy Ecosystem*, has a whole recipe dedicated to Gradle, so you may want to take a look at the *Integrating Groovy into the build process using Gradle* recipe to know more about this awesome tool. Furthermore, several recipes in this book will make use of Gradle to build the code examples.

The build process will download the required dependencies and compile the code. Upon successful compilation, the build will generate a ZIP file named `groovy-binary-2.x.x-SNAPSHOT.zip` that contains the binaries, under `/target/distributions`. Install the binaries in the same way as explained in the *Installing Groovy on Windows* and *Installing Groovy on Linux and OS X* recipes.

Note how two types of Groovy binaries are generated: a normal version and an `indy` version. The `indy` version will leverage the `invokedynamic` feature (see also the *Running Groovy with invokedynamic support* recipe).

Managing multiple Groovy installations on Linux

If a developer needs to work with different Groovy distributions on the same machine, chances are that he or she would be involved in a lot of environment variable fiddling, such as `PATH`, `JAVA_HOME`, and `GROOVY_HOME`.

Luckily, there is a tool that helps to manage those variables as well as to download the required setup files on demand.

The name of this goody is **GVM** (**Groovy enVironment Manager**). GVM was inspired by similar tools from the Ruby ecosystem, RVM, and rbenv.

In this recipe, we will demonstrate how to use the GVM tool and show the benefits it delivers.

Getting ready

Use the package manager available on your Linux distribution to install `curl`, `unzip`, and `java` on your machine. For example, on Ubuntu it can be achieved with the following command sequence:

```
sudo apt-get update
sudo apt-get install curl
sudo apt-get install zip
sudo apt-get install openjdk-6-jdk
```

The GVM installation script will not work without those packages. You can skip the OpenJDK package in case you have Java 5 or later distribution already installed.

Then you need to fetch the installation script from GVM's website (`http://get.gvmtool.net`) and pass it to bash using the following command:

```
curl -s get.gvmtool.net | bash
```

It will start the set up process as shown in the following screenshot:

To finalize the installation, open a new terminal and run the following command:

```
source ~/.gvm/bin/gvm-init.sh
```

How to do it...

As soon as GVM is installed and running, you can start putting it to use:

1. To install the latest Groovy distribution, you can issue the following command:

   ```
   > gvm install groovy
   Downloading: groovy 2.1.6

   ...

   Installing: groovy 2.1.6
   Done installing!
   ```

2. At the end of the installation, it will ask you whether to make it the default or not. Since we all like "the latest and greatest", type Y (yes):

   ```
   Do you want groovy 2.1.6 to be set as default? (Y/n): Y
   ```

3. To install different Groovy distribution (for example, v1.8.6, which is still rather popular) you can fire the following command:

   ```
   > gvm install groovy 1.8.6
   Downloading: groovy 1.8.6

   ...

   Installing: groovy 1.8.6
   Done installing!
   ```

4. Again it will ask about setting `1.8.6` as default Groovy distribution. Answer `n` (no) in this case since we would like to keep v2 as the primary one:

```
Do you want groovy 1.8.6 to be set as default? (Y/n): n
```

5. To set (or to ensure) Groovy version used by default, use the following command:

```
> gvm default groovy 2.1.6
Default groovy version set to 2.1.6
```

6. You can also verify that Groovy is running and is the requested version by typing:

```
> groovy --version
Groovy Version: 2.1.6 JVM: ...
```

7. To switch temporarily to a different Groovy distribution, just type:

```
> gvm use groovy 1.8.6
Using groovy version 1.8.6 in this shell.
```

8. Another way to check which version of Groovy is currently active is:

```
> gvm current groovy
Using groovy version 1.8.6
```

9. For example, this script will not run under 1.8.6:

```
> groovy -e "println new File('.').directorySize()"
Caught: groovy.lang.MissingMethodException:
    No signature of method:
        java.io.File.directorySize() is applicable ...
```

10. If we switch to the latest Groovy, the script will succeed as shown:

```
> gvm use groovy
Using groovy version 2.1.6 in this shell.
> groovy -e "println new File('.').directorySize()"
126818311
```

11. To remove the unnecessary distribution, we can just run:

```
> gvm uninstall groovy 1.8.6
Uninstalling groovy 1.8.6...
```

How it works...

The reason the `directorySize()` method (steps 9 and 10) didn't work for v1.8.6 of Groovy is simply because this method was only introduced in v2.

As we already mentioned, GVM manages the values of environment variables to direct your Groovy commands to the proper distribution. It also downloads, unpacks, and caches Groovy installation archives under the `~/.gvm/var` directory.

There's more...

GVM also can manage other popular Groovy-based products; for example, Gradle (to build a framework that we are going to discuss in the *Integrating Groovy into the build process using Gradle* recipe in *Chapter 2, Using Groovy Ecosystem*), Grails (a web application framework), Griffon (a desktop application framework), and so on in a similar way.

This recipe can also be applied to a Mac running OS X. You can enjoy GVM on Windows too, but you need to install and run Cygwin (a Linux environment simulation for Windows).

See also

Additional useful information can be found on the following product's home pages:

- GVM home page: `http://gvmtool.net/`
- Cygwin home page: `http://www.cygwin.com/`

Using groovysh to try out Groovy commands

Similar to many other languages (for example, Ruby or Perl), Groovy sports a so called **Read - Evaluate - Print loop** (**REPL**). REPL is a simple, interactive programming environment mostly used to quickly try out language features. Groovy's REPL is named `groovysh`, and in this recipe we are going to explore some of its features.

How to do it...

The `groovysh` command is a command-line tool available with the standard Groovy distribution. Install Groovy as described in one of the installation recipes (see the *Installing Groovy on Windows* recipe and *Installing Groovy on Linux and OS X* recipe) and you'll get the `groovysh` command available in your shell:

1. Open a shell on your operating system and type `groovysh`, as shown in the following screenshot:

2. The Groovy shell allows you to evaluate simple expressions, such as:

```
groovy:000> println "Hello World!"

Hello World

===> null
```

3. It is also possible to evaluate more complex expressions such as functions or closures, (closures are discussed in great length in the *Defining code as data in Groovy* recipe in *Chapter 3, Using Groovy Language Features*):

```
groovy:000> helloClosure = { println ""Hello $it"" }

===> groovysh_evaluate$_run_closure1@7301061

groovy:000> counter = 1..5

===> 1..5

groovy:000> counter.each helloClosure

Hello 1

Hello 2

Hello 3

Hello 4

Hello 5

===> 1..5
```

4. The Groovy shell also supports creating classes:

```
groovy:000> class Vehicle {
groovy:001> String brand
groovy:002> String type
groovy:003> String engineType
groovy:004> }
===> true
groovy:000> v = new Vehicle()
===> Vehicle@7639fabd
groovy:000> v.brand = 'Ferrari'
===> Ferrari
groovy:000> v.type = 'Car'
===> Car
===> null
groovy:000> println v.brand
Ferrari
===> null
```

5. The dynamic nature of Groovy allows us to quickly list all the methods on a class:

```
groovy:000> GString.methods.each { println it}
public java.util.regex.Pattern groovy.lang.GString.negate()
public boolean groovy.lang.GString.equals(java.lang.Object)
public boolean groovy.lang.GString.equals(groovy.lang.GString)
public java.lang.String groovy.lang.GString.toString()
public int groovy.lang.GString.hashCode()
```

How it works...

The groovysh command compiles and executes completed statements as soon as we press the *Enter* key. It then prints the result of that statement execution along with any output from the execution.

Autocompletion is supported through the JLine library that can be found at `http://jline.sourceforge.net/`. Pressing the *Tab* key automatically completes keywords and methods as we type:

```
groovy:000> string = "I'm a String!"
===> I'm a String!
groovy:000> string.
Display all 159 possibilities? (y or n)
groovy:000> string.toU
```

```
toURI()          toURL()          toUpperCase(     toUpperCase()
```

In step 2, the evaluated statement returned `null`. This is normal as `groovysh` is informing us that the last statement didn't return any value—hence `null`.

In step 4, we can see how `groovysh` supports code that spawns multiple lines. Note how the counter on the left of each statement increases at each line. The up and down arrows key will display the history of the typed commands. The history is preserved even across sessions so you can safely exit `groovysh` and you will still be able to access the history.

You may have noticed that in the previous examples, we didn't use any typed variables. A variable declared with `def` or a data type is not stored in the session and will be lost as soon as the command is issued:

```
groovy:000> def name = "Oscar"
===> Oscar
groovy:000> println name
ERROR groovy.lang.MissingPropertyException:
No such property: name for class: groovysh_evaluate
        at groovysh_evaluate.run (groovysh_evaluate:2)
```

This is a small gotcha you should remember when using `groovysh`.

There's more...

`groovysh` has a number of commands, which can be listed by typing `help` as shown in the following screenshot:

```
groovy:000> help

For information about Groovy, visit:
    http://groovy.codehaus.org

Available commands:
  help       (\h ) Display this help message
  ?          (\? ) Alias to: help
  exit       (\x ) Exit the shell
  quit       (\q ) Alias to: exit
  import     (\i ) Import a class into the namespace
  display    (\d ) Display the current buffer
  clear      (\c ) Clear the buffer and reset the prompt counter.
  show       (\S ) Show variables, classes or imports
  inspect    (\n ) Inspect a variable or the last result with the GUI object browser
  purge      (\p ) Purge variables, classes, imports or preferences
  edit       (\e ) Edit the current buffer
  load       (\l ) Load a file or URL into the buffer
  .          (\. ) Alias to: load
  save       (\s ) Save the current buffer to a file
  record     (\r ) Record the current session to a file
  history    (\H ) Display, manage and recall edit-line history
  alias      (\a ) Create an alias
  set        (\= ) Set (or list) preferences
  register   (\rc) Registers a new command with the shell

For help on a specific command type:
    help command
```

The `import` behaves like the standard `import` keyword in Groovy and Java. It allows to import packages from the JDK or the GDK:

```
groovy:000> import groovy.swing.SwingBuilder
===> [import groovy.swing.SwingBuilder]
groovy:000> swing = new SwingBuilder()
===> groovy.swing.SwingBuilder@6df59ac1
groovy:000> frame = swing.frame(title:'Frame') {
groovy:000>    textlabel = label(text:'hello world!')
groovy:000> }
===> javax.swing.JFrame[...]
groovy:000> frame.show()
===> null
```

The `display` command shows the current buffer and `save` allows to save it to a file:

```
groovy:000> display
Buffer is empty
groovy:000> class Person {
groovy:001> display
```

With `clear`, the buffer can be reset, in case you mistyped something.

The `record` command acts as a flying recorder. It saves the typed commands to a file as we type. Use `record start` and `record stop` to control the recording. It is preferable to specify a file to which you want the recorded commands to be stored:

```
groovy:000> record start Session1.txt
Recording session to: Session1.txt
===> Session1.txt
groovy:000> println 'hello world!'
hello world!
===> null
groovy:000> class Person {
groovy:001> String name
groovy:002> }
===> true
groovy:000> record stop
Recording stopped; session saved as: Session1.txt (202 bytes)
===> Session1.txt
```

A very useful feature of the Groovy shell is the `inspect` command that displays the content of the last evaluated expression inside a GUI application, named **Groovy Object Browser**.

The **Groovy Object Browser** shows a good deal of information about the latest stored object, such as the class name, the implemented interfaces, and all the methods exposed by the object. The following screenshot shows some of the methods visible in the `java.lang.String` class:

```
groovy:000> name = "Oscar"
===> Oscar
inspect
```

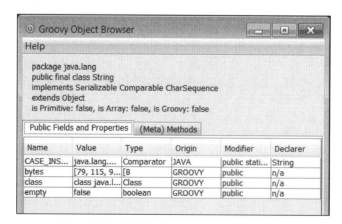

Starting groovyConsole to execute Groovy snippets

The Groovy distribution has another option for developers who are more familiar with a graphical interface and want to try out code snippets. The tool in question is `groovyConsole`, which is very similar to `groovysh` (see the *Using groovysh to try out Groovy commands* recipe) except that it provides a GUI with syntax highlighting and basic code editor features.

In this recipe, we are going to cover basic **GroovyConsole** usage scenarios.

How to do it...

Open your shell and let's dive in:

1. To start **GroovyConsole**, you just need to fire the `groovyConsole` command in your command line:

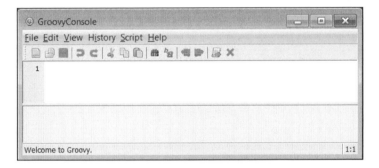

The **GroovyConsole** screen is divided into two logical parts. The top area is meant for script editing, and the bottom area displays the script execution output when a script is launched.

2. By pressing *Ctrl + R* (*CMD + R* on a Mac) or going to the **Script** menu and selecting **Run**, the script in the edit area will be executed:

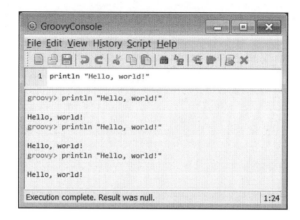

3. Press *Ctrl + W* (*CMD + W* on a Mac) to clean the output in the lower pane.

4. The bottom panel displays an output similar to the `groovysh` shell; that is, first the executed script is printed after the **groovy>** marker followed by the printed output and a result value, if any:

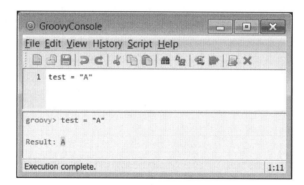

5. In the previous script, we set the value of the internal test property (this property is being stored within an instance of the `groovy.lang.Script` class that is used to execute all the code in the console). If you change that code to reuse the previous field value (for example, `+=`), you will actually notice that the value changes every time the code gets executed:

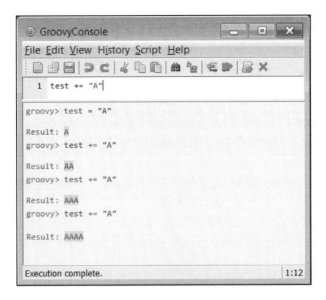

6. Similar to `groovysh`, if you define a variable using the `def` keyword, then you can't reuse the previous value. The `def` keyword is used to define locally scoped variables and in this case, it's bound only to single execution of the script:

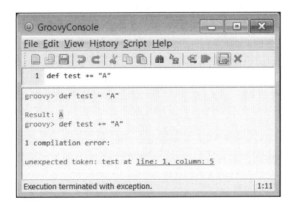

7. Let's go through the editor features of the **GroovyConsole** application. The **File** menu offers standard functions to start over by clicking on the **New File** menu item, to open a new **GroovyConsole** window, to open a previously saved Groovy script, to save or print contents of the editor, and to close the application as shown in the following screenshot:

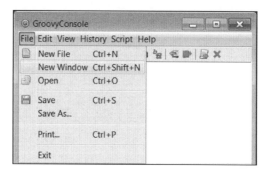

8. The **Edit** menu provides functionality available in any modern text editor such as copy, paste, and basic search functionality, as shown in the following screenshot:

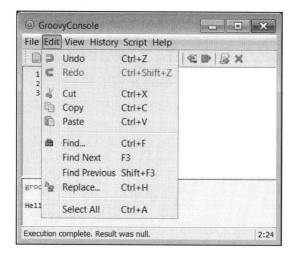

9. The **View** menu has some interesting features for manipulating what is displayed in the bottom output area, as shown in the following screenshot:

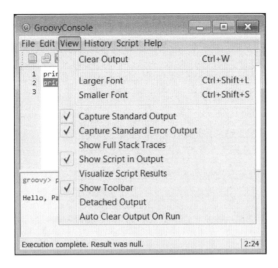

It is possible to increase or decrease the font size and configure the way the output panel displays information. For instance, you can disable the script output or clear the output screen at each run.

10. The **History** menu allows you to revive previous script versions that you have executed during your session with **GroovyConsole**, as shown in the following screenshot:

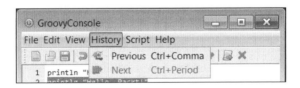

11. Since **GroovyConsole** is all about executing a script, the **Script** menu presents the most valuable options, as shown in the following screenshot:

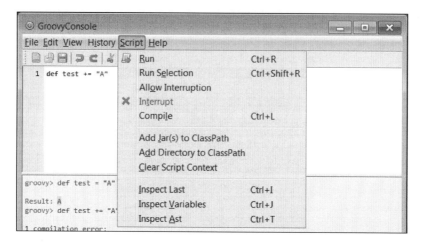

You can run or abort your script execution, force script compilation, and add additional libraries to the class path. Also, you can **Clear Script Context**, which will lead to clearing all the script's accumulated properties (for example, test).

12. Another useful feature is that you can select a part of your script in the editor and execute only that part by clicking on **Run Selection** in the **Script** menu, as shown in the following screenshot:

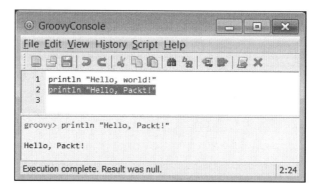

There's more...

The **GroovyConsole** tool comes with a handy **Object Browser** that graphically shows the fields and methods available for a given class.

Press *Ctrl + I* (*CMD + I* on a Mac) to launch the browser and display the last evaluated expression. The following simple class would appear like in the following screenshot:

```
class Person {
  String name
  String lastName
}

p = new Person()
```

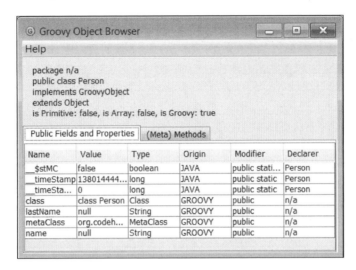

By pressing *Ctrl + J* (*CMD + J* on a Mac), we can display another view of the **Object Browser**, this time focused on the variables visible from within the script.

Configuring Groovy in Eclipse

Eclipse is a popular IDE that is taking up a big share of the IDE market for JVM-based technologies, as well as other languages and platforms. In fact, Eclipse is a huge ecosystem devoted to building tooling for different areas such as dynamic languages, reporting, testing, modeling, analysis, and so on.

Eclipse is distributed in various combinations featuring different areas. A special distribution exists that comes prepackaged with an Eclipse plugin for Groovy (code named GRECLIPSE), as well as various other useful plugins. It can be downloaded from `http://grails.org/products/ggts`.

However, in this recipe we will describe the installation instructions for the Eclipse plugin for Groovy assuming that it is not part of the distribution that you already have.

Getting ready

The steps in the following section have been tested against Eclipse Indigo 3.7, but are very similar when using previous or later versions of Eclipse. For information on different Eclipse versions, you can always check `http://groovy.codehaus.org/Eclipse+Plugin`.

How to do it...

The plugin installation in Eclipse usually starts with opening the **Install New Software...** menu item under the **Help** menu. Perform the following steps to configure Groovy support in Eclipse:

1. In the **Work with:** textbox, you need to type a plugin update site URL, which is `http://dist.springsource.org/release/GRECLIPSE/e3.7/` for the given version of Eclipse.

2. After you press *Enter*, Eclipse will load the updated site contents into the tree view.

3. You need to select the **Groovy-Eclipse** component and click on the **Next** button.

4. Then you will have to follow the standard Eclipse installation procedure by accepting the software license and restarting Eclipse workspace after the download and installation process is complete.

5. When your Eclipse instance starts again, it should be possible to create Groovy projects, as well as edit, compile, and execute Groovy source files.

6. To get started, let's create a new project first. Go to the **New** menu and select the **Other...** menu item.

7. In the **New** wizard window, you should select the **Groovy Project** item and then click on the **Next** button, as shown in the following screenshot:

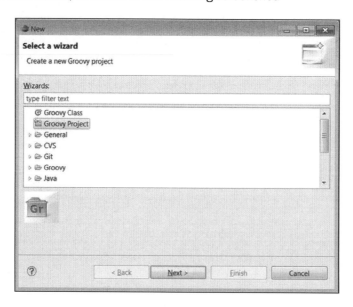

8. The following dialog shows the new project's options, which are very similar to the one for Java projects:

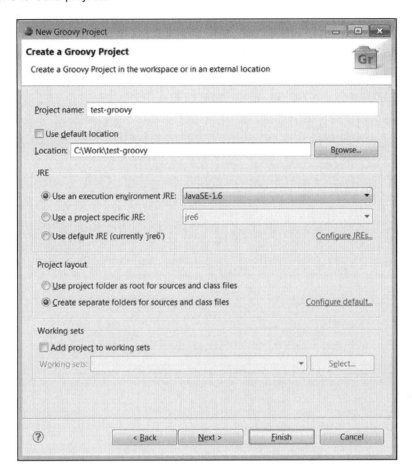

9. You need to choose a project name (for example, `test-groovy`), a project location (for example, `C:\Work\test-groovy`), a target JRE, and click on the **Finish** button for the project to be created in the current workspace, as shown in the following screenshot:

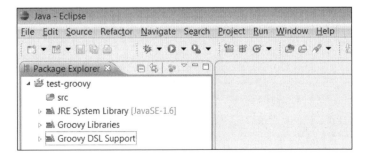

10. Now it's time to add some code. You can do it through the same **New** menu, and add a new **Groovy Class** to the recently created project.

11. The class creation dialog has many similarities to the one for Java classes:

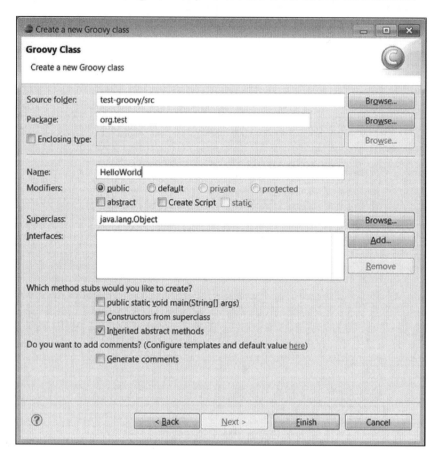

12. Groovy shares almost 100 percent of Java syntax; therefore, you can start creating Groovy classes in the same way you would do it in Java. You will also get all the syntax highlighting and other IDE goodies when editing Groovy source files, as shown in the following screenshot:

```
Package Explorer ☒        🗐 🕏 | 🏿 ▽ ⬜ 🗖     🗐 HelloWorld.groovy ☒
  ▲ 🗃 test-groovy                                 package org.test
    ▲ 🗁 src
      ▲ ⊞ org.test                                 class HelloWorld {
        ▷ 🗐 HelloWorld.groovy
    ▷ ➡ JRE System Library [JavaSE-1.6]                public static void main(String[] args) {
    ▷ ➡ Groovy Libraries                                  println "Hello world!"
    ▷ ➡ Groovy DSL Support                             }

                                                   }
```

How it works...

The code shown in the previous section is actually Groovy code (even though it looks very much like Java) since we omitted semicolons and used the `println` method. The reasons for that method to be available were described in the *Executing Groovy code from the command line* recipe.

With the Eclipse plugin for Groovy, you also get the possibility to execute Groovy code right from your IDE. For that, you need to use the **Run as...** menu item from the **Context Menu**, as shown in the following screenshot:

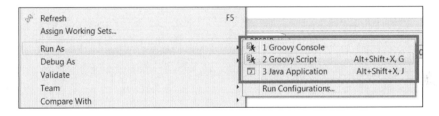

- ▶ The **Groovy Console** executor will send your code to the `groovyConsole` instance, which is described to a greater extent in the *Starting groovyConsole to execute Groovy snippets* recipe.

- ▶ The **Groovy Script** executor will run your code in the same way as `groovy HelloWorld.groovy` command would do it.

- ▶ The **Java Application** executor (similarly to how it works for Java classes) will try to invoke the main method of your class.

By running the example code with either the **Groovy Script** executor or **Java Application** executor, you should get the following output in Eclipse's **Console** view:

There's more...

Groovy can be used to write standard classes. But as we have seen in the previous recipes, Groovy is also a scripting language, and the Eclipse IDE plugin supports this feature as well.

To define a Groovy script in your project, simply create a plain empty text file with the `*.groovy` extension anywhere in your project. The new file is a Groovy script, so you can start by typing the line of code, as shown in the following screenshot:

When you run your script (`HelloWorld2.groovy`) with the **Groovy Script** executor, you will get the same output as the previously mentioned Groovy source file (`HelloWorld.groovy`).

Conversely, if you run your Groovy script (`HelloWorld2.groovy`) using the **Java Application** executor, it will complain about a missing class, as shown in the following screenshot:

```
Problems  @ Javadoc  Declaration  Console ✕
<terminated> HelloWorld2 [Java Application] C:\Program Files\Java\jre6\bin\javaw.exe (19/06/2012
java.lang.NoClassDefFoundError: org/test/HelloWorld2
Caused by: java.lang.ClassNotFoundException: org.test.HelloWorld2
        at java.net.URLClassLoader$1.run(Unknown Source)
        at java.security.AccessController.doPrivileged(Native Method)
        at java.net.URLClassLoader.findClass(Unknown Source)
        at java.lang.ClassLoader.loadClass(Unknown Source)
        at sun.misc.Launcher$AppClassLoader.loadClass(Unknown Source)
        at java.lang.ClassLoader.loadClass(Unknown Source)
Exception in thread "main"
```

The reason for the exception lies in how Groovy distinguishes between script files and classes. If you look at the way Groovy script and Groovy classes are compiled in the Eclipse **Navigator** view, you can also see that even though the script source file resides in the package folder `org.test` under the `src` directory, that information is erased when the actual script is compiled into a class file:

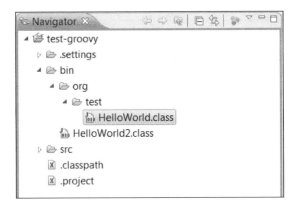

You can also spot the difference between scripts and classes by looking at the list of the class generated methods by activating **Package Explorer** view, as shown in the following screenshot:

As you can see, the Groovy script class has additional constructors as well as the `main` and `run` methods. The Groovy class has only the methods that were defined by the class definition.

This distinction makes Groovy a very powerful addition to a Java tool set. Groovy allows you to use an alternative and more concise syntax to extend your existing Java applications, as well as writing short and concise scripts that leverage the richness of the Java platform.

See also

 ▶   http://groovy.codehaus.org/Eclipse+Plugin

Configuring Groovy in IntelliJ IDEA

Since v8, IntelliJ IDEA, one of the most popular Java IDEs, has native support for Groovy. There is no need to install a plugin to start coding in Groovy and benefit from a number of interesting features such as code completion and refactoring. The latest iteration of IntelliJ IDEA, Version 12, has full support for Groovy 2.0.

In this recipe, we are going to show how to set up a Groovy project in IDEA and showcase some of the most interesting qualities of the integration.

Getting ready

To get started with this recipe, you need v12 of IntelliJ IDEA. The IDE comes in two versions, Community Edition and Ultimate. JetBrains, the company behind IDEA, offers the Community Edition for free, while it charges for the Ultimate version. The good news is that Groovy support is available in the free version of the IDE so you can start using it straight away. Download IntelliJ IDEA from http://www.jetbrains.com.

You also need to install Java and a Groovy distribution. Refer to the installation recipes from earlier in this chapter.

How to do it...

Let's start with the project creation:

1.   Click on the **Create New Project** link in the main **IntelliJ IDEA** start page, as shown in the following screenshot:

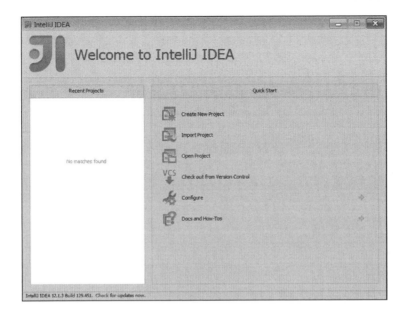

2. In the next wizard page, select **Groovy Module** and enter the name and location of your project, as shown in the following screenshot:

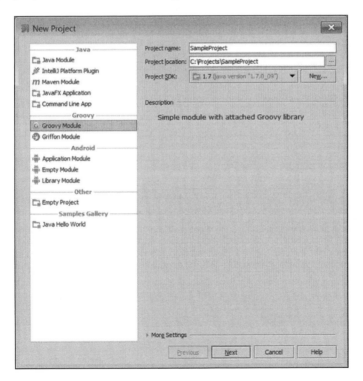

3. The **Project SDK** field should be set to the version of the JDK you want to use for this project. If the **Project SDK** is empty and there is nothing in the list, then click on the **New...** button, select **JDK** and locate the JDK installation directory in the open folder selection dialog.

4. After **JDK** is selected click on the **Next** button to get to the Groovy SDK selection page, as shown in the following screenshot:

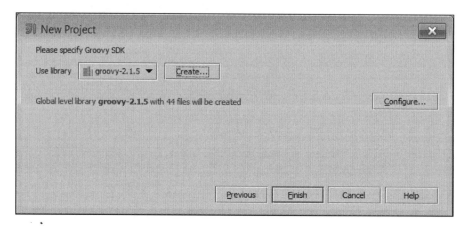

5. If it is a fresh installation, most likely the **Use library** drop-down list will be empty. Click on the **Create...** button and locate the Groovy installation directory. That's it, click on the **Finish** button.

6. Once the project is created, the IDE allows to create Groovy classes as well as Groovy scripts. Scripts can be used as scrapbooks for testing code snippets and can be later integrated into a class:

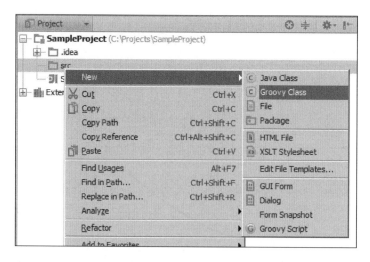

7. You can also create Java classes that call methods on Groovy classes. Let's create a simple Groovy class, named `MyGroovyClass`, as shown in the following screenshot:

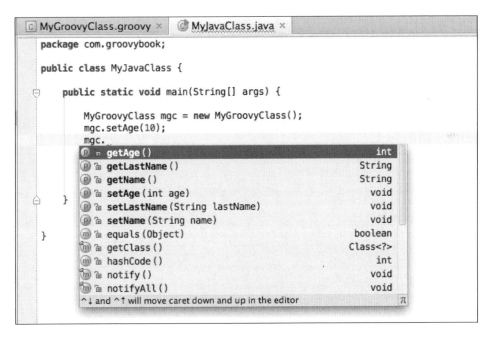

8. The class defines three attributes and uses the concise Groovy approach, with no need for getters and setters to access the variables.

9. Now let's create a Java class, `MyJavaClass`, as shown in the following screenshot:

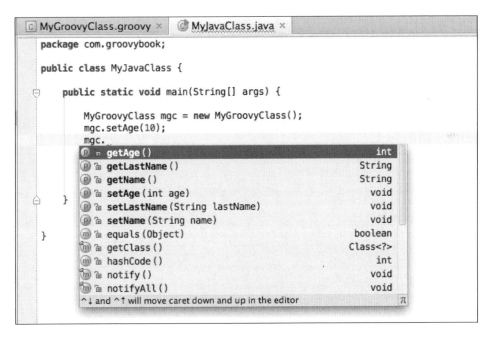

As you can see in the previous screenshot, the code autocompletion works perfectly and it's even able to propose synthetic methods that are generated by the Groovy compiler, such as getters and setters.

For a broader look at the integration between Java and Groovy, take a look at the *Using Java classes from Groovy* recipe in *Chapter 2, Using Groovy Ecosystem*.

There's more...

Several refactoring goodies are also available, including **Extract Parameter** that also works for closures (see the *Defining code as data in Groovy* recipe in *Chapter 3, Using Groovy Language Features*), as shown in the following screenshot:

The result of the refactoring will be as shown in the following screenshot:

```
def isMinimalAge = { int age, int minAge ->
    return age < minAge
}
```

2
Using Groovy Ecosystem

In this chapter, we will cover:

- ▶ Using Java classes from Groovy
- ▶ Embedding Groovy into Java
- ▶ Compiling Groovy code
- ▶ Simplifying dependency management with Grape
- ▶ Integrating Groovy into the build process using Ant
- ▶ Integrating Groovy into the build process using Maven
- ▶ Integrating Groovy into the build process using Gradle
- ▶ Generating documentation for Groovy code
- ▶ Checking Groovy code's quality with CodeNarc

Introduction

In this chapter, we will introduce the Groovy ecosystem: compilation, embedding, building, documentation, and analysis options that various, tools surrounding, Groovy offer to make your life smoother.

In the first three recipes, we will demonstrate how simple Java and Groovy interoperability is and what makes Groovy the perfect tool in a Java developer's hands. The following recipes will describe external dependency management possibilities and the most popular build tools (for example, Ant, Maven, and Gradle) integration options. Then there will be a recipe devoted to Groovydoc, which can be used to generate documentation for your sources. Finally, the last recipe will introduce a way to verify your Groovy code quality.

Using Java classes from Groovy

The Groovy language is designed in a way that it fully supports the Java syntax (there are only few minor exceptions; for example, `do..while` is not supported in Groovy). Most of the code that you can write in Java can automatically be considered Groovy code as well.

In this recipe, we will learn how simple it is to use existing Java classes and libraries from your Groovy code and we will explore some basic language features that makes Groovy—*groovy!*

How to do it...

This recipe has a rather simple setup. You can either start up the `groovyConsole`, as described in the *Starting groovyConsole to execute Groovy snippets* recipe in *Chapter 1, Getting Started with Groovy*, or you can create a new file with the `*.groovy` extension.

1. In the `groovyConsole` type the following code:

    ```
    import java.io.File;
    File currentDir = new File(".");
    System.out.println("Current directory: " +
                        currentDir.getAbsolutePath());
    File[] files = currentDir.listFiles();
    for (File file: files) {
       System.out.println(file.getName());
    }
    ```

2. Run the script to see the list of files found in the folder from where the `groovyConsole` was launched.

How it works...

The Groovy script from the previous section first prints the absolute path of the current directory and then the names of all the files contained in it by using the `java.io.File` API.

Since Groovy supports the Java syntax, you can import any class from the Java JDK in the same way you would do it in Java code.

As you can see, the code after the `import` statement can perfectly serve as a body of some Java method, but it is still Groovy code. On the other hand, we are still using the Java API directly.

There are several ways in which we can improve the previous script by using idiomatic Groovy syntax and without removing the `java.io.File` dependency.

First of all, Groovy automatically imports many classes from the Java JDK and the Groovy GDK into the scope of the script or class. The following packages do not need to be explicitly imported in Groovy, and you simply can refer to their classes:

- `java.io.*`
- `java.lang.*`
- `java.math.BigDecimal`
- `java.math.BigInteger`
- `java.net.*`
- `java.util.*`
- `groovy.lang.*`
- `groovy.util.*`

For this reason, we can omit the `import` statements from the example script. We still need to import a class which is not located in one of the packages previously listed.

As we discussed in *Chapter 1, Getting Started with Groovy*, the `Script` class, an instance of which is created for each Groovy script, exposes the `println` method; this is why all calls to `System.out.println` can be shortened to just `println`.

Another Groovy feature that can be applied to any imported class is the short notation for calling setters and getters. It allows you to write `file.name` instead of `file.getName` and `file.name = "poem.txt"` instead of `file.setName('poem.txt')`. This feature greatly simplifies working with Java Beans and makes code much more readable (see also the *Writing less verbose Java Beans with Groovy Beans* recipe in *Chapter 3, Using Groovy Language Features*).

Famously, Groovy doesn't require a semicolon (`;`) at the end of a statement, if the statement is the only one in the line. We can happily omit semicolons from our script.

One more facet we can resort to in order to *groovify* our script is interpolation. Groovy simplifies string concatenation with the help of the `${ }` operator, that is replaced with the value of the expression that appears inside it. If the expression is a simple reference to a variable or a dot expression (like in our case), then we can omit the curly brackets (`{ }`) and just write `$currentDir.absolutePath`. Or, for example, we can do the following:

```
def name = 'John'
println "My name is $name"
```

The previous code obviously yields the following:

```
My name is John
```

It is worth knowing that strings containing expression are actually `GString` in Groovy and not normal `java.lang.String`. String interpolation is only done for strings enclosed in double quotes (`"`). If you want to avoid string interpolation, then you can use single quotes (`'`) or escape the dollar sign; that is, `\$`:

```
def price = 8
println "Item price: \$${price}"
```

The previous code snippet will print:

```
Item price: $8
```

Thanks to the dynamic nature of the language, we can also omit specifying the variable type in the variable declaration. We can just use the `def` keyword instead.

Taking all the previous notes into account, the code can be shortened to:

```
def currentDir = new File('.')
println "Current directory ${currentDir.absolutePath}"
def files = currentDir.listFiles()
for (def file: files) {
  println file.name
}
```

There are a few other features of Groovy that can help to make this script even more concise such as closures and metaclass facilities, but those will be discussed in more detail in *Chapter 3*, *Using Groovy Language Features*.

Under the hood (either for dynamic scripts or Groovy classes compiled through `groovyc`), Groovy code is always compiled into Java bytecode. Every direct call to an imported Java class would act in the exact same way as it would if it were a Java code.

There's more...

For many standard JDK classes, Groovy provides API extensions. For example, instances of the `java.io.File` class have methods such as `append` or `getText`:

```
def textFile = new File('poem.txt')
textFile.append('What\'s in a name? ')
textFile.append('That which we call a rose\n')
textFile.append('By any other name would smell as sweet.\n')
println textFile.text
```

The previous code snippet adds two lines of William Shakespeare's poem at the end of the `poem.txt` file, and then it prints the file contents on the console. Even though we operate solely on the `java.io.File` object, we call methods that did not originally exist in the JDK. Additional utility methods that appear on standard classes are described in the Groovy JDK documentation located at `http://groovy.codehaus.org/groovy-jdk/`. Those methods can be called due to Groovy's metaclass functionality, which is discussed in more detail in *Chapter 9, Metaprogramming and DSLs in Groovy*, which allows to add your own methods to any Java class used within Groovy code.

See also

► *Chapter 4, Working with Files in Groovy*

► *Chapter 9, Metaprogramming and DSLs in Groovy*

► `http://groovy.codehaus.org/groovy-jdk/`

Embedding Groovy into Java

There are plenty of scripting languages available at the moment on the JVM. Some of them only offer expression language support for data binding and configuration needs, for example, MVEL (`http://mvel.codehaus.org/`) and SpEL (Spring Expression Language, `http://www.springsource.org/documentation`). Others provide a fully featured programming language. Examples of these are JRuby, Jython, Clojure, Jaskell, and of course, Groovy.

In this recipe, we will show you how to benefit from Groovy scripting from within your Java application.

Getting ready

To embed Groovy scripts into your Java code base, first of all, you need to add `groovy-all-2.x.x.jar` library to your class path. Or if you are using Java 7 and want to take advantage of the `invokedynamic` optimization, you should add `groovy-all-2.x.x-indy.jar` instead (see also the *Running Groovy with invokedynamic support* recipe in *Chapter 1, Getting Started with Groovy*).

These libraries are located inside the Groovy distribution archive under the `embeddable` folder. Another way to get those JAR files is from Maven Central Repository at `http://search.maven.org/`.

The `groovy-all` artifact contains all the required classes to run Groovy code. It also includes dependencies such as Antlr, ASM, and Apache Commons inside the archive to be able to run Groovy with only single JAR on the class path. However, you shouldn't worry about class version conflicts if you use one of these libraries because all foreign classes are placed under special packages inside the `groovy-all` library.

How to do it...

There are several ways in which a Groovy script can be invoked from your Java application, but the recommended one—and also the simplest—is using the `GroovyShell` class.

1. Let's start by creating a new Java class named `CallGroovyUsingGroovyShell` that has the following content:

```
import groovy.lang.GroovyShell;
import groovy.lang.Script;
import java.io.File;
import java.io.IOException;
import org.codehaus.groovy.control.CompilationFailedException;
public class CallGroovyUsingGroovyShell {
    public static void main(String[] args)
        throws CompilationFailedException,
                IOException {
        // Create shell object.
        GroovyShell shell = new GroovyShell();
        double result = (Double) shell.
            evaluate("(4/3) * Math.PI * 6370 " +
                    "// Earth volume in cubic killometeres ");
        System.out.println(result);
    }
}
```

The class instantiates a `GroovyShell` object and calls the `evaluate` method of the object by passing a `String` containing Groovy code.

2. Let's explore more methods of the `GrovyShell` class by adding the following Java code to the `main` method:

```
shell.evaluate("name = 'Andrew'");
shell.setVariable("name", "Andrew");
shell.evaluate("println \"My name is ${name}\"");
shell.evaluate("name = name.toUpperCase()");
System.out.println(shell.getVariable("name"));
System.out.println(shell.getProperty("name"));
shell.evaluate("println 'Hello from shell!'");
System.out.println(shell.evaluate(" 1 + 2 "));
```

3. In the same folder where the newly created Java class is located, place a Groovy script named `script.groovy`, with the following content:

```
def scriptName = 'external script'
name = scriptName

println "Hello from ${name} on ${currentDate}!"

def getCurrentDate() {
  new Date().format('yyyy-MM-dd')
}
```

4. Let's continue by adding a new line to the `main` method of our Java class:

```
shell.evaluate(new File("script.groovy"));
```

5. Now compile and run the class. The `groovy-all-2.x.x.jar` library must be located in the same folder as the Java and the Groovy file.

   On Linux/OS X:

```
javac -cp groovy-all-2.1.6.jar
  CallGroovyUsingGroovyShell.java
java -cp .:groovy-all-2.1.6.jar CallGroovyUsingGroovyShell
```

   On Windows:

```
javac -cp groovy-all-2.1.6.jar
  CallGroovyUsingGroovyShell.java
java -cp .;groovy-all-2.1.6.jar CallGroovyUsingGroovyShell
```

   The output should look as follows:

```
6682.593603822243
My name is Andrew
My name is Andrew
ANDREW
ANDREW
Hello from shell!
3
Hello from external script on 2013-08-31!
```

6. Let's add more examples to the `CallGroovyUsingGroovyShell` class. Append the following lines to the `main` method of the class:

```
Script script = shell.parse(new File("script.groovy"));
script.run();
System.out.println(script.
                    invokeMethod("getCurrentDate", null));
System.out.println(script.getProperty("name"));
// Calling internal script
```

```
script = shell.
          parse("println 'Hello from internal script!'");
script.run();
script = shell.parse(new File("functions.groovy"));
System.out.println(script.invokeMethod("year", null));
```

7. Add one more Groovy file to the list of files for this recipe, named `functions.groovy`:

```
def year() {
   Calendar.instance.get(Calendar.YEAR)
}

def month() {
   Calendar.instance.get(Calendar.MONTH)
}

def day() {
   Calendar.instance.get(Calendar.DAY_OF_MONTH)
}
```

8. Compile and run again; the additional output should look as follows:

```
Hello from external script on 2013-08-31!
2013-08-31
external script
Hello from internal script!
2013
```

How it works...

In the Java class example, the `GroovyShell` object is instantiated using the default constructor.

In step 1, the Groovy code passed to the `evaluate` method calculates the result of the simple arithmetical expression. No `return` statement is used, but still the expression evaluates correctly. The reason is that in Groovy, the `return` statement is optional, and an expression will always return the value of the last statement. The mathematical expression's result type is `java.lang.Double` as we only operate with floating numbers; this is why we can safely cast it.

Furthermore, the expression refers to a constant defined in the `java.lang.Math` class, without explicitly importing it. This is possible due to the fact that Groovy imports all `java.lang.*` classes automatically, just like Java.

There is also a comment at the end of the expression, which is safely ignored. Similar to Java, comments can appear anywhere in Groovy code.

The `GroovyShell` object supports defining global variables, which can be re-used by evaluated scripts, by using the `setVariable` method, as displayed in step 2.

The variable `name` is set and then used inside a script evaluated later. The variable will be available to all the scripts executed throughout the lifetime of the `GroovyShell` object.

The variable's value can also be changed during script execution and retrieved later using the `getVariable` method.

In step 3, we can observe another useful feature of the integration of Groovy with Java; the possibility of executing external Groovy scripts from Java by passing a `java.io.File` object to the `evaluate` method.

You can also create individual `Script` objects for repeated executions:

```
Script script = shell.parse(new File("HelloWorld2.groovy"));
script.run(); // run first time
script.run(); // run second time
```

In this case, the script code will be compiled by the `parse` method and the script execution will be faster than if we do repeated calls of the `evaluate` method.

Steps 6 and 7 show how you can also execute individual methods if they are defined by the code located in an external script. Once the script is successfully compiled, the `invokeMethod` can be used to call any function declared in the external script.

There's more...

If you are familiar with **JSR-223**, which provides the specification for the Java SE scripting API, you can also use it with Groovy. JSR-223 is recommended over the `GroovyShell` approach if you want to be able to switch to a different scripting language at any point. The next example shows how to get started with the scripting API:

```
import javax.script.ScriptEngine;
import javax.script.ScriptEngineManager;
import javax.script.ScriptException;

public class CallGroovyUsingJSR223 {

  public static void main(String[] args)
    throws ScriptException {

    ScriptEngineManager manager = new ScriptEngineManager();
    ScriptEngine engine = manager.getEngineByName("groovy");
```

```
        // Expression evalution.
        System.out
            .println(engine
                .eval("(4/3) * Math.PI * 6370 " +
                    "// Earth volume in cubic killometeres "));

        // Variable binding.
        engine.put("name", "Andrew");
        engine.eval("println \"My name is ${name}\"");

    }

}
```

The key to start using Groovy with JSR-233 is again to add the `groovy-all` artifact to the classpath. Adding the jar will automatically bind the Groovy script engine into JVM, which can be retrieved by a call to `manager.getEngineByName("groovy")` as shown in the previous example. Please note that the JSR-233 specification is only available from Java 6.

Another way to dynamically embed Groovy into Java code is by defining the Groovy classes and parsing them with `GroovyClassLoader`. For example, let's assume we have the following `TimePrinter.groovy` file:

```
class TimePrinter implements Runnable {
    void run() {
        (1..10).each {
            println Calendar.instance.time
            Thread.sleep(1000)
        }
    }
}
```

As you can see, it defines the `TimePrinter` class, which implements the `Runnable` interface. The method `run` prints the current time and then sleeps for one second, and it repeats that operation 10 times. This code also shows one way of looping in Groovy: the `(1..10)` expression under the hood creates an object of type `groovy.lang.IntRange`. This class implements the `java.lang.Iterable` interface, which in Groovy has an extension method called `each`. This takes a code block (`groovy.lang.Closure`) as an input parameter and executes it for every element of `java.lang.Iterable`. For more information about Groovy Ranges, please refer to `http://groovy.codehaus.org/api/groovy/lang/Range.html`.

In order to use the `TimePrinter` class dynamically at runtime, we need to create an instance of `GroovyClassLoader` and call the `parseClass` method on it in order to get the new class definition:

```
// Create class loader.
GroovyClassLoader gcl = new GroovyClassLoader();

// Parse and load class.
```

```
@SuppressWarnings("unchecked")
Class<? extends Runnable> runnableClass =
  gcl.parseClass(new File("TimePrinter.groovy"));
```

Then, by using the Java Reflection API and specifically the `newInstance` method, we can create an instance of our dynamically loaded class and use it inside our normal Java code:

```
// Create and use class instance.
new Thread(runnableClass.newInstance()).start();
```

In this way, you can define classes on the fly to change or enhance your application functionality.

To get even more configuration options and more control over security setup, you can also make use of the `GroovyScriptEngine` class, which is not in the scope of this recipe.

See also

 ▶ http://groovy.codehaus.org/Embedding+Groovy

 ▶ http://groovy.codehaus.org/JSR+223+Scripting+with+Groovy

 ▶ http://groovy.codehaus.org/api/groovy/lang/GroovyShell.html

 ▶ http://groovy.codehaus.org/api/groovy/lang/GroovyClassLoader. html

 ▶ http://groovy.codehaus.org/api/groovy/util/GroovyScriptEngine. html

Compiling Groovy code

Groovy scripts are normally executed by running the `groovy` command from the console; for example:

```
groovy someScript.groovy
```

The `groovy` command generates the JVM bytecode on the fly and immediately executes it. There are scenarios in which the Groovy code is required to be compiled to bytecode as a `*.class` file. A typical case is when Java and Groovy code have to be used side-by-side for building a mixed Groovy/Java application.

Groovy has an answer to that by offering a compiler command, `groovyc` (similarly to Java's `javac`), that can also be invoked from the command line or through a build tool such as Ant (see the *Integrating Groovy into the build process using Ant* recipe), Maven (see the *Integrating Groovy into the build process using Maven* recipe), or Gradle (see the *Integrating Groovy into the build process using Gradle* recipe).

In this recipe, we are going to show you the principal purposes of the `groovyc` command.

Getting ready

The best way to show the Groovy compiler in action is to actually invoke it on some Groovy code.

Let's create a file named `fizzbuzz.groovy` and add the following code to it:

```
1.upto(100) {
    ans = ''
    if (it % 3 == 0) { ans ='Fizz' }
    if (it % 5 == 0) { ans += 'Buzz' }
    if (ans == '') {
       println it
    } else {
       println ans
    }
}
```

The code prints numbers from 1 to 100. For numbers that are multiples of three, it prints `Fizz`, and for the multiples of five, it prints `Buzz`. For numbers which are multiples of both three and five, it prints `FizzBuzz`. This little coding exercise was made popular by *Jeff Atwood* back in 2007 in his *CODING HORROR* blog `http://www.codinghorror.com/blog/2007/02/why-cant-programmers-program.html`.

How to do it...

Once the file is ready, let's make sure it prints `Fizz` and `Buzz` where it has to:

1. Open the console and type:

   ```
   groovy fizzbuzz.groovy
   ```

2. And now, let's call the Groovy compiler from the same command line:

   ```
   groovyc fizzbuzz.groovy
   ```

3. The compiler should generate two `*.class` files:

   ```
   fizzbuzz$_run_closure1.class and fizzbuzz.class.
   ```

4. Finally, we can now try to run the compiled Groovy files using the standard Java command:

   On Windows:

   ```
   java -cp ".;%GROOVY_HOME%\lib\*" fizzbuzz
   ```

   On Linux/OS X type:

   ```
   java -cp ".:$GROOVY_HOME/lib/*" fizzbuzz
   ```

5. The output of our little program should be printed on the screen as follows:

```
1
2
Fizz
4
Buzz
Fizz
7
8
Fizz
Buzz
11
```

How it works...

The reason `groovyc` produces two class files lies in the dynamic nature of Groovy and the usages of special constructs—closures—in our code snippet. The code block that appears after the `each` statement is actually a closure that can be stored and passed as a data structure in Groovy. Closures are discussed in more detail in the *Defining code as data in Groovy* recipe in *Chapter 3*, *Using Groovy Language Features*. Groovy creates a separate internal class for each such dynamic code block. The main script code is placed in `fizzbuzz.class`.

Also, as you probably noticed, we added all the Groovy distribution libraries to the classpath since compiled Groovy code relies on their functionality.

See also

For single file compilation, `groovyc` is easy to use, though if you need to compile dozens or even hundreds of classes, then it would be better to use a build tool for that:

- ▶ *Integrating Groovy into the build process using Ant*
- ▶ *Integrating Groovy into the build process using Maven*
- ▶ *Integrating Groovy into the build process using Gradle*

Simplifying dependency management with Grape

Your nicely written and useful script can solve many interesting problems with the help of third-party libraries, and as long as it resides on your machine and has all the dependencies in place, it will work perfectly. However, at the point when you need to share it with your colleagues or community, you will realize that small and concise code requires several megabytes of additional libraries to be passed together with the script in order to make it work. Luckily, Groovy has a solution for that called **Grape**.

In this recipe, we will show you how to declare and automatically load Groovy script dependencies with the help of the wonderful Grape tool, which is integrated into Groovy.

Getting ready

Grape stands for the **Groovy Adaptable (Advanced) Packaging Engine**, and it is a part of the Groovy installation. Grape helps you download and cache external dependencies from within your script with a set of simple annotations.

How to do it...

If, in your script, you require an external dependency, that you know is available in a public repository as Maven Central Repository, you can use `@Grab` annotation to annotate your `import`, `class`, or `method` with a reference to that library, and Groovy will automatically download it, cache it, and put it on the class path of your script:

1. For example, the `search.groovy` script is dependent on Apache `Commons HttpClient` library for making a Google search and saving a result page to a local file:

   ```
   @Grab('org.apache.httpcomponents:httpclient:4.2.1')
   import org.apache.http.impl.client.DefaultHttpClient
   import org.apache.http.client.methods.HttpGet

   def httpClient = new DefaultHttpClient()
   def url = 'http://www.google.com/search?q=Groovy'
   def httpGet = new HttpGet(url)

   def httpResponse = httpClient.execute(httpGet)

   new File('result.html').text =
     httpResponse.entity.content.text
   ```

2. To execute the script, just use the usual invocation: `groovy search.groovy` mechanism. Groovy will automatically detect any external dependency requirements and tell Grape to fetch it before script execution.

How it works...

The first time the script gets executed, we experience a delay while the dependencies are downloaded. The second time, the script will execute faster because all libraries will be cached in Grape's cache directory, located in `.groovy\grapes`, in the user's home folder. Groovy also provides a command-line tool, `grape`, to overview and control Grape's library cache. If the Grape's cache was empty in the beginning, then after our script execution, grape's list command will output something as follows:

```
commons-codec commons-codec   [1.6]
commons-logging commons-logging   [1.1.1]
org.apache apache   [4, 9]
org.apache.commons commons-parent   [22, 5]
org.apache.httpcomponents httpclient   [4.2.1]
org.apache.httpcomponents httpcomponents-client   [4.2.1]
org.apache.httpcomponents httpcomponents-core   [4.2.1]
org.apache.httpcomponents httpcore   [4.2.1]
org.apache.httpcomponents project   [6]
org.ccil.cowan.tagsoup tagsoup   [1.2]

10 Grape modules cached
12 Grape module versions cached
```

You can put `@Grab` annotation preceding various elements of the code.

On `import`:

```
@Grab('org.apache.httpcomponents:httpclient:4.2.1')
import org.apache.http.impl.client.DefaultHttpClient

def httpClient = new DefaultHttpClient()
```

On variable:

```
@Grab('org.apache.httpcomponents:httpclient:4.2.1')
def httpClient =
  new org.apache.http.impl.client.DefaultHttpClient()
```

On method:

```
@Grab('org.apache.httpcomponents:httpclient:4.2.1')
def getHttpClient() {
  new org.apache.http.impl.client.DefaultHttpClient()
}
```

On `class`:

```
@Grab('org.apache.httpcomponents:httpclient:4.2.1')
class Searcher {
  def httpClient
  Searcher() {
    httpClient =
      new org.apache.http.impl.client.DefaultHttpClient()
  }
}
```

The only rule is that `@Grab` should appear before the first usage of the imported class; otherwise the Groovy compiler will complain about it.

There's more...

Additionally, the `@Grapes` annotation can be used to group several dependencies as follows:

```
@Grapes([
  @Grab('org.apache.httpcomponents:httpclient:4.2.1'),
  @Grab('org.ccil.cowan.tagsoup:tagsoup:1.2')])
class Searcher { ... }
```

By default, Grape is using the Maven Central Repository (located at `http://search.maven.org/`) for downloading libraries. If you need to add your own repository, then you can either change `grapeConfig.xml`, which is in fact, an Apache Ivy configuration, or you can use the `@GrabResolver` annotation inside the script itself to make it more portable:

```
@GrabResolver(name='codehaus',
              root='http://repository.codehaus.org/')
class Searcher { ... }
```

Like with any dependency management tool, sometimes you need to exclude certain dependencies from a dependency tree, and there, the `@GrabExclude` annotation comes to the rescue:

```
@GrabExclude(group='commons-codec',
             module='commons-codec')
class Searcher { ... }
```

Under the hood, Grape is using the Apache Ivy library for dependency management and resolution.

If you don't want to wait for the artifact download upon script start, you can use the `grape install` command to install artifacts before execution:

```
grape install org.apache.httpcomponents httpclient 4.2.1
```

You can also use the Grape API directly and prefetch the required dependencies using another Groovy script:

```
import groovy.grape.Grape

Grape.grab(group: 'org.apache.httpcomponents',
           module: 'httpclient',
           version: '4.2.1')
```

See also

▶ Grape documentation: `http://groovy.codehaus.org/Grape`

▶ Apache Ivy: `https://ant.apache.org/ivy/`

Integrating Groovy into the build process using Ant

Apache Ant (`http://ant.apache.org/`) was one of the first build tools that appeared within the Java ecosystem, and it is still widely used by many organizations around the globe.

In this recipe, we will cover how to compile and test a complete Groovy project using Apache Ant. At the end of the recipe, we will show you how to use Groovy from within Ant to add scripting to a build task.

Getting ready

For demonstrating the build tool integration, let's create the following folders and files:

```
src/main/groovy/org/groovy/cookbook
    DatagramWorker.groovy
    MessageReceiver.groovy
    MessageSender.groovy
src/test/groovy/org/groovy/cookbook
    MessageProcessingTest.groovy
```

The aim of the project is to create a very simple UDP client/server and accompany it with a unit test.

The base class for the server and the client, `DatagramWorker`, has the following code:

```
abstract class DatagramWorker {

  byte[] buffer = new byte[256]
  DatagramSocket socket = null
```

```
String lastMessage = null

DatagramPacket receive() {
  def packet = new DatagramPacket(buffer, buffer.length)
  socket.receive(packet)
  lastMessage = new String(packet.data, 0, packet.length)
  println "RECEIVED: $lastMessage"
  packet
}

def send(String message,
         InetAddress address,
         int port) {
  def output = new DatagramPacket(
              message.bytes,
              message.length(),
              address,
              port
            )
  socket.send(output)
}

def send(DatagramPacket inputPacket) {
  send('OK', inputPacket.address, inputPacket.port)
}
}
```

The class contains a field for holding the `socket` object, a temporary data `buffer` and the `lastMessage` received by the `socket`. Additionally, it exposes basic methods for sending and receiving data.

The server class, `MessageReceiver`, is implemented in the following way:

```
class MessageReceiver extends DatagramWorker {

def start() {
  socket = new DatagramSocket(12345)
  Thread.startDaemon {
    while(true) {
      send(receive())
    }
  }
}

}
```

Upon the `start` method call, it starts a daemon thread that listens to incoming messages on port `12345` and sends `OK` back to the client when a message is received.

The client class, `MessageSender`, looks as follows:

```
class MessageSender extends DatagramWorker {

  def send(String message) {
    socket = new DatagramSocket()
    send(message, InetAddress.getByName('localhost'), 12345)
    receive()
  }

}
```

It contains a single method `send`, which sends a given `message` to the server running at `localhost` on port `12345`.

Finally the unit test, `MessageProcessingTest`, verifies that both the server (`receiver`) and the client (`sender`) can successfully exchange messages:

```
import org.junit.Test

class MessageProcessingTest {

  MessageReceiver receiver = new MessageReceiver()
  MessageSender sender = new MessageSender()

  @Test
  void testMessages() throws Exception {
    receiver.start()
    sender.send('HELLO')
    assert receiver.lastMessage == 'HELLO'
    assert sender.lastMessage == 'OK'
  }

}
```

In this recipe, we also assume that you are familiar with Apache Ant, and you know how to install it. It also makes sense to use Apache Ivy for dependency management to simplify the dependencies download. So, we assume that Ant has the Ivy (`http://ant.apache.org/ivy/`) extension installed in `ANT_HOME/lib`.

How to do it...

At this point, we are going to create a fully functional Ant build for the project defined previously.

1. Let's start with the following partial `build.xml` that you need to place in the root directory of our project:

```
<project xmlns:ivy="antlib:org.apache.ivy.ant"
         basedir="."
         default="test"
         name="build-groovy">
  <property name="lib.dir"
            value="lib" />
  <property name="build.dir"
            value="output" />
  <property name="src.main.dir"
            value="src/main/groovy" />
  <property name="src.test.dir"
            value="src/test/groovy" />
  <property name="classes.main.dir"
            value="${build.dir}/main" />
  <property name="classes.test.dir"
            value="${build.dir}/test" />
  <property name="test.result.dir"
            value="${build.dir}/test-results" />
  <path id="lib.path.id">
    <fileset dir="${lib.dir}" />
  </path>
  <path id="runtime.path.id">
    <path refid="lib.path.id" />
    <path location="${classes.main.dir}" />
  </path>
  <path id="test.path.id">
    <path refid="runtime.path.id" />
    <path location="${classes.test.dir}" />
  </path>
  <!-- tasks -->
</project>
```

2. In order to start using Ivy, we need to define a dependency descriptor file, `ivy.xml`, and place it in the same directory as `build.xml`:

```
<ivy-module version="2.0">
  <info organisation="org.groovy.cookbook"
        module="build-groovy" />
```

```
<dependencies>
  <dependency org="org.codehaus.groovy"
              name="groovy-all"
              rev="2.1.6"
              transitive="false" />
  <dependency org="junit"
              name="junit"
              rev="4.10" />
</dependencies>
</ivy-module>
```

3. Once the dependencies are added, we can define the `clean` and `prepare` targets inside `build.xml`. Replace the `<!-- tasks -->` comment in the `build.xml` file with the following snippet:

```
<target name="clean"
        description="Clean output directory">
  <delete dir="${build.dir}" />
</target>
<target name="prepare"
        description="Get dependencies and create folders">
  <ivy:retrieve />
  <mkdir dir="${classes.main.dir}" />
  <mkdir dir="${classes.test.dir}" />
  <mkdir dir="${test.result.dir}" />
  <taskdef name="groovyc"
           classname="org.codehaus.groovy.ant.Groovyc"
           classpathref="lib.path.id" />
</target>
```

4. Now we are ready to define the `compile` target:

```
<target name="compile"
        depends="prepare"
        description="Compile Groovy code">
  <groovyc srcdir="${src.main.dir}"
           destdir="${classes.main.dir}"
           classpathref="lib.path.id" />
</target>
```

5. We can then define a similar target, `testCompile`, to compile our test code:

```
<target name="testCompile"
        depends="prepare, compile"
        description="Compile Groovy unit tests">
  <groovyc srcdir="${src.test.dir}"
           destdir="${classes.test.dir}"
           classpathref="runtime.path.id" />
</target>
```

6. And finally we define a target for running unit tests:

```
<target name="test"
        depends="testCompile"
        description="Run unit tests">
  <junit>
    <classpath refid="test.path.id" />
    <batchtest todir="${test.result.dir}">
      <fileset dir="${classes.test.dir}" includes="**/*" />
      <formatter type="plain" />
    </batchtest>
  </junit>
</target>
```

7. In order to build and test the project, we can just call the declared Ant targets:

```
ant clean test
```

You should get an output similar to the following:

```
Buildfile: build.xml
clean:
    [delete] Deleting directory output
prepare:
[ivy:retrieve] <...skipped part...>
    [mkdir] Created dir: output\main
    [mkdir] Created dir: output\test
    [mkdir] Created dir: output\test-results
compile:
    [groovyc] Compiling 3 source files to output\main
testCompile:
    [groovyc] Compiling 1 source file to output\test
test:
BUILD SUCCESSFUL
Total time: 3 seconds
```

How it works...

There are several properties and paths defined in Ant's `build.xml` script:

- The `lib.dir` property refers to a directory where Apache Ivy puts all the downloaded dependencies

- `build.dir` will contain all the files we produce during the compilation and build

- `src.main.dir` and `src.test.dir` refer to the directories holding the Groovy main and test code respectively

- ▶ `classes.main.dir` and `classes.test.dir` hold the compiled classes for the main and test code
- ▶ `test.result.dir` will contain the JUnit test results
- ▶ `lib.path.id` is reference to all the libraries imported by Ivy
- ▶ `runtime.path.id` appends all the compiled classes to `lib.path.id`
- ▶ `test.path.id` also appends the compiled test classes to `runtime.path.id`

Step 2 shows the Ivy dependencies file: there are only 2 dependencies declared for this project: `groovy-all` library for actually running the Groovy code and `junit` library for tests. The `groovy -all` artifact has the `transitive` property set to `false`, because the main Groovy library is enough for running this project and we don't need to download other dependencies.

Now let's go into more detail of our Ant script targets. The `clean` target just deletes the output folder. The `prepare` target does several things:

- ▶ Downloads all the dependencies specified in the `ivy.xml` file,
- ▶ Creates all output folders,
- ▶ Holds the definition of the `groovyc` task that we will use for compiling Groovy code.

As you can notice we specify the location of Groovy sources through the `srcdir` attribute, and the output folder of compiled classes through `desdir` attribute. `classpathref` is pointing to the classpath variable, `lib.path.id`, which contains the `groovy-all` library that holds the Groovy compiler.

The `groovyc` task has a number of options, including the initial and maximum memory size (`memoryInitialSize`, `memoryMaximumSize`) and the file encoding (`encoding`). A more exhaustive explanation of these attributes can be found in the documentation.

Finally, the testing target does not differ from what you would normally do for running Java unit tests. That is possible only because Groovy code is actually compiled into Java byte code.

There's more...

If the same source folder contains both Java and Groovy code, the `groovyc` Ant task can run in joint compilation mode. In this mode, the Groovy compiler creates Java files out of the Groovy source code and feeds them directly to the Java `javac`, which proceeds to compile them along with the standard Java files. In order to enable the joint compilation, a `javac` nested element must be added to the `groovyc` task:

```
<target name="compile"
        depends="prepare"
        description="Compile Groovy and Java code">
  <groovyc srcdir="${src.main.dir}"
           destdir="${classes.main.dir}"
```

```
            classpathref="lib.path.id">
    <javac source="1.6" target="1.6" debug="on" />
  </groovyc>
</target>
```

So far, this recipe has demonstrated how to compile Groovy code using Ant. However, the integration between Groovy and Ant can go further than that: Groovy can be used to extend Ant capabilities by calling embedded or external Groovy scripts from an Ant build file.

Ant can call Groovy scripts with the `groovy` task that is also part of the `groovy-all` library. To show how this can work, we can extend the `prepare` target with another `taskdef` as follows:

```
<taskdef name="groovy"
         classname="org.codehaus.groovy.ant.Groovy"
         classpathref="lib.path.id" />
```

The `taskdef` declaration should be placed between properties and targets definitions.

Once the `taskdef` is declared, the `groovy` task can be called from within any target. For example, the following target, `info`, prints the project name and the list of dependencies using a Groovy embedded script:

```
<target name="info"
        depends="prepare"
        description="Print project information">
  <groovy>
    println "Name: $project.name"
    println 'Dependencies: '
    project.references."lib.path.id".each { println it.name }
  </groovy>
</target>
```

The embedded Groovy script has access to the Ant API and script variables from within the script body. The output of running the `ant info` command will display an output similar to the following:

```
info:
   [groovy] Name: build-groovy
   [groovy] Dependencies:
   [groovy] groovy-all-2.1.6-javadoc.jar
   [groovy] groovy-all-2.1.6-sources.jar
   [groovy] groovy-all-2.1.6.jar
   [groovy] hamcrest-core-1.1.jar
   [groovy] junit-4.10-javadoc.jar
   [groovy] junit-4.10-sources.jar
   [groovy] junit-4.10.jar

BUILD SUCCESSFUL
Total time: 2 seconds
```

You can also externalize your scripts and run them by specifying the `src` attribute of the `groovy` task:

```
<groovy src="info.groovy"/>
```

See also

▶ The Groovy Compile Ant task documentation:
  `http://groovy.codehaus.org/The+groovyc+Ant+Task`

▶ The Groovy Ant task documentation:
  `http://groovy.codehaus.org/The+groovy+Ant+Task`

Integrating Groovy into the build process using Maven

Apache Maven (`http://maven.apache.org/`) is a software project build tool that uses the **POM** (**Project Object Model**) to describe project artifacts, dependencies, and rules in a declarative form.

Apache Maven was an important milestone in Java build tool evolution. Together with important features such as organized dependency management and declarative build scripts, it also brought a variety of standards and conventions that have been widely adopted by the Java community, even if Maven itself is not used.

In this recipe, we are going to look into how to compile, test, and run a fully blown Groovy project using the Apache Maven build tool.

Getting ready

We are going to re-use the same Groovy project presented in the *Integrating Groovy into the build process using Ant* recipe. We also assume that you are familiar with Apache Maven and that it is installed on your machine and is ready for use. The steps of this recipe were tested against Maven 3. For those who don't have it yet, download and installation instructions can be found at `http://maven.apache.org/download.cgi`.

How to do it...

As we already mentioned, Maven uses POM. The POM definition is stored in `pom.xml`.

1. Let's start with the following partial `pom.xml`:
   ```
   <?xml version="1.0" encoding="UTF-8"?>
   <project>
     <modelVersion>4.0.0</modelVersion>
   ```

```
      <groupId>org.groovy.cookbook</groupId>
      <artifactId>build-groovy</artifactId>
      <version>1.0-SNAPSHOT</version>
      <!-- dependencies -->
      <!-- build -->
</project>
```

It's not much different from the standard POM you would use for any Maven project.

2. Then we can add the dependencies needed to inject Groovy functionality into the Maven build. Just replace `<!-- dependencies -->` comment line with the following:

```
<dependencies>
  <dependency>
    <groupId>junit</groupId>
    <artifactId>junit</artifactId>
    <version>4.10</version>
    <scope>test</scope>
  </dependency>
  <dependency>
    <groupId>org.codehaus.gmaven.runtime</groupId>
    <artifactId>gmaven-runtime-2.0</artifactId>
    <version>1.4</version>
  </dependency>
</dependencies>
```

3. The last step of the configuration is to add the extensions to build goals to let Maven compile the Groovy code. Replace the `<!-- build -->` comment with the following snippet:

```
<build>
  <plugins>
    <plugin>
      <groupId>org.codehaus.gmaven</groupId>
      <artifactId>gmaven-plugin</artifactId>
      <version>1.4</version>
      <executions>
        <execution>
          <goals>
            <goal>compile</goal>
            <goal>testCompile</goal>
          </goals>
        </execution>
      </executions>
      <dependencies>
        <dependency>
          <groupId>org.codehaus.gmaven.runtime</groupId>
```

```
        <artifactId>gmaven-runtime-2.0</artifactId>
        <version>1.4</version>
      </dependency>
    </dependencies>
  </plugin>
 </plugins>
</build>
```

4. Then, in order to compile and test the project, we just use the standard Maven command line:

```
mvn clean test
```

5. The output of the command should look similar to the following screenshot:

```
[INFO] Scanning for projects...
[INFO]
[INFO] ------------------------------------------------------------------------
[INFO] Building build-groovy 1.0-SNAPSHOT
[INFO] ------------------------------------------------------------------------
[INFO]
```

```
-------------------------------------------------------
 T E S T S
-------------------------------------------------------
Running org.groovy.cookbook.MessageProcessingTest
RECEIVED: HELLO
RECEIVED: OK
Tests run: 1, Failures: 0, Errors: 0, Skipped: 0, Time elapsed: 0.597 sec

Results :

Tests run: 1, Failures: 0, Errors: 0, Skipped: 0

[INFO] ------------------------------------------------------------------------
[INFO] BUILD SUCCESS
[INFO] ------------------------------------------------------------------------
[INFO] Total time: 5.227s
```

How it works...

We have chosen to use the GMaven plugin to integrate Groovy and Maven. The gmaven-runtime-2.0 library is part of that plugin, and it contains transitive references to required Groovy distribution libraries including the groovy-all library.

We instruct GMaven to execute during the standard compile and testCompile goals. Unfortunately, due to the nature of the GMaven plugin, we need to list the gmaven-runtime-2.0 library in the plugin dependencies once again.

After command execution, Maven (with the help of GMaven) compiles and tests the Groovy classes and reports the status in the console. Files produced during the build will be placed under the target directory, which will contain the .class files and JUnit reports.

There's more...

If you want to use the latest Groovy release, which may not yet be referenced by `gmaven-runtime`, then you can override the `groovy-all` dependency in the following way (both for project and plugin configuration):

```
<dependencies>
  <dependency>
    <groupId>org.codehaus.gmaven.runtime</groupId>
    <artifactId>gmaven-runtime-2.0</artifactId>
    <version>1.4</version>
    <exclusions>
      <exclusion>
        <groupId>org.codehaus.groovy</groupId>
        <artifactId>groovy-all</artifactId>
      </exclusion>
    </exclusions>
  </dependency>
  <dependency>
    <groupId>org.codehaus.groovy</groupId>
    <artifactId>groovy-all</artifactId>
    <version>2.1.6</version>
  </dependency>
</dependencies>
```

There is also a possibility to use Groovy to supply additional logic to Maven goals. The same GMaven plugin can be used for that. For example, the following snippet executes Groovy script after the `compile` phase is finished, and it prints a list of dependencies:

```
<execution>
  <id>compile</id>
  <phase>compile</phase>
  <goals>
    <goal>execute</goal>
  </goals>
  <configuration>
    <source>
      println "Name: $project.name"
      println 'Dependencies: '
      project.dependencies.each { println it.artifactId }
    </source>
  </configuration>
</execution>
```

This snippet has to be added inside the GMaven plugin configuration under the `<executions>` tag. Also, please note that if you use GMaven for Groovy code compilation, then you need to set unique the `<id>` of your `<execution>` elements.

The output of the snippet will appear in the build output and will look as follows:

```
[INFO] --- gmaven-plugin:1.4:execute (compile) @ build-groovy ---
Name: build-groovy
Dependencies:
junit
gmaven-runtime-2.0
```

As an alternative to GMaven, there's also the Eclipse Groovy Compiler plugin for Maven that can be used instead of GMaven. They are very similar in functionality, and it's hard to recommend one over the other.

See also

- ▸ Maven homepage: `http://maven.apache.org/`
- ▸ GMaven homepage: `http://docs.codehaus.org/display/GMAVEN/Home`
- ▸ Maven's Groovy Eclipse Compiler plugin documentation: `http://groovy.codehaus.org/Groovy-Eclipse+compiler+plugin+for+Maven`

Integrating Groovy into the build process using Gradle

Gradle (`http://www.gradle.org/`) is a build and automation tool written in Java/Groovy, which makes use of a Groovy-based DSL for defining declarative and imperative build scripts. Gradle brings a lot of innovation into the Java/Groovy build tool space, and at a fast pace is replacing other popular tools. At the same time, it builds upon the best practices and foundations of those tools, such as project conventions standardization and dependency management.

In this recipe, we will demonstrate how Gradle can simplify the compilation and testing of a complete Groovy project.

Getting ready

We will build the same example Groovy project defined in the *Integrating Groovy into the build process using Ant* recipe. We assume that you have at least some familiarity with Gradle, and it is already installed on your system. Otherwise, you can refer to the installation page (http://www.gradle.org/docs/current/userguide/installation.html) of the Gradle User Guide.

How to do it...

At first glance, a Gradle script may seem too simple to be actually functional. This is one of the strengths of the product: simplicity and power.

1. You can achieve compilation and test of a project with just the following simple `build.gradle` script:

```
apply plugin: 'groovy'

group = 'org.groovy.cookbook'

repositories {
  mavenCentral()
}

dependencies {
  compile 'org.codehaus.groovy:groovy-all:2.1.6'
  testCompile 'junit:junit:4.10'
}
```

2. Then in order to compile and test the project, we just use standard Gradle command line:

```
gradle clean test
```

3. The output of the command should look similar to the following:

```
:clean
:compileJava UP-TO-DATE
:compileGroovy
:processResources UP-TO-DATE
:classes
:compileTestJava UP-TO-DATE
:compileTestGroovy
:processTestResources UP-TO-DATE
:testClasses
:test
BUILD SUCCESSFUL
Total time: 9.989 secs
```

How it works...

As you can probably guess, all the logic required for Groovy integration is built into the `groovy` plugin declared on the first line of the build script. The remaining content of the script has the following functions:

- ▶ Define the project's `groupId` in case we decide to build a JAR and deploy it to some repository
- ▶ Tell Gradle to load dependencies from Maven Central Repository by using the special `mavenCentral` method
- ▶ Declare the required libraries for the `compile` and for `testCompile` configurations, which are defined by the `groovy` plugin and which are used at respective build stages

Upon build completion, the code will be compiled and tested. The result of the build activity including compiled classes and JUnit report files will be located in the automatically created `build` directory.

There's more...

The Gradle build script language is actually a Groovy DSL. That's why you can define tasks directly using Groovy. For example, you can add an `info` task that prints the project test code dependencies:

```
task info << {
  println "Name: $project.name"
  println 'Dependencies: '
  project.configurations.testCompile.allDependencies.each {
    println it.name
  }
}
```

To execute the task, you can just type `gradle info`.

A more detailed introduction to Gradle features is out of scope for this recipe, and it's actually worth a separate book.

See also

- ▶ Gradle's Groovy plugin documentation:
  http://gradle.org/docs/current/userguide/groovy_plugin.html
- ▶ Gradle homepage: http://www.gradle.org/

Generating documentation for Groovy code

All Java developers are familiar with Javadoc comment style and the `javadoc` command-line tool, which is well integrated into all major IDEs and build tools.

Unfortunately, you will not be able to run the `javadoc` tool against Groovy source code, just because `javadoc` does not recognize the Groovy language syntax - unless your Groovy classes or scripts are written in Java. This is why Groovy has a tool, which for obvious reasons is called **Groovydoc**. It shares a lot of features with its predecessor but also has some significant differences. For example, `groovydoc` does not implement the Doclet extension feature, which was used mainly for code generation but since the introduction of annotations in Java 5, its usage has decreased dramatically. Also, unlike `javadoc`, which is a standalone executable originally written in C++ with its extension points (that is, Doclets) written in Java, Groovydoc's core functionality is fully implemented in Groovy and is available as a command line script.

In this recipe, we will present the basic features of the `groovydoc` command-line tool.

Getting ready

For our experiments, we are going to use the `VehicleUtils.groovy` class, which should be placed under the `src/org/groovy/cookbook` directory inside your current folder. The class contains several Javadoc-like comments in order to demonstrate Groovydoc's capabilities:

```groovy
package org.groovy.cookbook

/**
 * This class contains vehicle related
 * calculation utility methods.
 *
 * @author Groovy Writer
 * @since 2013
 *
 */
class VehicleUtils {

    /**
     * Returns average fuel consumption per 100 km.
     * More information about involved calculations
     * can be found in the
     * <a
     *  href="http://en.wikipedia.org/wiki/Fuel_efficiency"
     * >respected source</a>.
     *
```

```
 * @param distance
 *             the distance driven by the vehicle.
 * @param liters
 *             the amount of fuel spent in liters.
 *
 * @return calculated fuel consumption.
 *
 */
static fuelConsumptionPer100Km(distance, liters) {
  (liters * 100) / distance
}
}
```

As you can see, there is not much difference in the formatting of comments compared to javadoc.

If we try to use the javadoc command (executed from your current directory) to generate documentation for that class, it will not find any source files:

```
> javadoc -sourcepath src org.groovy.cookbook
Loading source files for package org.groovy.cookbook...
javadoc: warning -
   No source files for package org.groovy.cookbook
Constructing Javadoc information...
javadoc: warning -
   No source files for package org.groovy.cookbook
javadoc: error -
   No public or protected classes found to document.
1 error
2 warnings
```

Even if you rename VehicleUtils.groovy to VehicleUtils.java, javadoc will still complain about unrecognized syntax (since javadoc is re-using javac functionality):

```
./src/org/groovy/cookbook/VehicleUtils.java:1:
   ';' expected
package org.groovy.cookbook
                           ^
./src/org/groovy/cookbook/VehicleUtils.java:25:
   <identifier> expected
  static def fuelConsumptionPer100Km(distance, liters) {
                                    ^

...

5 errors
```

This all leads to the necessity of using Groovydoc for generating documentation. Groovydoc is installed together with Groovy, and if you followed one of the installation recipes (see the *Installing Groovy on Linux and OS X* or the *Installing Groovy on Windows* recipes in *Chapter 1, Getting Started with Groovy*) correctly, the `groovydoc` command should already be available in your shell.

How to do it...

By simply typing the `groovydoc` command, you'll get default help message with parameter description.

1. To produce the HTML documentation for `VehicleUtils.groovy`, you need to launch the following command from your current folder:

   ```
   groovydoc -d doc -sourcepath src org.groovy.cookbook
   ```

2. The generated documentation will be located under the `doc` folder, and if you launch `index.html` in our browser you should get the following view:

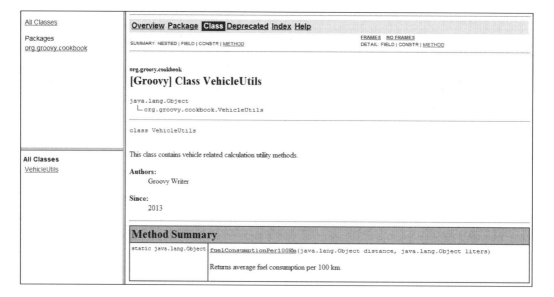

How it works...

Under the hood, `groovydoc` acts similar to `javadoc` by parsing the source files and navigating internally to the **AST (Abstract Syntax Tree)** to extract comment information and convert it to a set of HTML files.

Groovydoc supports all the standard Javadoc tags such as `@author`, `@see`, `@since`, `@param`, `@return`, and some others.

There's more...

Groovydoc can also be used to generate documentation for Java source code since by design, Groovy fully supports Java syntax. This is very handy since, in the case of a combined code base, which contains both Java and Groovy source code files, you can take advantage of using the same tool to produce joint documentation.

For example, we can add the `Vehicle.java` source file inside the `src/org/groovy/cookbook` folder:

```
package org.groovy.cookbook;

/**
 * This class contains vehicle data structure.
 *
 * @author Groovy Writer
 * @since 2013
 *
 */
public class Vehicle {

  final double maxSpeed;

  public Vehicle(double maxSpeed) {
    this.maxSpeed = maxSpeed;
  }

  /**
   * Returns vehicle's maximum speed.
   */
  public double getMaxSpeed() {
    return maxSpeed;
  }

}
```

If we run the `groovydoc` tool again, it will happily create documentation for both classes:

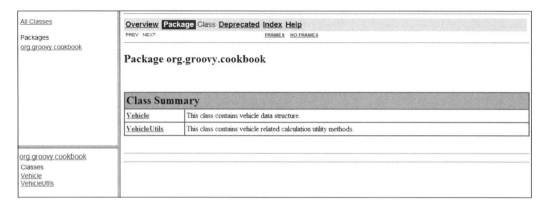

Groovydoc is also well integrated with the build tools described in the *Integrating Groovy into the build process using Ant* and *Integrating Groovy into the build process using Gradle* recipes.

See also

▶ Javadoc's home page: `http://www.oracle.com/technetwork/java/javase/documentation/index-jsp-135444.html`

▶ Groovydoc's Ant task: `http://groovy.codehaus.org/api/org/codehaus/groovy/ant/Groovydoc.html`

▶ Gradle's Groovydoc integration: `http://www.gradle.org/docs/current/dsl/org.gradle.api.tasks.javadoc.Groovydoc.html`

Checking Groovy code's quality with CodeNarc

As soon as you finish writing your first Groovy scripts or classes, you will probably start wondering how Groovy pros write their code and what are the best practices they are using. One way would be to learn by peeking at the best Groovy code bases (for example, Groovy itself: `https://github.com/groovy/groovy-core/tree/master/src/main/groovy`). Another way can be using code analysis tools that let you catch common coding mistakes that are already well-known in the community.

In the Java language world, there are many open source static code analysis tools such as PMD (Project Mess Detector) (`http://pmd.sourceforge.net/`), Checkstyle (`http://checkstyle.sourceforge.net/`), FindBugs (`http://findbugs.sourceforge.net/`), and so on. There are also many commercial products and IDEs that support various types of Java source code analysis.

In that regard, Groovy is less rich, though it has one library called **CodeNarc** (`http://codenarc.sourceforge.net`). The library is already integrated into the most popular build tools including Ant (see the *Integrating Groovy into the build process using Ant* recipe), Maven (see the *Integrating Groovy into the build process using Maven* recipe), and Gradle (see the *Integrating Groovy into the build process using Gradle* recipe). Also, some IDEs have plugins for CodeNarc.

In this recipe, we will cover the typical use case for the CodeNarc command-line tool and show how it can help to improve your Groovy code and boost your skills with the language.

Getting ready

For the sake of demonstration, we will use the following Groovy script, which on purposely violates several coding rules that CodeNarc inspects:

```groovy
import java.io.*;

public class DirListing {

  public static void main(String[] args) throws IOException {
    String path;
    if (args.length > 0) {
      path = args[0];
    } else {
      path = ".";
    }
    File directory = new File(path);
    File[] files = directory.listFiles();
    System.out.println("Directory of "
      + directory.getCanonicalFile().getAbsolutePath());
    for (int i = 0; i < files.length; i++) {
      if (files[i].isFile()) {
        File file = files[i];
        System.out.println(file.getName());
      }
    }
  }

}
```

In fact, the previous code is actually plain Java, but since Groovy almost fully supports Java syntax, the code will run under Groovy as well.

The task that is performed by the script is a simple directory file listing. The program takes a directory path as its first argument. If the argument is omitted, the current directory is used. All first-level file (not directory) names are printed to the standard output.

We assume that the script is placed in the `src` directory located in your current working folder.

How to do it...

We can launch the CodeNarc command-line interface using Groovy script with a little help from Grape (see the *Simplifying dependency management with Grape* recipe).

1. Create a `codenarc.groovy` script in the current directory:

    ```groovy
    @Grab('org.codenarc:CodeNarc:0.18.1')
    import org.codenarc.CodeNarc

    CodeNarc.main(args)
    ```

2. Now you can start CodeNarc to get its default help message:

    ```
    groovy codenarc.groovy -help
    ```

3. To get CodeNarc to generate a report for our poorly coded script, we need to pass more parameters to the `codenarc.groovy` script:

    ```
    groovy codenarc.groovy
        -rulesetfiles="rulesets/unnecessary.xml"
        -title="Directory Listing"
        -basedir=src
    ```

4. This will generate an HTML report inside the current directory that looks like the following screenshot:

CodeNarc Report

Report title:	Directory Listing
Date:	16-07-2013 15:44:15
Generated with:	CodeNarc v0.18.1

Summary by Package

Package	Total Files	Files with Violations	Priority 1	Priority 2	Priority 3
All Packages	1	1	-	-	16
<Root>	1	1	-	-	16

Package: <Root>

↳ DirListing.groovy

Rule Name	Priority	Line #	Source Line / Message
UnnecessarySemicolon	3	1	[SRC] import java.io.*; [MSG] Semi-colons as line endings can be removed safely
UnnecessaryPublicModifier	3	3	[SRC] public class DirListing { [MSG] The public keyword is unnecessary for classes
UnnecessaryPublicModifier	3	5	[SRC] public static void main(String[] args) throws IOException { [MSG] The public keyword is unnecessary for methods
UnnecessarySemicolon	3	6	[SRC] String path; [MSG] Semi-colons as line endings can be removed safely
UnnecessarySemicolon	3	8	[SRC] path = args[0]; [MSG] Semi-colons as line endings can be removed safely
UnnecessaryGString	3	10	[SRC] path = " "; [MSG] The String '' can be wrapped in single quotes instead of double quotes

How it works...

The violations that are reported are easy to fix, and most of them are self-explanatory.

As you probably noticed, we specified only one rule set file (`rulesets/unnecessary.xml`) as an input parameter to CodeNarc. That specific rule-set groups rules for redundant code and can be omitted or simplified. Writing redundant, non-idiomatic code is exactly what Java programmers will face during their early days of Groovy programming since Groovy accepts Java syntax.

As of writing CodeNarc has 300+ rules split into 21 major group (rule set). Each group has its own name that can be referred to in the form of `rulesets/<name>.xml`. All those rule files are part of the CodeNarc library, and you don't need to download them separately. More information on the existing rules can be found at `http://codenarc.sourceforge.net/codenarc-rule-index.html`.

Let's go through a few violations to give the reader a taste of Groovy:

▸ The `UnnecessarySemicolon` violation indicates that we terminated our statement with a semicolon and that statement is the only statement on the line. In Groovy, you can omit the `;` (semicolon) in these cases.

▸ The `UnnecessaryPublicModifier` violation says that in Groovy, you can omit the public modifier for classes and methods since it's there by default.

▸ The `UnnecessaryGString` violation warns you of the fact that you are using heavy `GString` to define `String` constants. `GString`, which is defined by the `"` (double quote), is useful when you need to insert variable expression (for example, `${name}`) into the `String`. We discussed variable interpolation in the *Using Java classes from Groovy* recipe. In order to fix this warning, you just need to use a `'` (single quote), which will create a normal `String` without further processing.

▸ The `UnnecessaryGetter` warning simply notifies you about the fact that in Groovy, you can refer to a getter using a field notation; for example, `x.name` instead of `x.getName()`.

If we just fix all those violations, our Groovy code will look as follows:

```groovy
import java.io.*

class DirListing {

    static void main(String[] args) throws IOException {
        String path
        if (args.length > 0) {
            path = args[0]
        } else {
            path = '.'
        }
        File directory = new File(path)
        File[] files = directory.listFiles()
        def dirPath = directory.canonicalFile.absolutePath
        System.out.println("Directory of ${dirPath}")
        for (int i = 0; i < files.length; i++) {
            if (files[i].isFile()) {
                File file = files[i]
                System.out.println(file.name)
            }
        }
    }

}
```

There's more...

Similarly to spelling or grammar checkers, CodeNarc does not detect all possible styling/coding mistakes. So, there is still room for manual code reviews that may improve your code even more. CodeNarc can be an early indicator for the parts of the code base that need deeper analysis and refactoring.

By using some of the knowledge we've learned in this chapter, as well as the information that we will learn in *Chapter 3, Using Groovy Language Features* and *Chapter 4, Working with Files in Groovy*, we can rewrite the original code in a more idiomatic way:

```groovy
def path = args.size() > 0 ? args[0] : '.'
def directory = new File(path)
def dirPath = directory.canonicalFile.absolutePath
println "Directory of ${dirPath}"
directory.eachFile { File file ->
  if (file.isFile()) {
    println file.name
  }
}
```

The previous code will produce the same result as our original and modified scripts.

See also

- CodeNarc's home page: http://codenarc.sourceforge.net/
- List of CodeNarc rules:
  http://codenarc.sourceforge.net/codenarc-rule-index.html
- CodeNarc's Ant task:
  http://codenarc.sourceforge.net/codenarc-ant-task.html
- Maven's plugin for CodeNarc:
  http://mojo.codehaus.org/codenarc-maven-plugin/
- Gradle's plugin for CodeNarc: http://www.gradle.org/docs/current/userguide/codenarc_plugin.html

3
Using Groovy Language Features

In this chapter, we will cover:

- ▶ Searching strings with regular expressions
- ▶ Writing less verbose Java Beans with Groovy Beans
- ▶ Inheriting constructors in Groovy classes
- ▶ Adding the cloning functionality to Groovy Beans
- ▶ Defining code as data in Groovy
- ▶ Defining data structures as code in Groovy
- ▶ Implementing multiple inheritance in Groovy
- ▶ Adding a functionality to the existing Java/Groovy classes
- ▶ Defining type-checking rules for dynamic code
- ▶ Adding automatic logging to Groovy classes

Introduction

This chapter is all about what makes Groovy a very productive and fun programming language.

Groovy popularity builds on certain features of the language that are simply done right, such as closures or builders and are particularly appealing for Java programmers.

The recipes found in this chapter show the different facets of the Groovy language that allows to write a more terse, readable, and less ceremonious code in comparison to Java.

In this chapter, the reader will find—among others—recipes about the incredibly productive Groovy-enhanced collection framework, closures, builders, and the fancy annotations that makes code shorter and to the point.

For the most geeks among the readers, we have also added some recipes about advanced language features such as regular expressions, mixins, and extension methods.

Searching strings with regular expressions

The regular expression API became part of JDK since v1.4. `Pattern`, `Matcher`, and `String` classes contain functionality for regular expression matching and replacement that may not always be obvious, especially for complex use cases.

Luckily, Groovy adds some syntax sugar and functionality to support regular expressions in a more native fashion that will be demonstrated in this recipe.

Getting ready

We assume that you already have familiarity with regular expressions. This recipe will only focus on the features added by Groovy to the already rich infrastructure offered by Java to deal with regular expressions.

How to do it...

To begin with, Groovy offers a simple way to create `Pattern` objects using the `~/pattern/` notation:

```
Pattern pattern = ~/^.*?groovy.*$/
```

The previous pattern will match any text that contains the word `groovy` in it.

In fact, slashes at the beginning and the end of a pattern represent an alternative way to define strings in Groovy. The following code will have the same effect:

```
Pattern pattern = ~"^.*?groovy.*\$"
```

The important difference between using slashes and quotes is that, in the former case, you omit escaping backslashes and some other special characters, for example, `"\\s\\d"` can just be written as `/\s\d/`.

You can use `Pattern` objects in the same way you would do in Java, but there are other goodies that Groovy offers. There is the `==~` operator that you can use to directly match your input string against a regular expression:

```
def input = 'Probably the easiest way to get groovy' +
            ' is to try working with collections.'
```

```
if (input ==~ /^.*?groovy.*$/) {
   println 'Found groovy'
}
```

In fact, the `==~` operator is equivalent to calling the `matches` method of the `String` class.

Another operator that you can use in a similar way is `=~` (note the single `=` sign):

```
if (input =~ /^.*?groovy.*$/) {
   println 'Found groovy'
}
```

Actually, the `input =~ /^.*?groovy.*$/` expression just creates a `Matcher` object under the hood. According to Groovy Truth, a `Matcher` object is equivalent to true if it has at least one match. That's why if the `input` string contains the `groovy`, the body of the `if` statement will be executed. That's also why you can assign this expression to a variable:

```
def matcher = input =~ /^.*?groovy.*$/
```

You can use all the standard JDK methods of the `Matcher` class as well as the additional ones added by Groovy JDK.

It is also possible to refer to `matcher's` occurrences and internal regular expression groups using the array index notation:

```
def matcher =
   'The Groovy Cook Book contains Groovy recipes' =~ /(.oo.)\s/

println "<${matcher[0][0]}>"
println "<${matcher[0][1]}>"
println "<${matcher[1][0]}>"
println "<${matcher[1][1]}>"
```

The previous code will print:

```
<Cook >
```

```
<Cook>
```

```
<Book >
```

```
<Book>
```

To better explain the previous example, we can rewrite this code using closures and the `each` method:

```
matcher.each { match ->
   match.each { group ->
      println "<$group>"
   }
}
```

This will produce the same output as the first code snippet. As you can see, the first dimension of `matcher` is our regular expression occurrences, and the second dimension is a list of groups inside the regular expression. The group with index 0 corresponds to a fully matched string, and the next indexes refer to internal groups.

There's more...

A more advanced way to use regular expressions is to use them with replacement patterns. That's where Groovy provides very interesting extensions. For example, you can apply a closure to matching strings:

```
def input = 'The Groovy Cook Book contains Groovy recipes'
println input.replaceAll(/\b\w*?oo\w*?\b/) { match ->
  match.toUpperCase()
}
```

The previous code will print:

```
The GROOVY COOK BOOK contains GROOVY recipes
```

We just called the `toUpperCase` method for every string that matched the `/\b\w*?oo\w*?\b/` expression in the original input. As you can guess, the regular expression in the snippet matches any word containing a double small "o" letter.

See also

- ▶ http://groovy.codehaus.org/Regular+Expressions
- ▶ http://www.regular-expressions.info/groovy.html
- ▶ http://docs.oracle.com/javase/6/docs/api/java/util/regex/Pattern.html
- ▶ http://groovy.codehaus.org/groovy-jdk/java/util/regex/Matcher.html
- ▶ http://docs.codehaus.org/display/GROOVY/Groovy+Truth

Writing less verbose Java Beans with Groovy Beans

Java Beans are very popular among Java developers. A Java Bean is essentially data with little or no behavior (depending on the implementation). Formally, a Java Bean is a Java class that is serializable, has a public no-argument constructor, private fields, and getter and setter methods for accessing the fields. Often, **POJO** (**Plain Old Java Object**) and a Java Bean are used interchangeably.

In this recipe, we will show how Groovy can save you from a lot of typing by offering several features for bean class creation built into the language and API.

Getting ready

A typical Java Bean looks like the following code snippet:

```
public class Student implements Serializable {

    private Long id;
    private String name;
    private String lastName;

    // more attributes

    public Student() {
        // NO-ARGS CONSTRUCTOR
    }

    // more constructors

    public void setId(final Long id) {
        this.id = id;
    }

    public Long getId() {
        return id;
    }

    public void setName(final String name) {
        this.name = name;
    }

    public Long getName() {
        return name;
    }

}
```

This is quite a lot of code for a simple object without any business logic. The bean is instantiated as with any other Java class, and properties are set either through setters or one of the constructors.

```
Student student = new Student();
student.setId(23892);
student.setName("Charlie");
```

How to do it...

Let's check out how Groovy simplifies the writing of such objects with Groovy Beans.

1. Groovy makes the creation of a Java Bean way less verbose. Let's convert the above Java class `Student` into a Groovy Bean:

```
class Student {
    Long id
    String name
    String lastName
}
```

2. Yes. That's it. The bean only has to declare the properties. Both getters and setters and constructors are created at compilation time (through an AST transformation).

How it works...

Now let's check out how to interact with our newly created Groovy Bean:

```
def student = new Student()
student.setName('Charlie')
student.lastName = 'Parker'

assert student.name == 'Charlie'
assert student.lastName == 'Parker'

def student2 = new Student(
                id: 100,
                name: 'Jack',
                lastName: 'Shepard'
            )

assert student2.name == 'Jack'
assert student2.id == 100
assert student2.lastName == 'Shepard'
```

Mutators (or setters) can be invoked by either using the familiar Java syntax `student.setName("John")` or by a handy shortcut `student.name = 'John'` (note that the shortcut doesn't use the actual field, but the generated mutator). The Groovy Bean has also a constructor that uses a `Map` for quick initialization. The `Map` parameters can be set in any order and do not need to set all the properties of the bean:

```
def customer2 = new Customer(id:100)
def customer3 = new Customer(id:100, lastName:'Shepard')
```

A requirement that is often needed is that a bean has one or more fields that are read-only. To define a field as immutable, add the `final` keyword to it and add an explicit constructor:

```
class Student {
  final Long id
  String name
  String lastName
  Student(Long id) {
    this.id = id
  }
}


def c = new Student(100)
```

Unfortunately, the explicit constructor replaces the Groovy-generated one so that named parameters constructors are no longer available. Another way to make a Groovy Bean completely immutable is to use the `@Immutable` AST transformation:

```
import groovy.transform.Immutable

@Immutable
class Student {
  String name, lastName
  Long id
}

def student = new Student(
                  lastName: 'Hogan',
                  id: 200,
                  name: 'Mark'
                )
student.name = 'John'
```

Executing the previous code yields the following exception:

```
groovy.lang.ReadOnlyPropertyException:
Cannot set read-only property: name
for class: Customer
```

The `@Immutable` annotation makes the class final, all the fields become final, and also the default `equals`, `hashCode`, and `toString` methods are provided based on the property values. Furthermore, along with the standard Map constructor, a tuple-style constructor is provided which allows you to set properties in the same order as they are defined.

```
def c1 = new Student('Mark', 'Hogan', 100)
```

There's more...

We just encountered the `@Immutable` annotation that conveniently adds a number of default methods to the Groovy Bean. But what if we want to automatically generate these rather common methods and have the class mutable? Groovy has a number of AST transformations (based on annotations) that just do that.

The first annotation that we look at is `@ToString`, used to add a `toString` method to a bean.

```
import groovy.transform.ToString

@ToString
class Student {
   String name
}

def s = new Student(name:'John')
assert s.toString() == 'Student(John)'
```

To include the field names in the output of `toString` add the `includeNames=true` attribute.

```
@ToString(includeNames = true)
class Student {
   ...
}
```

To exclude some fields from the computation of the `String`, use the `excludes` attribute.

```
@ToString(includeNames = true, excludes = 'lastName,age')
class Student {
   ...
}
```

The `toString` method is conventionally accompanied by two other methods, `hashCode` and `equals`. The first method is important to the performance of hash tables and other data structures that store objects in groups (buckets) based on their computed hash values. The `equals` method checks if the object passed to it as an argument is equal to the object on which this method is invoked.

To implement both methods on a Groovy Bean, simply add the `@EqualsAndHashCode` annotation to it:

```
import groovy.transform.EqualsAndHashCode

@EqualsAndHashCode
class Student {
    String name
    String lastName
}

def s1 = new Student(
            name: 'John',
            lastName: 'Ross'
        )

def s2 = new Student(
            name: 'Rob',
            lastName: 'Bell'
        )

assert !s1.equals(s2)

def copyOfS2 = new Student(
                name: 'Rob',
                lastName: 'Bell'
            )

Set students = [:] as Set
students.add c1
students.add c2
students.add copyOfC2

assert users.size() == 2
```

Similar to the `@ToString` annotation, the `excludes` property can be used to exclude properties from the computation. If the bean extends from a second bean, the property `callSuper` set to true can be used to include the properties of the superclass.

The `@TupleConstructor` annotation deals with Groovy Bean constructors and creates constructors that do not require named parameters (Java-style constructors). For each property in the bean, a parameter with a default value is created in the constructor in the same order as the properties are declared. As the constructor is using default values, we don't have to set all the properties when we build the bean.

```groovy
import groovy.transform.TupleConstructor

@TupleConstructor
class Student {
    String name
    String lastName
    Long age
    List favouriteSubjects
}

def s1 = new Student('Mike','Wells',20,['math','phisics'])
def s2 = new Student('Joe','Garland',22)

assert s1.name == 'Mike'
assert !s2.favouriteSubjects
```

The `@TupleConstructor` annotation has also some additional attributes that can be set to modify the behavior of the generated constructor. The `force=true` property instructs the annotation to generate a constructor even if a different constructor is already defined. Naturally, the property will fail in the case of a constructor conflict.

If the class annotated with `@TupleConstructor` extends another class and we wish to include the properties or fields of the superclass, we can use the attributes `includeSuperProperties` and `includeSuperFields`. Finally, the `callSuper=true` attribute instructs the annotation to create a code in the constructor to call the super constructor of the superclass with the properties.

A Groovy Bean can be annotated with more than one of the previous annotations:

```groovy
@EqualsAndHashCode
@ToString
class Person {
    def name, address, pets
}
```

Furthermore, all the annotations we discussed in this recipe can be combined in a single annotation, `@Canonical`. The `@Canonical` annotation instructs the compiler to execute an AST transformation which adds positional constructors, `hashCode`, `equals`, and a pretty print `toString` to a class.

The @Canonical annotation has only two parameters, includes and excludes, to select which properties to include or exclude in the computation. Since @Canonical doesn't take any additional parameters and uses some sensible defaults, how can we customize certain aspects of the code generation? For example, if you want to use @Canonical but customize the @ToString behavior, then annotate the class with both @Canonical and @ToString. The @ToString definition and parameters take precedence over @Canonical.

```
@Canonical
@ToString(excludes='age')
class Person {
  String name
  int age
}
```

Inheriting constructors in Groovy classes

In Java, class inheritance doesn't support the inheriting of constructors for a number of good reasons (leaving the details of constructing an object to the programmer is generally a good idea). There are times when automatically inheriting the constructors of a class would be really useful and make the code less verbose. One of these cases is when inheriting from a class that extends Exception, where all the constructors are just calling super. Groovy has a convenient annotation for doing just that, @InheritConstructors.

In this recipe, we will explore how to use this annotation.

How to do it...

Let's demonstrate the features that the @InheritConstructors annotation gives:

1. Create an Exception class: one of the classes that are used to communicate that something is horribly wrong with the code or the data:

    ```
    class BusinessException extends Exception {

    }
    ```

2. Try to instantiate the class using one of the default constructors of the Exception class, for instance:

    ```
    def be = new BusinessException('missing resource')
    ```

    The code fails at runtime with the following error:

    Could not find matching constructor for:

    BusinessException(java.lang.String)

3. Add the `groovy.transform.InheritConstructors` annotation to the `BusinessException` and try to instantiate the class again with a `String` message. This time, the code will execute without errors:

```
@groovy.transform.InheritConstructors
class BusinessException extends Exception {


}
```

How it works...

The `@InheritConstructors` annotation removes the boilerplate of writing matching constructors for a superclass. By adding the `@InheritConstructors` annotation to the class, we can create the `BusinessException` by using any of the constructors exposed by `java.lang.Exception`:

```
import groovy.transform.InheritConstructors

@InheritConstructors
class BusinessException extends Exception { }

assert new BusinessException('hello').message == 'hello'

def b1 = new BusinessException('missing resource')
def b2 = new BusinessException('catastrophic failure', b1)
assert b2.cause.message == 'missing resource'
```

The annotation is smart enough to detect your existing constructors, if any, and avoid overriding them during the constructor generation phase.

Adding the cloning functionality to Groovy Beans

There are several strategies to clone an object in Java. To clone an object means the ability to create an object with the same state as the original object.

A widely used strategy to clone an object is for the class to be cloned to implement the `Cloneable` interface, and implement a method, `clone`, in which the cloning code is executed. Naturally, Groovy supports this semantic but makes it even easier to implement with the `@AutoClone` annotation, which will be demonstrated in this recipe.

How to do it...

The following steps will show the power of the `@AutoClone` annotation:

1. Let's define an object `Vehicle` and annotate the class with the `@AutoClone` annotation:

   ```
   import groovy.transform.AutoClone

   @AutoClone
     class Vehicle {
     String brand
     String type
     Long wheelsNumber
   }
   ```

2. In the same script where the `Vehicle` object is defined, add the following code:

   ```
   def v1 = new Vehicle()
   v1.brand = 'Ferrari'
   v1.type = 'Testarossa'
   v1.wheelsNumber = 4
   def v2 = v1.clone()

   assert v1 instanceof Cloneable
   assert v1.brand == v2.brand
   ```

   The script should execute without errors.

3. Let's add a second object to the mix:

   ```
   class Engine {
     int horseEngine
     Number liter
   }
   ```

4. Let's add the `engine` property to the `Vehicle` class:

   ```
   Engine engine
   ```

5. Modify the test code, so that the vehicle is created with an engine:

   ```
   def v1 = new Vehicle(
             brand: 'Ferrari',
             type: 'Testarossa',
             wheelsNumber: 4
           )
   def e1 = new Engine(
             horseEngine: 390,
   ```

```
                liter: 4.9
            )
    v1.engine = e1 // assign engine to car
    def v2 = v1.clone() // clone

    println 'Original vehicle engine liters: ' +  v1.engine.liter
    println 'Cloned vehicle engine liters: ' + v2.engine.liter
    v2.engine.liter = 8
    println 'Original vehicle engine liters: ' + v1.engine.liter
```

6.   The result of the modified script yields:

Original vehicle engine liters: 4.9

Cloned vehicle engine liters: 4.9

Original vehicle engine liters: 8

How it works...

The snippet in step 2 shows how easy is to clone an object without having to implement any interface. The default cloning strategy implemented by the annotation will call `super.clone` before calling `clone` on each `Cloneable` property of the class. If a field or property is not cloneable, it is simply copied in a bitwise fashion. If some properties don't support cloning, a `CloneNotSupportedException` is thrown.

The decompiled `Vehicle` class has the following aspect (the code is cleaned up a bit for the sake of readability, as the Groovy-generated bytecode uses reflection heavily):

```
public class Vehicle implements Cloneable, GroovyObject {

    public Object clone() throws CloneNotSupportedException {
        Object result = super.clone()
        if (brand instanceof Cloneable) {
            result.brand = brand.clone()
        }
        if (type instanceof Cloneable) {
            result.type = type.clone()
        }
        if (wheelsNumber instanceof Cloneable) {
            result.wheelsNumber = wheelsNumber.clone()
        }
        return result
    }

}
```

In step 6, we can observe that the cloning process didn't quite work as expected. An attribute of the cloned object is modified, and the same attribute on the original object gets modified as well. Not surprisingly, the reason for this behavior is that the `Engine` class is not annotated with the `@AutoClone` annotation; therefore, the cloning process only clones the reference to the object, not the actual object. Simply annotate the `Engine` object with `@AutoClone` to have the actual object cloned.

There's more...

The `@AutoClone` annotation supports some additional cloning styles. The first cloning style is based on the `Copy Constructor` pattern:

```
import groovy.transform.*

@AutoClone(style=AutoCloneStyle.COPY_CONSTRUCTOR)
class Vehicle {
    ...
}
```

The `clone` method implementation is moved into the body of a constructor that takes a parameter of the same type as the class. Then, calls to `clone` simply return the result of calling this constructor. Enabling the COPY_CONSTRUCTOR pattern produces Java code similar to the following code snippet:

```
public class Vehicle implements Cloneable {

    private String brand;
    private String type;
    private Long wheelsNumber;

    protected Vehicle(Vehicle other) {
        brand = other.brand;
        type = other.type;
        wheelsNumber = other.wheelsNumber;
    }

    public Object clone() throws CloneNotSupportedException {
        return new Vehicle(this);
    }

}
```

If a class already implements `Serializable`, the `@AutoClone` annotation can be configured to use the `Serialization` style. This feature performs a deep copy automatically, attempting to copy the entire tree of objects including array and list elements. The `AutoCloneStyle.SERIALIZATION` style has some limitations; it is generally slower and it doesn't support fields marked with `final`.

Defining code as data in Groovy

One of the things that attracted the Java crowd to Groovy has been the presence of closures in the language since its creation in 2003. Closures are a very powerful feature of Groovy and one of the most widely used. It is important to understand them well to take full advantage of the language. In this recipe, we will try to demonstrate the beauty that closures add to the language.

Getting ready

At its core, a closure is an anonymous block of code, such as:

```
{ -> }
```

The previous snippet is actually a closure without body. It is, in fact, an object of type `groovy.lang.Closure`. As with every other object, a closure can be passed to other methods or even to other closures. However, a closure is also a method—a method with no associated class; therefore, it may have arguments and can return a value (yes, it can also return a closure). A closure always returns the value of the last statement in the body; the `return` keyword is not needed. The body of a closure is not executed until it gets called.

This is what a closure definition with an argument looks like:

```
def doubling = { arg1 -> println arg1 * 2 }
```

This closure just prints the doubled value of the argument. The closure is assigned to the variable `doubling`. The argument is not typed, and it gets used in the body of the closure, the statement after the `->` symbol. The closure object can be passed to other methods as a parameter. For example, if we try to print it, we will actually call the `toString` method of the `Closure` class:

```
println doubling
```

The previous line of code will yield something like the following:

closures$_run_closure1@76bb5e95

We can also pass closures to many methods (for example, `each`, `collect`, `find`, and so on) that Groovy makes available on collections and arrays:

```
[1,2,3,4].each(doubling)
```

The preceding code snippet will apply the passed closure to every element in the collection:

2

4

6

8

Now that we have a general idea about closures, we can look at how to use them to write more elegant and concise code. Closures normally contain less code, have little or no repetition, and can be re-used easily . This is because a closure can also be defined code as data.

How to do it...

A common way to display the conciseness of Groovy closures is to show some looping and iteration methods from the Groovy Collection API:

```
[1,2,3].each { println it }
```

The previous snippet is a great example of the power of closures. The code prints all the elements of a list by iterating on each element of the array, and calls the `println` command on each element. The astute reader is probably wondering what the `it` keyword is for; `it` is simply a reference to the current element. The snippet can be also expressed in a slightly more verbose way if we choose not to use `it`:

```
[1,2,3].each { element -> println element }
```

The `it` keyword is an implicit variable that works on closures, accepting a single argument. A very welcome syntactic sugar!

The `each` is a method from the enhanced `java.lang.Object` of the Groovy JDK and takes a closure a parameter. The closure contains the code that does actual stuff on each member of the list.

The Java equivalent of the former snippet would look as follows:

```
List<Integer> list = Arrays.asList(1,2,3);
for (Integer it :list) {
  System.out.println(it);
}
```

Another example of how a closure can help with refactoring the code is that it deals with resources that have to be disposed of once out of scope.

Let's create a class, `ExpensiveResource`, and assume that this resource has to be explicitly opened and closed once it has been used (very much like a JDBC connection):

```
class ExpensiveResource {
    def open() { println 'opened!' }
    def writeData(data) { println "data written! $data" }
    def close(){ println 'closed!'}
}
```

To use this class, we would write something like the following:

```
def e = new ExpensiveResource()
try {
  e.open()
  println e.data
} finally {
  e.close()
}
```

The `open` and `close` methods must be called every time we deal with the resource. Let's see how a closure simplifies and makes the code more polished:

```
def safeResource(Closure closure) {
    def resource = new ExpensiveResource()
    try {
      resource.open()
      closure(resource)
    } finally {
      resource?.close()
    }
}


safeResource { it -> it.writeData('hello world!') }
```

The method `safeResource` accepts a closure and encapsulates the resource management code, leaving the calling code to show its intent much more clearly.

Groovy provides a similar approach when dealing with file access by automatically handling resource management code such as opening, closing, and handling exceptions behind the scenes. For instance, the method `file.eachLineMatch(pattern) { ... }` opens a file, iterates over each line trying to find the lines that match the specified pattern, and then invokes some code passed in form of a closure for the matching line(s), if any, before eventually closing the file.

There's more...

Once you get familiar with Groovy closures, it will not take long before you'll encounter the need to curry your closures. The term *currying* comes from the functional programming domain, and it defines a way to apply default values to a closure by defining a complete new closure. Here is an example:

```
def multiply = { x, y -> x * y }
multiply 3, 5


Result: 15


def closureByFour = multiply.curry(4)
```

The previous code snippets shows a standard closure that multiplies two numbers and returns the result (remember, no `return` is needed). The second closure calls the `curry` method on the first closure and specifies the value 4. The second closure, `closureByFour`, can then be invoked with one argument only, and that argument will be multiplied by 4, the value passed to the `curry` method. The limitation of the `curry` method is that arguments are bound from left to right in the argument list. In other words, in two arguments-closures, only the left argument can be used with the `curry` function.

The following example shows an interesting use case for currying. Let's define a closure that filters the elements of a list. The `filter` argument is a closure:

```
def filterList = { filter, list -> list.findAll(filter) }
```

Now let's define a couple of closures that can be used as filters:

```
def even = { it % 2 == 0 }
def odd = { !even(it) }
```

Finally, we create two new closures by applying the `curry` function to the original closure, and passing one of the closure filters:

```
def evenFilterList = filterList.curry(even)
def oddFilterList = filterList.curry(odd)
```

The new closures can now be invoked autonomously to filter out odd and even numbers:

```
assert [0,2,4,6,8] == evenFilterList(0..8)
assert [1,3,5,7] == oddFilterList(0..8)
```

Defining data structures as code in Groovy

An important and powerful part of Groovy is its implementation of the **Builder** pattern. This pattern was made famous by the seminal work *Design Patterns: Elements of Reusable Object-Oriented Software*; *Erich Gamma, Richard Helm, Ralph Johnson*, and *John Vlissides*.

With builders, data can be defined in a semi-declarative way. Builders are appropriate for the generation of XML, definition of UI components, and anything that is involved with simplifying the construction of object graphs. Consider:

```
Teacher t = new Teacher('Steve')
Student s1 = new Student('John')
Student s2 = new Student('Richard')
t.addStudent(s1)
t.addStudent(s2)
```

There are a few issues with the previous code; verbosity and the lack of a hierarchical relationship between objects. This is what we can do with a Builder in Groovy:

```
teacher ('Jones') {
  student ('Bob')
  student ('Sue')
}
```

Out of the box, Groovy includes a suite of builders for most of the common construction tasks that we might encounter:

- ▶ `MarkupBuilder` for building an XML-style tagged output (see the *Constructing XML content* recipe in *Chapter 5, Working with XML in Groovy*)

- ▶ `DOMBuilder` for constructing a WC3 DOM tree in memory from the GroovyMarkup-like syntax (`http://groovy.codehaus.org/GroovyMarkup`)

- ▶ `JsonBuilder` for building data structures using the JSON format (see the *Constructing JSON messages with JsonBuilder* recipe in *Chapter 6, Working with JSON in Groovy*)

- ▶ `SwingBuilder` to build Swing-based UIs

- ▶ `ObjectGraphBuilder` to construct a graph of objects that follow the Java Beans rules

Builders are the fundamental blocks for creating **DSLs** (**Domain Specific Languages**) in Groovy. *Martin Fowler*, in his book *Domain-Specific Languages*, defines a DSL as *a computer programming language of limited expressiveness focused on a particular domain*. The limits of a DSL are not bound to its usefulness, but rather to its scope within the domain. A typical example of this contraposition is SQL: the language has enough expressiveness to operate on a database, but it lacks the eloquence to write an operating system.

A DSL is a small scale, specifically-focused language, rather than a general purpose language like Java. *Chapter 9, Metaprogramming and DSLs in Groovy*, contains two recipes that show how you to create DSLs in great detail.

In this recipe, we are going to explore how builders can simplify the creation of an object hierarchy for testing purposes.

Getting ready

Generating test data is a tedious task, especially when we need realistic data that can be used to simulate different situations in our code. Normally, it all starts from a domain model that has to be manually built and fed to some function:

```
Book book1 = new Book()
book.id = 200
book.title = 'Twenty Thousand Leagues Under the Sea'
book.author = 'Jules Verne'
Book book2 = new Book()
book.id = 201

. . .
```

...you get the idea. Test cases quickly become an endless list of hard-to-read object graph definitions and before you know it, your tests are very hard to maintain.

In this recipe, we want to create a simple DSL mainly based on Builders to draw our domain model without the Java Bean ceremony and, as a bonus, be able to generate random data using different strategies.

This is our domain model:

```
import groovy.transform.*

@Canonical
class ShoppingCart {
    List<Book> items = []
    User user
    Address shippingData
}

@Canonical
class Book {
    Long id
    String title
    BigDecimal price
}
```

```
@Canonical
class User {
    Long id
    String name
    Address address }

@Canonical
class Address {
    String street
    String city
    String country
}
```

It's a simplistic domain model for a books e-commerce site. Our goal is to build a DSL that uses the metaprogramming features of Groovy to express the object graph in a concise way.

```
def shoppingCart = new ECommerceTestDataBuilder().build {
    items(2) {
        title RANDOM_TITLE
        id RANDOM_ID, 100, 200000
        price 100
    }
    user {
        id RANDOM_ID, 1,500
        firstName RANDOM_STRING
        lastName RANDOM_STRING
        address RANDOM_US_ADDRESS
    }
}
```

The preceding snippet generates a `ShoppingCart` object containing two books. Each book has a random title fetched from the amazing Gutenberg project (http://www.gutenberg.org/), a random unique ID with values ranging from 100 to 200000, and a fixed price, set to 100.

How to do it...

First of all, let's create a new Groovy file named `randomTestData.groovy` and paste the domain model classes defined in the previous paragraph.

1. In the same file, following the domain classes, add the definition for the new builder:

   ```
   class ECommerceTestDataBuilder {

   }
   ```

2. Add the main builder method, `build`, to the body of the class:

```
ShoppingCart shoppingCart
def books = []

ShoppingCart build(closure) {
   shoppingCart = new ShoppingCart()
   closure.delegate = this
   closure()

   shoppingCart.items = books
   shoppingCart
}
```

3. The next method to add is the one for defining the number of books to add to the shopping cart:

```
void items (int quantity, closure) {
   closure.delegate = this
   quantity.times {
      books << new Book()
      closure()
   }
}
```

4. Add the `methodMissing` method, which is a key part of the DSL architecture, as explained in the next section:

```
def methodMissing(String name, args) {
   Book book = books.last()
   if (book.hasProperty(name)) {
      def dataStrategy = isDataStrategy(args)
      if (dataStrategy) {
         book.@"$name" = dataStrategy.execute()
      } else {
         book.@"$name" = args[0]
      }
   } else {
      throw new MissingMethodException(
            name,
            ECommerceTestDataBuilder,
            args)
   }
}
```

5. The last method to add for the `ECommerceTestDataBuilder` class is required for adding random data generation strategies to our DSL:

```groovy
def isDataStrategy(strategyData) {
  def strategyClass = null
  try {
    if (strategyData.length == 1) {
      strategyClass = strategyData[0].newInstance()
    } else {
      strategyClass = strategyData[0].
                      newInstance(*strategyData[1,-1])
    }
    if (!(strategyClass instanceof
              DataPopulationStrategy)) {
      strategyClass = null
    }
  } catch (Exception e) {
  }
  strategyClass
}
```

6. The builder code is complete. Now let's add a couple of strategy classes to the script and the main strategy interface:

```groovy
interface DataPopulationStrategy {
  def execute()
}

class RANDOM_TITLE implements DataPopulationStrategy {

  def titleCache = []

  def ignoredTitleWords = ['Page', 'Sort', 'Next']

  void getRandomBookTitles() {
    def slurper = new XmlSlurper()
    slurper.setFeature(
      'http://apache.org/xml/features/' +
      'nonvalidating/load-external-dtd',
      false)
    def dataUrl = 'http://m.gutenberg.org' +
                  '/ebooks/search.mobile'
    def orderBy = '/?sort_order=random'
    def htmlParser = slurper.parse("${dataUrl}${orderBy}")
    htmlParser.'**'.findAll{ it.@class == 'title'}.each {
      if (it.text().tokenize().disjoint(ignoredTitleWords)) {
```

```
          titleCache << it.text()
        }
      }
    }

  def execute() {
    if (titleCache.size==0) {
      randomBookTitles
    }
    titleCache.pop()
  }

}

class RANDOM_ID implements DataPopulationStrategy {

  Long minVal
  Long maxVal

  RANDOM_ID (min, max) {
    minVal = min
    maxVal = max
  }

  def execute() {
    double rnd = new Random().nextDouble()
    minVal + (long) (rnd * (maxVal - minVal))
  }

}
```

7. It is time to put our code to the test:

```
def shoppingCart = new ECommerceTestDataBuilder().build {
  items(5) {
    title RANDOM_TITLE
    id RANDOM_ID, 100, 200000
    price 100
  }
}

assert shoppingCart.items.size == 5
shoppingCart.items.each {
  assert it.price == 100
  assert it.id > 100 && it.id < 200000
}
```

How it works...

The domain model's classes are standard Groovy Beans annotated with the `@Canonical` annotation. The annotation is discussed in detail in the *Writing less verbose Java Beans with Groovy Beans* recipe. In short, it adds an implementation of `equals`, `hashCode`, and `toString`, along with a tuple constructors, to a bean.

```
@Canonical
class Book {
    Long id
    String title
    BigDecimal price
}
Book b = new Book(2001, 'Pinocchio', 22.3)
println b.toString()
```

The preceding code snippet will print:

Book(2001, Pinocchio, 22.3)

The method `build` that was displayed at step 2 is the builder's entry method:

```
def shoppingCart = new ECommerceTestDataBuilder().build {
    ...
}
```

The `build` method takes a closure as only argument. The closure is where most of the magic happens. Let's dig into the closure code:

```
items(5) {
    title RANDOM_TITLE
    id RANDOM_ID, 100, 200000
    price 100
}
```

The `items` method that was defined at step 3 is invoked with two arguments: the number of books to create, and another closure where the random data strategies are defined. In Groovy, if the last argument of a method is a closure, it does not need to be inside the parentheses of the invoked method:

```
def doSomething(int i, Closure c) {
    c(i)
}
something(i) {
    // closure code
}
```

You may have noticed that both methods, `build` and `item`, have a call to the `delegate` method of the closure just before the closure is invoked:

```
closure.delegate = this
closure()
```

The `delegate` method allows you to change the scope of the closure so that the methods invoked from within the closure are delegated directly to the builder class.

Inside the `items` block, we define the (random) values that we want to be assigned to each property of the `Book` object. The properties are only defined in the `Book` object but are not visible by the Builder. So how is the Builder able to resolve a call to the `title` or `price` property of `Book` and assign a value? Every method invoked from inside the `items` block, in fact, does not exist.

Thanks to Groovy's metaprogramming capabilities, we can intercept method calls and create methods on the fly. In particular, the most common technique for intercepting calls in Groovy is to implement the `methodMissing` method on a Groovy class. This method can be considered as a net for undefined functions in a class. Every time a call is executed against a missing method, the runtime routes the call to the `methodMissing` routine, just before throwing a `MissingMethodException` exception. This offers a chance to define an implementation for these ghost methods.

Let's take a closer look:

```
title RANDOM_TITLE
```

The method `title` does not exist in the Builder code. When an invocation to this method is executed from within the closure, the dispatcher, before giving up and throwing a `MissingMethodException`, tries to see if `methodMissing` can be used to resolve the method.

 Groovy allows you to call a method and omit the parentheses if there is at least one parameter and there is no ambiguity. This is the case for the `title` method, which can be written as `title(RANDOM_TITLE)`, but obviously the DSL is much more readable without parentheses.

Inside the Builder's `methodMissing` method, the code does the following:

1. Fetches the last book created by the `items` method.
2. Checks that the book has a property named as the missing method, using the `hasProperty` method on the object itself.
3. If the missing method is named as one of the book's properties, the code either directly assigns the parameter passed after the missing method to the appropriate property of `Book`, or tries to resolve a random strategy through the `isDataStrategy` method (step 7).

The object property is accessed through the @ operator, which accesses the field directly bypassing the mutators (getters and setters):

```
book.@"$name" = (dataStrategy) ? dataStrategy.execute() : args[0]
```

In the previous code snippet, the field is populated with the value defined in the DSL (for example, `price 100`, or by the result of the random data strategy call). The random data strategy classes must implement the `DataPopulationStrategy` (step 8). The interface exposes only one `execute` method. If a strategy requires more arguments, these have to be passed through the constructor (see `RANDOM_ID` strategy, where the minimum and maximum values are set via the class' constructor). The method `isDataStrategy` is invoked for each field specified in the `items` block. The class accesses the argument passed after the field specification:

```
title RANDOM_TITLE
```

It tries to instantiate the class as a `DataPopulationStrategy` instance. The argument passed to the property must match the class name of the strategy class in order for the strategy resolution to work.

The `isDataStrategy` method employs a small trick to instantiate the random data strategy class in case the DSL specifies additional arguments, such as:

```
id RANDOM_ID, 1,500
```

In the previous snippet, the `id` field will be populated by the result of the `RANDOM_ID` strategy that will generate a random number between `1` and `500`. If the strategy has no arguments, the class is instantiated with `newInstance`:

```
strategyClass = strategyData[0].newInstance()
```

The `strategyData` variable corresponds to the `args` variable of the `methodMissing` function, which is the caller. `args` is a list of arguments containing whatever values are passed from the DSL. For instance, `id RANDOM_ID, 1, 500` corresponds to calling a method with the following signature:

```
def id(Object... args) { }
```

This is why we call `newInstance` on the first element of the `strategyData` variable. If the `args` list contains more than one argument, we assume that the strategy class requires the additional values, so the strategy class is instantiated in this fashion:

```
strategyClass = strategyData[0].newInstance(*strategyData[1,-1])
```

In this one-liner, we take advantage of several features of Groovy. The first one is the possibility of calling `newInstance` with an array of objects. Java makes creating classes dynamically with a constructor much more cumbersome. The second feature is the spread operator. The spread operator (`*`) is used to tear a `List` apart into single elements.

This can be used to call a method that has more than one argument and automatically assigns each element of the list to the values for the parameters. We know that strategyData contains the list of arguments specified in the DSL, and that the first item of the list should be ignored because it is the actual strategy class to instantiate. The remaining elements of the list must be used as arguments for the class' constructor. The spread does exactly that in conjunction with Groovy ranges, strategyData[1,-1].

The two strategies defined in the code (step 5) are outside the scope of this recipe. The first strategy simply fetches random book titles from the Internet. The second strategy generates random Long values between a specified range. In real life, random data would be probably pulled from a database or an existing source.

You may have also noticed that this recipe doesn't fully implement the DSL specified at the beginning. The code doesn't support creating users and addresses. We will leave this for the reader as an exercise to further understand builders and DSLs in Groovy.

See also

- ▶ *Defining code as data in Groovy*
- ▶ *Writing less verbose Java Beans with Groovy Beans*
- ▶ *Chapter 9, Metaprogramming and DSLs in Groovy*
- ▶ http://groovy.codehaus.org/Builders

Implementing multiple inheritance in Groovy

Java classes are only allowed to inherit from a single parent class. Multiple inheritance is only available for interfaces that do not carry any state or implementation details. This is not a drawback, but rather a design choice that allows you to avoid several problems. An example of this is the **diamond problem** that arises in languages which do employ multiple inheritance. Basically, there is an ambiguity (which method implementation to call) if classes B and C inherit from class A and class D inherits from both B and C. The diamond name comes from the shape of the class diagram formed by the A, B, C, and D.

Groovy still does not allow multiple class inheritance, but offers another approaches for injecting logic that is spread over multiple classes into a single entity.

This recipe will demonstrate a simple use case for the @Mixin and @Delegate annotations that can help you simulate multiple inheritance.

Using Groovy Language Features

Getting ready

We'll start with a simple project that models a publishing house. We are going to build the code with the Gradle build tool that we touched in the *Integrating Groovy into the build process using Gradle* recipe in *Chapter 2, Using Groovy Ecosystem*. The following directory structure is what we are aiming for:

```
src/main/groovy/org/groovy/cookbook
    Publication.groovy
    OnlinePublication.groovy
    PeriodicPublication.groovy
    PrintedPublication.groovy
src/test/groovy/org/groovy/cookbook
    PublicationTest.groovy
build.gradle
```

The `Publication` class is the base class for describing the properties and behavior of all the published items our publishing agency is dealing with:

```
package org.groovy.cookbook

abstract class Publication {
  String id
  String title
  Date issueDate
}
```

Then we have to define the specializations of our publications. For example, the `PrintedPublication` class exists to denote items printed on paper:

```
package org.groovy.cookbook

class PrintedPublication {
  int pageCount
}
```

On the other hand, the `OnlinePublication` class may represent items published electronically:

```
package org.groovy.cookbook

class OnlinePublication {
  URL url
}
```

The `PeriodicPublication` class refers to items issued daily, weekly, monthly, or repeatedly after any other period:

```
package org.groovy.cookbook

class PeriodicPublication {
  Duration issuePeriod
}
```

As you can guess, these three classes can be combined in a number of ways to properly satisfy the publishing business needs. For instance, our publishing house may have an electronic, monthly magazine, or a printed and online publication. Implementing all of these combinations with a single inheritance hierarchy is clearly impossible. In the course of the next section of this recipe, we'll show how Groovy deals with this situation.

We also have to define an empty unit test, which we are going to fill in soon:

```
package org.groovy.cookbook

import org.junit.Test
import groovy.time.DatumDependentDuration

class PublicationTest {

  @Test
  def testPublications() { ... }

}
```

Before we can start, `build.gradle` also goes here, which is the simplest possible in this situation:

```
apply plugin: 'groovy'

repositories {
  mavenCentral()
}

dependencies {
  compile 'org.codehaus.groovy:groovy-all:2.1.6'
  testCompile 'junit:junit:4.11'
}
```

How to do it...

At this stage, we are ready to introduce multiple inheritance in our code base:

1. Let's create the `Newspaper` class (in the `src/main/groovy/org/groovy/cookbook/Newspaper.groovy` file), which obviously represents the printed periodic publication:

    ```
    package org.groovy.cookbook

    @Mixin([PeriodicPublication,
            PrintedPublication])
    class Newspaper extends Publication {

    }
    ```

2. The next step is to create a class representing the online magazine, `OnlineMagazine.groovy`:

    ```
    package org.groovy.cookbook

    @Mixin([OnlinePublication,
            PeriodicPublication])
    class OnlineMagazine extends Publication {

    }
    ```

3. And finally, we create a class that shares all the publication features we have: `MultimediaMagazine.groovy`:

    ```
    package org.groovy.cookbook

    @Mixin([PeriodicPublication,
            PrintedPublication,
            OnlinePublication])
    class MultimediaMagazine extends Publication {

    }
    ```

4. Let's extend the unit test to verify that our hierarchy actually works:

    ```
    @Test
    def testPublications() {

        def monthly = new DatumDependentDuration(0, 1, 0, 0, 0, 0, 0)
        def daily = new DatumDependentDuration(0, 0, 1, 0, 0, 0, 0)

        def groovyMag = new OnlineMagazine(
    ```

```
                      id: 'GRMAG',
                      title: 'GroovyMag'
                  ).with {
                  url = new URL('http://grailsmag.com/')
                  issuePeriod = monthly
                  it
              }

      def time = new MultimediaMagazine(
                  id: 'TIME',
                  title: 'Time'
              ).with {
              pageCount = 60
              url = new URL('http://www.time.com')
              issuePeriod = monthly
              it
          }

      def pravda = new Newspaper(
                  id: 'PRVD',
                  title: 'Pravda'
              ).with {
              pageCount = 8
              issuePeriod = daily
              it
          }

  }
```

5. To verify that our code compiles and our test works, we just ran the standard `Gradle` command:

   ```
   gradle clean build
   ```

6. The result should be a normal successful build output:

   ```
   ...

   BUILD SUCCESSFUL

   ...
   ```

How it works...

The @Mixin annotation that we placed in our source code informs Groovy to perform a transformation of the target class and add behavior (methods) of mixed-in classes into that. The annotation accepts a single class name or an array of class names. Mixing in behavior is done exclusively at runtime, since (as we already noted) under the hood, JVM does not allow multiple parent classes. This is also the reason that the instanceof operator will not work for mixed-in classes. For example, you can't check that groovyMag is an instance of the PeriodicPulication class. But you can still use the groovyMag and other variables to call the features of the mixed-in classes at runtime.

In the test class, we used the Groovy Bean constructor syntax (we discussed Groovy Beans in more details in the *Writing less verbose Java Beans with Groovy Beans* recipe) to refer to the fields that are available in the base class, but the fields we mixed-in from different sources can only be accessed in a dynamic way. In fact, they are not just fields but also a pair of getter and setter automatically defined by Groovy for all the bean classes. So, we really mix the behavior (that is, methods) in, not the state of the class. That's also the reason we used another Groovy feature here—the with method. This method is defined for all objects in Groovy; it takes a closure (see the *Defining code as data in Groovy* recipe) as a parameter, and the object itself is passed to the closure's context. That's why you can easily refer to an object's methods and properties in a short form. In fact, you could have used the with method to define all the properties of our object:

```
def groovyMag = new OnlineMagazine().with {
        id = 'GRMAG'
        title = 'GroovyMag'
        url = new URL('http://grailsmag.com/')
        issuePeriod = monthly
        it
    }
```

But we used different syntax to show the distinction between base class properties and mixed-in properties.

There's more...

Another way to add behavior from other classes is to use Groovy's @Delegate annotation. To give an example, we can define a new Book class:

```
package org.groovy.cookbook

class Book extends Publication {

  @Delegate
  PrintedPublication printedFeatures = new PrintedPublication()

}
```

The @Delegate transformation makes all the methods available on the PrintedPublication class also accessible from instances of the Book class. It delegates all those method calls to the specific PrintedPublication's instance created upon book object construction.

```
def groovy2cookbook = new Book(
                id: 'GR2CBOOK',
                title: 'Groovy 2 Cookbook',
                pageCount: 384
            )
```

This is similar in the result it achieves compared to the @Mixin annotation, but the implementation is quite different. The @Delegate annotation is a compile-time transformation and influences the way Groovy constructs the bytecode for this class. This is also the reason that the map-based constructor syntax worked for the pageCount property. If we'd used the @Mixin annotation for the Book class, it would not have worked due to the runtime nature of the @Mixin transformation.

It's hard to vote for any of these approaches and decide which one would be better to handle your multiple inheritance needs. The @Mixin definition is less verbose and automatically creates instances of all mixed-in classes, but on the other hand, managing the state of those instances may not be so obvious. The @Delegate transformation has a more verbose definition due to an additional variable declaration, but it also gives your target class direct access and control over the way your mixed-in state is created.

In general, mixins and delegates can also be handy for splitting long classes into several code units.

See also

▶ http://groovy.codehaus.org/Category+and+Mixin+transformations
▶ http://groovy.codehaus.org/Delegate+transformation

Adding a functionality to the existing Java/Groovy classes

How many times have you dreamed of adding a new method to a final class or to a class that you don't even have sources for? With Groovy, you are given the ability to do so. That's all possible thanks to Groovy's extension methods. The original class stays untouched and Groovy takes care of catching extended method calls.

In fact, we have already seen examples of this feature in some of the recipes in *Chapter 2, Using Groovy Ecosystem*, for example, the *Using Java classes from Groovy* and *Embedding Groovy into Java* recipes, and we'll see more in coming recipes of this book. Groovy extends many of the standard JDK classes (for example, `java.io.File`, `java.lang.String`, `java.util.Collection`, and so on). It's one of the many cool Groovy features that makes working with some old Java APIs a pleasant business.

In this recipe, we are going to cover the mechanism of creating an extension module to an existing Java class, and then using that class inside Groovy with added functionality.

Getting ready

For our demonstration, we are going to extend the `java.util.Date` class with a new method. To build the extension, we will use the Gradle build tool that we already encountered in the *Integrating Groovy into the build process using Gradle* recipe in *Chapter 2, Using Groovy Ecosystem*. Let's assume we have the following simple project structure:

- `src/main/groovy/org/groovy/cookbook`
- `src/main/resources/META-INF/services`
- `build.gradle`

The `build.gradle` looks as simple as is:

```
apply plugin: 'groovy'

dependencies {
  compile localGroovy()
}
```

How to do it...

Let's define the extension module contents and verify that it works with a sample script:

1. Inside the `src/main/groovy/org/groovy/cookbook` directory, we need to create the `DateExtentions.groovy` file with the following content:

    ```
    package org.groovy.cookbook

    import static java.util.Calendar.*
    import java.text.DateFormatSymbols

    class DateExtensions {

      static String getMonthName(Date date) {
        def dfs = new DateFormatSymbols()
    ```

```
            dfs.months[date[MONTH]]
         }

    }
```

2. In order for the extension to become active when it is added to the classpath, we
   need to create a special descriptor file called `org.codehaus.groovy.runtime.`
   `ExtensionModule` and place it under the `src/main/resources/META-INF/`
   `services` directory:

```
moduleName=groovy-extension
moduleVersion=1.0
extensionClasses=org.groovy.cookbook.DateExtensions
staticExtensionClasses=
```

3. Now you are ready to compile the extension JAR with the following standard command:

```
gradle clean build
```

4. At this point, we can create a test script to verify that our extension actually works
   and that the `Date` class actually has the `getMonthName` method. Define a `date.`
   `groovy` file in the project's root directory with the following content:

```
def now = new Date()
println now.monthName
```

5. Run the script from the same directory with the `groovy` command:

```
groovy -cp ./build/libs/* date.groovy
```

6. Depending on your locale and date, the script should print the name of the
   current month:

```
July
```

How it works...

Groovy dynamically loads all extension modules upon startup and makes the methods
defined by those available on instances of the target classes. In our case, it's the same
old `Date` class.

If we try to execute the `date.groovy` script without the classpath containing the extension
module, we'll get an ugly error:

```
Caught: groovy.lang.MissingPropertyException:
   No such property: monthName for class: java.util.Date
groovy.lang.MissingPropertyException:
   No such property: monthName for class: java.util.Date
       at date.run(date.groovy:2)
```

There's more...

Extension methods existed in Groovy before v2.0. Most of the magical GDK functionality (for example, additional methods available on the `java.lang.String` or `java.io.File` classes) is implemented in that way. But since Groovy 2.0, creating and packaging your own extension modules became possible.

Extension modules also work if you use the `@Grab` annotations to append classpath dependencies to your scripts (see the *Simplifying dependency management with Grape* recipe in *Chapter 2, Using Groovy Ecosystem*).

You can also append static methods to the classes. The mechanism works in the exactly same way with the only small exception that you need to use `staticExtensionClasses` in the module descriptor to refer to the class implementing those extensions. Also, if your module defines both static and non-static extension points, then those should be located in different classes.

That's not the only way to extend existing classes. Another approach is to use metaclass facilities at runtime. This technique is discussed in more detail in *Chapter 9, Metaprogramming and DSLs in Groovy*.

See also

▶ Groovy's User Guide pages about extension modules: `http://docs.codehaus.org/display/GROOVY/Creating+an+extension+module`

Defining type-checking rules for dynamic code

The defining characteristic of Groovy is probably the dynamic nature of the language. Dynamic languages possess the capacity to extend a program at runtime, including changing types, behaviors, and object structures. With these languages, the things that static languages do at compile time can be done at runtime; we can even execute program statements that are created on the fly at runtime. Another trait of Groovy, typical of other dynamic languages such as Ruby or Python, is dynamic typing. With dynamic typing, the language automatically tests properties when expressions are being (dynamically) evaluated (that is, at runtime).

In this recipe, we will present how Groovy can be instructed to apply static typing checks to code elements to warn you about potential violations at compiletime; that is, before code is executed.

Getting ready

Let's look at some script as follows:

```
def name = 'john'
printn naame
```

The Groovy compiler `groovyc` is perfectly happy to compile the previous code. Can you spot the error?

But, if we try to execute the code we get, not surprisingly, the following exception:

```
Caught: groovy.lang.MissingPropertyException:
  No such property: naame
  for class: DynamicTypingExample
```

Dynamic typing is a very controversial topic. Proponents of static typing argue that the benefits of static typing encompass:

1. Easier to spot programming mistakes (for example, preventing assigning a Boolean to an integer).
2. Self-documenting code thanks to type signatures.
3. The compiler has more opportunities to optimize the code (for example, replacing a virtual call with a direct one when the receiver's type is statically known).
4. More efficient development tools (for example, autocompletion of members of a class).

Defenders of dynamic typing return fire by claiming that static typing is inflexible and has a negative impact on prototyping systems with volatile or unknown requirements. Furthermore, writing code in dynamic languages requires more discipline than writing in statically typed languages. This is often translated into a greater awareness for testing—and unit testing in particular—among developers who decide to produce code with dynamic languages.

It is worth noting that Groovy also supports optional static typing, even though the name is slightly misleading. In Groovy, we can declare a variable's type as follows:

```
int var = 10
```

or

```
String computeFrequency(List<String> listOfWords) {  }
```

Still, the compiler would not catch any compilation error if we assigned the wrong type to a typed variable:

```
int var = "Hello, I'm not a number!"
```

Groovy has optional typing mostly for Java compatibility and to support better code readability.

To mitigate some of the criticism inherent to dynamic typing, the Groovy team has introduced static type-checking since v2.0 of the language. Static type-checking enables the verification of the proper type and ensures that the methods we call and properties we access are valid for the type at compile time, hence decreasing the number of bugs pushed to the runtime.

How to do it...

Forcing the compiler to enable static type-checking it is simply a matter of annotating the code that we want to be checked with the `@groovy.transform.TypeChecked` annotation. The annotation can be placed on classes or individual methods:

1. Create a new Groovy file (with the `.groovy` extension) with the following code:

    ```groovy
    def upperInteger(myInteger) {
      println myInteger.toUpperCase()
    }


    upperInteger(10)
    ```

2. From the shell, compile the code using the Groovy compiler `groovyc`. The compiler shouldn't report any error.

3. Now, run the script using `groovy`. The runtime should throw an exception:

    caught: groovy.lang.MissingMethodException:

    No signature of method: java.lang.Integer.toUpperCase()

    is applicable for argument types: () values: []

4. Add the type-checking annotation to the `upperInteger` function:

    ```groovy
    @groovy.transform.TypeChecked
    def upperInteger(myInteger) {
      println myInteger.toUpperCase()
    }
    ```

5. Compile the code again with `groovyc`. This time, the compiler reports the type error:

    DynamicTypingExample.groovy: 3: [Static type checking] -

    Cannot find matching method java.lang.Object#toUpperCase().

    Please check if the declared type is right

    and if the method exists.

    @ line 3, column 11.

    println myInteger.toUpperCase()

    ^

How it works...

If we place the annotation on a class, then type-checking is performed on all the methods, closures, and inner classes in the class. If we place it on a method, the type-checking is performed only on the members of the target method, including closures.

Static type-checking is implemented through an AST Transformation (see more on AST Transformations in *Chapter 9, Metaprogramming and DSLs in Groovy*) and can be used to enforce proper typing for a number of different cases. The following list shows a collection of bugs that would not be caught by the compiler but are caught by the `TypeChecked` annotation.

1. Variable names:

   ```
   @TypeChecked
   def variableName() {
      def name = 'hello'
      println naame
   }
   ```

   The variable named `name` is misspelled in the second line. The compiler outputs: **MyClass.groovy: 7: [Static type checking] - The variable [naame] is undeclared.**.

2. GStrings:

   ```
   @TypeChecked
   def gstring() {
      def name = 'hello'
      println "hello, this is $naame"
   }
   ```

   Similar to the previous bug, the compiler complains about the undeclared variable `naame`.

3. Collections:

   ```
   @TypeChecked
   def collections() {
      List myList = []
      myList = "I'm a String"
   }
   ```

   Here, the compiler detects that we are assigning a `String` to a `List` and throws an error: [Static type checking] - Cannot assign value of type java. lang.String to variable of type java.util.List.

4. Collection type:

```
@TypeChecked
def moreCollections() {
  int[] array = new int[2]
  array[0] = 100
  array[1] = '100'
}
```

Similarly to the previous example, the compiler detects the invalid assignment of a `String` to an element of an array of `ints`.

5. Return type:

```
@TypeChecked
int getSalary() {
  'fired on ' + new Date().format('yyyy-MM-dd')
}
```

Return types are also verified by the static type-checking algorithm. In this example, the compiler throws the following error:

```
[Static type checking] - Cannot return value of type java.lang.
String on method returning type int
```

6. Return type propagation:

```
boolean test() {
  true
}
@TypeChecked
void m() {
  int x = 1 + test()
}
```

Wrong return types are also detected when the type is propagated from another method. In the previous example, the compiler fails with:

```
Static type checking] - Cannot find matching method
int#plus(void). Please check if the declared type is right and if
the method exists
```

7. Generics:

```
@TypeChecked
def generics() {
  List<Integer> aList = ['a','b']
}
```

Generics are supported as well. We are not allowed to assign the wrong type to a typed `List`.

There's more...

As you may have suspected, static type-checking doesn't play very nice with a dynamic language. Metaprogramming capabilities are effectively shut down when using the `@TypeChecked` annotation on a class or method.

Here is an example that uses metaprogramming to inject a new method into the class `String` (the *Dynamically extending classes with new methods* recipe in *Chapter 9, Metaprogramming and DSLs in Groovy* has more information about method injections):

```
class Sample {
  def test() {
    String.metaClass.hello = { "Hello, $delegate" }
    println 'some String'.hello()
  }
}
new Sample().test()
```

When executed, this script yields the following output:

Hello, some String

If we add the `@TypeChecked` annotation to the class and try to run the script, we get the following error from the compiler:

[Static type checking] -

Cannot find matching method java.lang.String#hello().

**Please check if the declared type is right
and if the method exists.**

The reason for the error is that the compiler doesn't see the new dynamic method and therefore fails. Another case where static type-checking is too picky is when using implicit parameters in closures. Let's take an example:

```
class Sample {
  def test() {
    ['one','two','three'].collect { println it.toUpperCase() }
  }
}
new Sample().test()
```

This example, when executed, prints the following output:

ONE

TWO

THREE

If the `Sample` class is annotated with `@TypeChecked`, the compiler will return:

```
[Static type checking] -
Cannot find matching method java.lang.Object#toUpperCase().
Please check if the declared type is right
and if the method exists.
@ line 77, column 44.
wo','three'].collect { println it.toUpper
                                          ^
```

What is happening here? Simply, the compiler has no idea of the type of the implicit variable it, which is often used inside closures to make the code even more terse. This compilation error can be solved by explicitly declaring the closure variable as follows:

```
['one','two','three'].collect {
    myString -> println myString.toUpperCase()
}
```

Adding automatic logging to Groovy classes

In the *Writing less verbose Java Beans with Groovy Beans*, *Adding the cloning functionality to Groovy Beans*, and *Inheriting constructors in Groovy classes* recipes, we met some of the annotation-based AST transformations available in Groovy. An AST transformation is a process in which a programmer is able to hook into the bytecode generation process and influence the final shape of the resulting bytecode. Groovy ships with many useful transformations and in this recipe, we are going to look at the family of logging annotations.

How to do it...

The transformation we are going to demonstrate is the `@groovy.util.logging.Log` annotation that injects `java.util.logging.Logger` into a Groovy class:

1. Let's apply the annotation to a Groovy class:

   ```
   @groovy.util.logging.Log
   class UserService {
       def createUser(String username, String password) {
           log.info("creating user with name ${username}")
       }
   }
   ```

2. And call the method of the new class:

   ```
   def userService = new UserService()
   userService.createUser('john', 'secret')
   ```

3. The output will be:

```
INFO: creating user with name john
```

How it works...

The annotation takes a number of steps. First, it creates a logger with the variable name `log` and injects it in the class as a static final variable. Then it surrounds every call to the logger with a conditional check to verify whether the log level is enabled. No need to pollute your code with hard-to-read `if` statements just to check whether the log statement should be evaluated.

The variable that holds the logger can be modified by using an attribute on the annotation:

```
@groovy.util.logging.Log('someLogger')
class UserService { ... }
```

There's more...

The logging transformation is not limited to use only one logging framework but it also allows to use the following logging facilities by changing the annotation class:

- `@groovy.util.logging.Commons`: It injects an Apache Commons logger and initializes it using `LogFactory.getLog(class)`.
- `@groovy.util.logging.Log4j`: It injects Log4J `org.apache.log4j.Logger` into the class and initializes it using `Logger.getLogger(class)`.
- `@groovy.util.logging.Slf4j`: It injects a Slf4J logger into the annotated class and initializes it using `org.slf4j.LoggerFactory.getLogger(class)`. Slf4J is the underlying logger used by the newer framework Logback. If you wish to use that framework you should use the `@Slf4j` annotation.

See also

- http://groovy.codehaus.org/api/groovy/util/logging/Log.html
- http://docs.oracle.com/javase/7/docs/api/java/util/logging/Logger.html
- http://commons.apache.org/proper/commons-logging/
- http://logging.apache.org/log4j
- http://www.slf4j.org/

4
Working with Files in Groovy

In this chapter, we will cover:

- ▶ Reading from a file
- ▶ Reading a text file line by line
- ▶ Processing every word in a text file
- ▶ Writing to a file
- ▶ Replacing tabs with spaces in a text file
- ▶ Filtering a text file's content
- ▶ Deleting a file or directory
- ▶ Walking through a directory recursively
- ▶ Searching for files
- ▶ Changing file attributes on Windows
- ▶ Reading data from a ZIP file
- ▶ Reading an Excel file
- ▶ Extracting data from a PDF

Introduction

Groovy offers many shortcuts for dealing with files and directories. Mundane tasks such as listing, copying, renaming, and deleting files are elegantly executed by Groovy, thanks to the methods added to the standard JDK classes such as `java.io.File`. This chapter's recipes are all about I/O with Groovy, from simple cases such as reading a file to more complex endeavors, such as mining data from a PDF file or an Excel spreadsheet. The Java build tool Ant makes a cameo appearance in this chapter as well. Groovy and Ant are tightly integrated and we will discover some of the tasks made available through this marriage.

Reading from a file

Groovy makes dealing with files a very pleasant business, thanks to a number of helper methods that work with standard Java's `Reader` and `Writer`, `InputStream` and `OutputStream` and `File` classes.

In this recipe, we are going to look at the options available for reading a file in Groovy and accessing its content, mainly through the Groovy-enhanced `File` class.

Getting ready

Let's assume we have a script that defines the following `java.io.File` object:

```
def file = new File('poem.txt')
```

Of course, in order to be read, the `poem.txt` file needs to exist in the same directory where our script is.

How to do it...

Let's explore some different ways to read the content of the `poem.txt` file.

1. In order to get the full text file content as a `java.lang.String`, you can use the `getText` method provided by the Groovy JDK extension:

    ```
    String textContent = file.text
    ```

    `file.text` is equivalent to `file.getText`, thanks to Groovy's special property getter handling syntax.

2. You can also read it into memory as a byte array by using the `getBytes` method:

    ```
    byte[] binaryContent = file.bytes
    ```

3. If you want to have more control over the reading process, then you can use the `withReader` method, which takes a closure as an input parameter:

```
file.withReader { Reader reader ->
  def firstLine = reader.readLine()
  println firstLine
}
```

4. In a similar way, you can read the file with the help of the `withInputStream` method, which is similar to `withReader` with the exception that the closure operates on a `java.io.BufferedInputStream` instance:

```
file.withInputStream { InputStream stream ->
  def firstByte = stream.read()
  println firstByte
}
```

How it works...

The `getText` method displayed in step 1 can also be called by passing the `charset` name, in order to specify the character encoding:

```
String textContent = file.getText('UTF-8')
```

The `withReader` method in step 3 is an example of how Groovy can make the code much more concise and unceremonious. In Java, readers and writers have to be explicitly closed after we finish with them. Groovy has several `with...` methods for `File`, `URL`, streams, readers and writers, where `...` is the name of the stream, reader or writer class. We pass a closure to these methods and Groovy makes sure all streams, readers and writers are closed correctly, even if exceptions are thrown in the closure (Java 7 now has a similar feature via the `java.lang.AutoCloseable` interface). The `withReader` method creates a new `java.io.BufferedReader` instance for the given file and passes the reader into the closure. It also ensures that the reader object gets closed after the method returns.

There's more...

To get even more control, you can just use the `newReader` method to get the `reader`:

```
Reader reader = file.newReader()
```

Or the `newInputStream` method to get the `stream`:

```
InputStream stream = file.newInputStream()
```

Naturally, that means that you need to manually control the resource life cycle and close them properly.

The Groovy's extensions for `java.io.File` also offer methods to create standard Java input streams. You can use `newDataInputStream` or `newObjectInputStream` to create streams for reading Java primitives and serialized Java objects. To get those streams automatically closed you can also use the `withDataInputStream` and `withObjectInputStream` methods.

All the methods described above shorten your path to reading a file's content compared to what you would need in pure Java.

Additionally, many of the methods (for example, `getText`, `getBytes`, and others described in later recipes) that we find on `java.io.File` are also available in `java.io.Reader` and `java.io.InputStream` Groovy extensions.

See also

- ▶ *Reading a text file line by line*
- ▶ *Processing every word in a text file*
- ▶ *Writing to a file*
- ▶ `http://docs.oracle.com/javase/6/docs/api/java/io/File.html`
- ▶ `http://groovy.codehaus.org/groovy-jdk/java/io/File.html`
- ▶ `http://groovy.codehaus.org/groovy-jdk/java/io/Reader.html`
- ▶ `http://groovy.codehaus.org/groovy-jdk/java/io/InputStream.html`

Reading a text file line by line

You may often find yourself with the need to read a file line-by-line and extract information from each processed line; think of a logfile. In this recipe, we will learn a quick way to read text files line-by-line using the efficient Groovy I/O APIs.

Getting ready

For the following code snippets, please refer to the *Getting Ready* section in the *Reading from a file* recipe, or just assume you have the file variable of the `java.io.File` type defined somewhere in your script.

How to do it...

Let's see how to read all the text file's lines and echo them to the standard output.

1. To read all the lines at once, you can use the `readLines` method:

```
def lines = file.readLines()
```

2. The lines is a collection (`java.util.ArrayList`) that you can iterate over with the usual collection iterator:

```
lines.each { String line ->
  println line
}
```

3. There is also the `eachLine` method, which allows doing the above without keeping an intermediate variable:

```
file.eachLine { String line ->
  println line
}
```

There's more...

The `java.io.Reader` and `java.io.InputStream` class extensions also have the `readLines` and `eachLine` methods. For example, consider the following code:

```
file.withReader { Reader reader ->
  reader.eachLine { String line ->
    ...
  }
}
```

This actually makes it possible for any `Reader` or `InputStream` to be processed line-by-line.

In a similar way, you can also read files, readers, or streams byte by byte with the help of the `eachByte` method:

```
file.eachByte { int b ->
  ...
}
```

See also

The *Processing every word in a text file* recipe contains additional approaches to a text file content processing.

You can also find the following Javadoc and Groovydoc references useful:

- http://docs.oracle.com/javase/6/docs/api/java/io/File.html
- http://groovy.codehaus.org/groovy-jdk/java/io/File.html
- http://groovy.codehaus.org/groovy-jdk/java/io/Reader.html
- http://groovy.codehaus.org/groovy-jdk/java/io/InputStream.html

Processing every word in a text file

Sometimes, you may need to make a word-based analysis of a text file, for example, for spell checking or statistics. This recipe shows how a file can be read word-by-word in Groovy.

Getting ready

For this recipe, you can create a new Groovy script file and download a large text file for testing purposes. The *Project Gutenberg* website has thousands of text files that can be used for text analysis, for example, *William Shakespeare's Macbeth*, available at `http://www.gutenberg.net/cache/epub/2264/pg2264.txt`.

How to do it...

We assume that the `pg2264.txt` file containing Shakespeare's masterpiece Macbeth has been downloaded, but any large text file will do for this example.

1. Add the following code to the Groovy script:

```
def file = new File('pg2264.txt') // Macbeth
int wordCount = 0
file.eachLine { String line ->
  line.tokenize().each { String word ->
    wordCount++
    println word
  }
}
println "Number of words: $wordCount"
```

2. After the execution, the script should terminate with the following output:

```
. . .
FINIS.
THE
TRAGEDIE
OF
MACBETH.
Number of words: 20366
```

How it works...

The snippet in the previous paragraph prints every word in the file on a separate line, and at the end, it outputs a total number of words. The simplest way to pick all the words from a file is by reading the file line by line with the help of the `eachLine` method (described in the *Reading a text file line by line* recipe) and then splitting each line into words. The `java.lang.String` class already provides a `split` method that takes a regular expression for a word separator. There is also a `tokenize` method added by the Groovy JDK. This splits a given string into a collection of strings by using a whitespace separator (`[\s\t]+`).

The `tokenize` method is equivalent to the following `split` method call:

```
line.split(/[\s\t]+/).findAll{ it.trim() }.each { String word ->
    ...
}
```

Note that we filtered the empty words from the result of the `split` method using the `findAll` method available in all collections in Groovy. The `tokenize` method does this cleaning automatically for us.

There's more...

Another way to split words in a text file is to use the `splitEachLine` method from `java.io.File` Groovy's extension. Like `String`'s `split` method, it also takes a regular expression as an input, as well as a closure to which it passes the collection of strings received from a line split. With the help of this method, our original code snippet can be rewritten in the following way:

```
int wordCount = 0
file.splitEachLine(/[\s\t]+/) { Collection words ->
  words.findAll{ it.trim() }.each { String word ->
    wordCount++
    println word
  }
}
println "Number of words: $wordCount"
```

Also, similar to the `split` method, we need to filter empty words to get the same number of words.

See also

▶ http://groovy.codehaus.org/groovy-jdk/java/io/File.html
▶ http://groovy.codehaus.org/groovy-jdk/java/lang/String.html

Writing to a file

Java's I/O API demands a lot of "ceremony code" to cover the file output operations (and actually any other I/O resource). Groovy adds several extensions and syntax sugar to hide Java's complexity and make the code more concise than its Java counterpart. In this recipe, we will cover the file writing methods that are available in Groovy.

Getting ready

To start writing to a file, you just need to create an instance of `java.io.File`, for example:

```
File file = new File('output.txt')
```

How to do it...

Now let's see which writing operations we can perform on a `File` object.

1. To replace the full text of the file content with a `String` you can use the `setText` extension method of the `java.io.File` (or just Groovy's syntax for property assignment):

   ```
   file.text = 'Just a text'
   ```

2. This also gives you the possibility of assigning multiple text lines at once:

   ```
   file.text = '''What's in a name? That which we call a rose
   By any other name would smell as sweet.'''
   ```

3. You can also assign binary content with the help of the `setBytes` method:

   ```
   file.bytes = [ 65, 66, 67, 68 ] as byte[]
   ```

4. If you just want to append some text at the end of the file, you can use the append method:

   ```
   file.append('What\'s in a name? That which we call a rose,\n')
   file.append('By any other name would smell as sweet.')
   ```

5. A more idiomatic way to append text to a file is by using the `leftShift` operator (`<<`).

   ```
   file << 'What\'s in a name? That which we call a rose\n'
   file << 'By any other name would smell as sweet.'
   ```

6. You can also take advantage of the `java.io.Writer` with the help of the `withWriter` method:

```
file.withWriter { Writer writer ->
  writer << 'What\'s in a name? That which we call a rose\n'
  writer << 'By any other name would smell as sweet.'
}
```

7. And if you prefer working with streams, you can also do it with the help of the `withOutputStream`:

```
file.withOutputStream { OutputStream stream ->
  stream << 'What\'s in a name? That which we call a rose\n'
  stream << 'By any other name would smell as sweet.'
}
```

How it works...

In the first and second code snippets, we used the `setText` method. It is actually absolutely equivalent to the `write` method that also replaces the file content with the string that is passed. Those methods exist to give the developer the freedom to choose the best wording to describe his or her intent.

The functionality of the `leftShift` method is exactly the same as for the `append` method. We used both in steps 4 and 5. There are other special method names in Groovy such as `plus` for + or `minus` for - , which you can add to your own classes to be able to write more concise expressions with the help of well-known arithmetical operators.

Each call to the `append` or `leftShift` methods opens and closes the file every time you execute them. That's, of course, not very efficient if you need to perform many write operations. To get more control, you can operate on the `java.io.Writer` object within a closure passed to the `withWriter` method that we used in the sixth example.

As you might have noticed, we also make use of the left shift (<<) operator on the `writer` object. That operator is made available by Groovy on all the `java.io.Writer` instances, just like with `java.io.File`, and even with `java.io.OutputStream`.

The `withWriter` method creates a new instance of `java.io.BufferedWriter` and ensures it is flushed and closed upon return. The file content will be fully replaced. In a similar way, you can use the `withWriterAppend` method to use the `writer` object to add content to the end of the file. Another available method is `withPrintWriter`, which gives you access to the `java.io.PrintWriter` instance within a closure.

Another way of writing to a file implies using the `withOutputStream` method, which is similar to `withWriter` with the exception that the closure operates on the `java.io.BufferedOutputStream` instance as you can see in the seventh snippet.

The leftShift operator is used again to append data to a stream. The stream object will be opened and closed automatically in a similar way to the withWriter method.

There's more...

You can also wrap file access using the withDataOutputStream and withObjectOutputStream methods. This gives you access to the java. io.DataOutputStream and java.io.ObjectOutputStream instances within a closure that allows you to write out primitive and serialized Java types respectively.

If you want to control the writer or stream instances yourself, you can use convenient constructor methods such as newWriter, newOutputStream, newDataOutputStream, and newObjectOutputStream.

Many of the writing methods of java.io.File are also available in the java.io.Writer and java.io.OutputStream classes that allow using Groovy goodies for virtually any output target.

See also

- ► *Reading from a file*
- ► http://groovy.codehaus.org/groovy-jdk/java/io/File.html
- ► http://groovy.codehaus.org/groovy-jdk/java/io/Writer.html
- ► http://groovy.codehaus.org/groovy-jdk/java/io/OutputStream.html
- ► http://groovy.codehaus.org/groovy-jdk/java/io/PrintWriter.html
- ► http://groovy.codehaus.org/groovy-jdk/java/io/PrintStream.html

Replacing tabs with spaces in a text file

Searching and replacing file content is an often needed routine that can be automated with the help of Groovy scripts, one of which will be shown in this recipe.

Getting ready

Let's assume that we have an input.txt file that contains some tabulation characters. We want to replace the tabulation characters with spaces and save the results into a output.txt file.

To perform any action on these files (similar to the *Filtering a text file's content* recipe), we need to create two instances of `java.io.File` objects:

```
def inputFile = new File('input.txt')
def outputFile = new File('output.txt')
```

How to do it...

Let's go through several ways to achieve the desired result:

1. First of all, we will take advantage of the `transformLine` method available in the `java.io.Reader` class, as well as the `withWriter` and `withReader` methods that are described in more detail in the *Writing to a file* and *Reading from a file* recipes:

```
outputFile.withWriter { Writer writer ->
  inputFile.withReader { Reader reader ->
    reader.transformLine(writer) { String line ->
      line.replaceAll('\t', '  ')
    }
  }
}
```

2. A more concise form of the above code snippet looks like this:

```
inputFile.withReader { reader ->
  reader.transformLine(outputFile.newWriter()) { line ->
    line.replaceAll('\t', '  ')
  }
}
```

3. Another way to do this is with the help of the `getText` and `setText` extension methods of `java.io.File`:

```
outputFile.text = inputFile.text.replaceAll('\t', '  ')
```

Although this approach is the shortest one, it has some complications, which we will describe in the next section.

How it works...

Groovy adds an extension method, `transformLine`, to the `java.io.Reader` class. We used this method in the first and second examples. The method takes two input parameters, a `Writer` and a `Closure`. The closure expects a `String` and it should return a transformed `String` back. The writer is used to output the transformed lines. This means that by having a reader and a writer, we can use `transformLine` to perform a line-based data transformation.

Since the `transformLine` method automatically closes the writer, we can omit the outer method call to `withWriter` and just pass a new `Writer` instance to the `transformLine` method. That's what we've shown in the second example we just described.

The previous code snippet, of course, looks more concise; but this approach has one disadvantage. The whole file content will be loaded into the memory, and, in the case of a very large file, we are at risk of getting an `OutOfMemoryError` exception. With the first and second approaches, we don't risk incurring any memory problems.

You have to choose which approach is more appropriate based on your input file sizes.

There's more...

In a similar way as we used `transformLine`, you can also use the `transformChar` method to make character-based input transformations. For example, this code will transform a TAB character with a single space character:

```
inputFile.withReader { Reader reader ->
  reader.transformChar(outputFile.newWriter()) { String chr ->
    chr == '\t' ? ' ' : chr
  }
}
```

See also

The following recipes give an introduction to I/O operations in Groovy:

- ▸ *Reading from a file*
- ▸ *Writing to a file*

Also, it's worth looking at what additional functionality Groovy offers in the `java.io.Reader` class:

- ▸ `http://groovy.codehaus.org/groovy-jdk/java/io/Reader.html`

Filtering a text file's content

Filtering a text file's content is a rather common task. In this recipe, we will show how it can be easily achieved with Groovy.

Getting ready

Let's assume we want to filter out comment lines from a Bash script stored in the `script.sh` file and we want to save it into the `new_script.sh` file. First of all, we need to define two variables of the `java.io.File` type that point to our `inputFile` and `outputFile`:

```
def inputFile = new File('script.sh')
def outputFile = new File('new_script.sh')
```

How to do it...

File filtering can be implemented in several ways:

1. We can make use of the closure-based methods (that is `eachLine` and `withPrintWriter`) that we have got familiar with in the *Reading a text file line by line* and *Writing to a file* recipes:

```
outputFile.withPrintWriter { writer ->
  inputFile.eachLine { line ->
    if (!line.startsWith('#')) {
      writer.println(line)
    }
  }
}
```

2. Another way to achieve the same result is to use a `filterLine` method. It takes a `Writer` and a `closure` as input parameters. The closure gets a string line as an input and should return true or false depending on whether line is filtered in or out. We can rewrite the original code snippet in the following way:

```
outputFile.withWriter { writer ->
  inputFile.filterLine(writer) { line ->
    !line.startsWith('#')
  }
}
```

3. Actually, the `filterLine` method also closes the given writer automatically. So, we can omit one closure from the previous code and just pass a new `Writer` instance to the method:

```
inputFile.filterLine(outputFile.newWriter()) { line ->
  !line.startsWith('#')
}
```

How it works...

In the first code example above, we have first called a method `withPrintWriter` to which we passed a closure in which we iterated through text lines with the help of the `eachLine` method. The inner closure passed to `eachLine` has access to both the `writer` and the `line` objects. Inside that closure, we added a simple conditional statement to write out only those lines that do not start with #.

In the second snippet, we passed a closure to the `filterLine` method. That closure gives you access to the line and expects to return a `boolean` that indicates whether that line should be written to the final output (writer) or not.

All code examples achieve the same result. The filtered Bash script should contain no comments after execution of the Groovy code demonstrated in the previous section.

There's more...

There is another overloaded version of the `filterLine` method that returns an instance of `groovy.lang.Writable`. `Writable` has only one method that is, `writeTo(java.io.Writer writer)`. It's a Groovy abstraction that allows postponing the content creation until it is actually streamed to the final output target. Instances of `Writable` can be used in most of the output operations such as `print`, `write`, `append`, and `leftShift`. That's why this `filterLine` version does not need any `Writer`. Taking it all into account, we can rewrite the previous code as a one-liner:

```
outputFile << inputFile.filterLine { !it.startsWith('#') }
```

The `Writable` result of the `filterLine` method is sent to `outputFile` with the help of the `leftShift` operator (you can read more about it in *Writing to a file* recipe). We also omitted the line variable and simply referred to Groovy's default it closure parameter. In this way, the code looks almost similar to an OS command; short and clear.

See also

Check the following recipes for some additional insights:

- *Reading a text file line by line*
- *Writing to a file*

The following Groovydoc links may be of interest for the reader:

- http://groovy.codehaus.org/api/groovy/lang/Writable.html
- http://groovy.codehaus.org/groovy-jdk/java/io/File.html

Deleting a file or directory

Deleting a file or directory may seem a trivial task and it often is, but it has some hidden quirks that Groovy may help you with. This recipe will enlist and give details about several methods to delete a file or a directory.

Getting ready

Let's assume that we have two `java.io.File` variables: one pointing to a normal file and another to a nonempty directory with several subdirectories in it. For example:

```
def dir = new File('./tmp1')
def file = new File('./tmp2/test.txt')
```

As you know from Java, the `java.io.File` class has a `delete` method and it works perfectly in many situations. But it will only delete a normal file or an empty directory. So, to delete a nonempty directory you need to write a recursive function in Java. Also, in most of the situations, the `delete` method will not throw any exceptions; it will just return false if it fails to delete a file or directory.

How to do it...

Let's explore several ways to delete things on the file system.

1. To delete the nonempty directories, Groovy provides an extension method `deleteDir` in the `java.io.File` class. Let's try to delete our `file` and `directory` with both the `delete` and `deleteDir` methods and print the result:

   ```
   println file.deleteDir()
   println file.delete()
   println dir.delete()
   println dir.deleteDir()
   ```

2. The previous code snippet should give the following output:

   ```
   false
   true
   false
   true
   ```

How it works...

The first method call returns `false`, because the given `file` is not a directory. The second one successfully deletes the `file` and returns `true`. The third one returns `false` because we try to delete a nonempty directory. The last one returns `true`, because we recursively delete the root folder and its subfolders with the Groovy's `deleteDir` method.

In order to ensure that a file or a directory is deleted, you always need to check the result of the `delete` or `deleteDir` method. In a scenario where several files or folders have to be deleted, you may end up with a lot of noisy conditional statements. Not pretty. An elegant solution to the issue posed above is possible by resorting to Groovy's metaprogramming features. The `java.io.File` class can be enhanced with a new method, `safeDelete`:

```
File.metaClass.safeDelete = {
    if (exists()) {
        if (isDirectory()) {
            if (!deleteDir()) {
                def msg = "Unable to delete a directory: ${name}"
                throw new IOException(msg)
            }
        } else {
            if (!delete()) {
                def msg = "Unable to delete a file: ${name}"
                throw new IOException(msg)
            }
        }
    }
}
```

Groovy metaprogramming and the `metaClass` object are discussed in more detail in *Chapter 9, Metaprogramming and DSLs in Groovy*. In short, the previous code adds a new method to the `java.io.File` class called `safeDelete`. The new method ensures that the file exists; then it checks if the `File` is a directory, and calls a recursive delete on it. If the `File` object points to a file, it calls a normal `delete`. If either the `delete` or `deleteDir` operations return `false`, the method throws an `IOException`.

After you have extended the `java.io.File` class, then you can simply call the method on any `File` instance:

```
file.safeDelete()
dir.safeDelete()
```

By using this method, you can avoid many conditional statements and implement simpler exception handling.

There's more...

One more way to manipulate files is by using Groovy's built-in Apache Ant support. Through the `groovy.util.AntBuilder` class, you can get access to all the common Ant tasks including the `delete` task.

```
def ant = new AntBuilder()
ant.delete(dir: file.absolutePath, failonerror:false)
```

Ant's file-handling capabilities are quite extended, especially when it comes to copying files around.

See also

▶ *Chapter 9, Metaprogramming and DSLs in Groovy*

▶ `http://groovy.codehaus.org/Using+Ant+from+Groovy`

▶ `http://groovy.codehaus.org/api/groovy/util/AntBuilder.html`

Walking through a directory recursively

Hierarchical file systems are the way we store most of our data. Groovy can help to build code that needs to go through a dense forest of directory trees.

In this recipe, we will cover different ways of walking through a directory tree using Groovy I/O awesomeness.

Getting ready

Let's assume that we need to walk through the current working directory. We can define the `currentDir` variable of `java.io.File` type that points to it:

```
def currentDir = new File('.')
```

To test this recipe, you can use either a script file that you launch with the `groovy` command or the `groovysh/groovyConsole` prompt.

How to do it...

As you probably know, the `java.io.File` class already provides the `list` and `listFiles` methods that return a collection of first-level elements (files and directories) in a directory represented by a `File` object. Using a recursive function, you can easily traverse the subfolders found in the first-level folders.

1. However, Groovy already provides more concise methods that use recursion internally to traverse a directory. One of them is the `eachFileRecurse` method. It takes a closure as an input parameter, which is called for every file or directory entry that is found:

```
currentDir.eachFileRecurse { File file ->
  println file.name
}
```

2. If you need to walk recursively only through the directories, then you can use the eachDirRecurse method instead:

```
currentDir.eachDirRecurse { File dir ->
  println dir.name
}
```

3. If you only need to go through the files, then you can pass an additional parameter to eachFileRecurse, which is a value of a groovy.io.FileType enumeration (you'll need to add an additional import at the beginning of your script or groovysh/ groovyConsole prompt):

```
import groovy.io.FileType
...


currentDir.eachFileRecurse(FileType.FILES) { File file ->
  println file.name
}
```

How it works...

The previous code recursively prints the names of all the files and/or directories in the current directory tree. The recursive walk performs a depth-first search. That means that when the search goes through a list of children and encounters a directory, then it goes (deeper) inside that directory first before returning to process the remaining children. The order in which files and directories are processed depends on the implementation of the file system.

There's more...

Groovy also adds the eachFile and eachDir methods to a java.io.File class that you can use to iterate through the first-level elements only (just like listFiles). As other each-methods, they take a closure as an input parameter. You can use that to build a recursive function in a similar way as you would use it with the listFiles method. But instead of defining a separate function, you can also make use of Groovy's closure that is capable of creating a copy of itself with the help of the trampoline method:

```
currentDir.eachFile { File file ->
  println file.name
  if (file.isDirectory()) {
    file.eachFile( trampoline() )
  }
}
```

The code snippet above does exactly the same thing as the previous code examples. The "magic" trampoline method passes a copy of the parent closure to the nested eachFile call, a copy of the parent closure and makes it behave like a recursive function.

The previous example is very condensed, but it's not as obvious and easy to read compared to the initially described methods.

Since v1.7.1, Groovy has also introduced a very powerful `traverse` method in the `java.io.File` class. In its simplest form, it does the same as `eachFileRecurse`:

```
currentDir.traverse { File file ->
  println file.name
}
```

The `traverse` method has an overloaded version that also accepts a `Map` of additional parameters, which allows you to control various aspects of directory traversing behavior.

More advanced traverse options are described in the *Searching for files* recipe.

See also

The following recipes contain some additional information on the topics discussed in this recipe:

▶ *Searching for files*

▶ The *Defining code as data in Groovy* recipe in *Chapter 3, Using Groovy language features*

Also, it's worth examining the Groovydoc for the `File`, `FileType`, and `Closure` classes:

▶ http://groovy.codehaus.org/groovy-jdk/java/io/File.html

▶ http://groovy.codehaus.org/api/groovy/io/FileType.html

▶ http://groovy.codehaus.org/api/groovy/lang/Closure.html

Searching for files

In this recipe, we will show how easy it is to filter out files and folders during a search operation on the file system.

Getting ready

Let's assume that we are searching for files in a current working directory. For that, we need to define a variable of the `java.io.File` type that points to the `.` path:

```
def currentDir = new File('.')
```

How to do it...

As we already mentioned in the *Walking through a directory recursively* recipe, Groovy adds a powerful `traverse` method for helping us with our searching task. Let's explore the options that are given by that method:

1. The simplest way to search for specific files is to apply some filtering logic within a closure that we pass to the `traverse` method:

```
currentDir.traverse { File file ->
  if (file.name.endsWith('.groovy')) {
    println file.name
  }
}
```

2. The `traverse` method has another overloaded version that accepts a `Map` of the parameters. One of those parameters is `nameFilter`, which should be of the `java.util.regex.Pattern` type. So, our initial code snippet can be written in the following way:

```
currentDir.traverse(nameFilter: ~/.*\.groovy/)
  { File file ->
  println file.name
}
```

3. The `traverse` method has even more tricks up its sleeve. By specifying the type of the entries (you need to import the `groovy.io.FileType` class beforehand), we can search for the pattern of the names we want to exclude (`excludeNameFilter`):

```
import static groovy.io.FileType.*

...

currentDir.traverse(
  type: FILES,
  nameFilter: ~/.*\.groovy/,
  excludeNameFilter: ~/^C.*$/) { File file ->
    println file.name
}
```

4. A closure that is passed as a final input argument can also be passed through a `visit` parameter in the `map`:

```
currentDir.traverse(
  type:              FILES,
  nameFilter:        { it.matches(/.*\.groovy/) },
  excludeNameFilter: { it.matches(/^C.*$/)      },
  visit:             { println it.name          }
)
```

5. You can also filter on file attributes, other than name, by using the `filter`/ `excludeFilter` closure parameters, which are given on `java.io.File` objects:

```
def today = new Date()

currentDir.traverse(
    filter:            {
                           it.lastModified() < (today-5).time &&
                           it.name.endsWith('.groovy')
                       },
    excludeFilter: { it.isDirectory() },
    visit:             { println it.name   }
)
```

6. You can prune some directory tree branches by using the `preDir` (or `postDir`) closure parameters:

```
import static groovy.io.FileVisitResult.*

...

currentDir.traverse(
    preDir:                {
                               if (it.name == '.svn') {
                                   return SKIP_SUBTREE
                               }
                           },
    nameFilter:            { it.matches(/.*\.groovy/) },
    excludeNameFilter: { it.matches(/^C.*$/)          },
    visit:                 { println it.name           }
)
```

How it works...

As you can guess, the first code snippet will walk through all the subdirectories and print all Groovy (`*.groovy`) source file names that are found.

In the *Searching strings with regular expressions* recipe in *Chapter 3, Using Groovy Language Features*, we mentioned the `~//` operator, which constructs a `Pattern` object. That's what we use in the second example to match the `*.groovy` files and print their name again.

In the third step, we add a bit more logic to the code, since we only go through normal files by specifying `FileType.FILES` in the type parameter. Other possible values are `FileType. ANY` and `FileType.DIRECTORIES`. The search also excludes all files starting with `C` with the help of a regular expression passed to the `excludeNameFilter` parameter.

The fourth example is identical to the third one, except that all filtering logic is passed through named parameters in a map.

The fifth code snippet prints the names of the files having the `*.groovy` extension, which are older than 5 days and which are not directories.

The last code example behaves in the same way as the third snippet, but it also excludes the `.svn` directory and all subdirectories from searching. The closure passed to `preDir` returns an instance of the `groovy.io.FileVisitResult` enumeration, which controls the traversing behavior. Other possible enumeration values are `CONTINUE`, `SKIP_SIBLINGS`, and `TERMINATE`. In general, `preDir` and `postDir` can execute any code, and it's not mandatory to return `FileVisitResult`.

There's more...

There are other useful options available for the `traverse` method:

- ▶ `maxDepth`: It says how deep should we go in our search.
- ▶ `sort`: It is a closure that sets the sorting order in which files and directories will be processed.
- ▶ `visitRoot`: It indicates that the `visit` closure should also be called for the target search directory.
- ▶ `preRoot`: It indicates that the `preDir` closure should also be called for the target search directory.
- ▶ `postRoot`: It indicates that `postDir` closure should also be called for the target search directory.

If you just want to search in the current directory without visiting its subdirectories, you can use the `eachFileMatch` method instead:

```
currentDir.eachFileMatch(~/.*\.groovy/) { File file ->
  println file.name
}
```

There is also an `eachDirMatch` method, in case you only need to walk through the matching first-level directories.

See also

An initial introduction to walking through directory trees was given in the *Walking through a directory recursively* recipe.

Also pay your attention to the following Groovydoc references:

- ▶ `http://groovy.codehaus.org/groovy-jdk/java/io/File.html`
- ▶ `http://groovy.codehaus.org/api/groovy/io/FileType.html`
- ▶ `http://groovy.codehaus.org/api/groovy/io/FileVisitResult.html`

Changing file attributes on Windows

Groovy is widely used as a scripting language for automating repetitive tasks. While working with files, it occurs sometime that one has to change the attributes of a file in Windows. For example, you may need to set the file as read-only, archived, and so on.

In this recipe, we will learn how to change file attributes in Windows using Groovy.

Getting ready

Let's start by creating a file and adding some content to it. Open your shell, start `groovysh` and type the following code:

```
f = new File('test.txt')
f << 'hello, this is a test file'
```

You should now see a file named `test.txt` in the same directory where you started `groovysh`.

On a DOS console, type:

```
attrib test.txt
```

The output should be as follows:

```
A        I     C:\hello.txt
```

The initial on the left stands for the first letter of the enabled attribute: `A` for "archive", `S` for "system", `H` for "hidden" and `R` for "read-only".

How to do it...

With the exclusion of the read-only attribute; in Java, there is no way to set the Windows file attributes through the File API. To make a file read-only:

```
f.setReadOnly()
```

This will change the R attribute:

```
attrib test.txt

A    R   I     C:\hello.txt
```

1. In order to change other file attributes, we have to resort to executing an external process with Groovy, using the `execute` method of `String`. The external process is the `attrib` DOS command that can be used to set and read file attributes.

2. To make a file "Hidden":

   ```
   'attrib +H C:/hello.txt'.execute()
   ```

3. And to remove the "Hidden" attribute:

   ```
   'attrib -H C:/hello.txt'.execute()
   ```

4. You can use the same approach for the other file attributes, S and A.

How it works...

Groovy provides a simple way to execute command line processes. Simply write the command line as a string and call the `execute` method. The `execute` method returns a `java.lang.Process` instance, which will subsequently allow the `in/err/out` streams to be processed and the exit value from the process to be inspected.

This snippet executed from `groovish` will output the directory listing on a UNIX machine:

```
println 'ls -al'.execute().text
```

Alternatively, we can access the stream resulting from the process and print the result line-by-line:

```
p = 'ls -al'.execute().text
p.in.eachLine { line -> print line }
```

There's more...

If you run Groovy using JDK 7, you can leverage the new NIO API to set the Windows file attributes. The following example shows you how to do it:

```
import java.nio.file.*
import java.nio.file.attribute.*
def f = new File('hello.txt')
f << 'hello, hello'
def path = Paths.get('C:\\groovybook\\hello.txt')
def dosView = Files.getFileAttributeView(
                path, DosFileAttributeView
            )
```

```
dosView.hidden = true
dosView.archive = true
dosView.system = true
```

This code will fail if it is executed in an environment other than Windows.

Reading data from a ZIP file

Reading from a ZIP file with Groovy is a simple affair. This recipe shows you how to read the contents of a ZIP file without having to extract the content first.

Getting ready

Groovy doesn't have any GDK class to deal with ZIP files so we have to approach the problem by using one of the JDK alternatives. Nevertheless, we can "groovify" the code quite a lot in order to achieve simplicity and elegance.

How to do it...

Let's assume we have a ZIP file named `archive.zip` containing a bunch of text files.

1. The following code iterates through the ZIP entries and prints the name of the file as well as the content:

```
def dumpZipContent(File zipFIle) {
  def zf = new java.util.zip.ZipFile(zipFIle)
  zf.entries().findAll { !it.directory }.each {
    println it.name
    println zf.getInputStream(it).text
  }
}
dumpZipContent(new File('archive.zip'))
```

2. The output may look as follows:

```
a/b.txt
This is text file!
c/d.txt
This is another text file!
```

How it works...

The `dumpZipContent` function takes a `File` as an argument and creates a JDK `ZipFIle` out of it. Finally, the code iterates on all the entries of the ZIP file, filtering out the folders. The iteration is done through a couple of nested closures, the second of which prints the content of the ZIP file using the handy `text` property added to the Java's `InputStream` class by Groovy JDK.

There's more...

We have already encountered the `AntBuilder` class in the *Deleting a file or directory* recipe. This class is a gateway to the enormous amount of tasks exposed by the Ant build system. Among them, we can find the unzip task that allows us to decompress a `ZIP`, `JAR`, `WAR`, and `EAR` file:

```
def ant = new AntBuilder()
ant.unzip (src: 'zipped.zip', dest: '.')
```

The previous snippet unzips a file named `zipped.zip` into the same folder where the code is executed. For a complete list of properties of the unzip task, refer to Ant documentation (`https://ant.apache.org/manual/Tasks/unzip.html`).

See also

▶ `http://docs.oracle.com/javase/7/docs/api/java/util/zip/ZipFile.html`

▶ `https://ant.apache.org/manual/Tasks/unzip.html`

Reading an Excel file

In this recipe, you will learn how to read and extract data from an Excel file. If you are a Windows or Mac user, changes are that you have worked in some capacity with Microsoft Excel, the *de facto* standard for spreadsheets. Excel files are often the default data interchange format of the enterprise. Entire departments are run using incredibly complex Excel files with thousands of rows and absurdly convoluted formulas. As a programmer, it is often the case that you are asked to interact with such files.

Getting ready

Groovy (and Java) does not offer any out-of-the-box ingredient to manipulate Excel files. Fortunately, there is no shortage of third-party libraries that are able to deal with Microsoft documents. The undisputed king of this realm is Apache POI, the Java API for Microsoft documents. With Apache POI, it is possible to parse as well as write Excel 2007 OOXML documents (.xlsx) and older formats (.xls).

How to do it...

Let's start with a simple Excel file with only a few columns:

1. The script that follows, extracts the content of the Excel file depicted in the previous screenshot and prints it on the console:

```
@Grab('org.apache.poi:poi:3.8')
@Grab('org.apache.poi:poi-ooxml:3.8')
@GrabExclude('xml-apis:xml-apis')
import org.apache.poi.xssf.usermodel.XSSFWorkbook
import org.apache.poi.xssf.usermodel.XSSFSheet
def excelFile = new File('Workbook1.xlsx')
excelFile.withInputStream { is ->
  workbook = new XSSFWorkbook(is)
  (0..<workbook.numberOfSheets).each { sheetNumber ->
    XSSFSheet sheet = workbook.getSheetAt( sheetNumber )
    sheet.rowIterator().each { row ->
      row.cellIterator().each { cell ->
        println cell.toString()
      }
    }
  }
}
```

2. Running this script displays the following output:

```
100.0
A
200.0
B
300.0
C
400.0
D
```

How it works...

The recipe's code uses Grape (see the *Simplifying dependency management with Grape* recipe in *Chapter 2, Using Groovy Ecosystem*) to fetch the necessary dependencies: Apache POI and POI OOXML, the latter required to deal with the post-2007 Excel files. The `GrabExclude` explicitly excludes the `xml-apis` library to avoid conflicts with the Groovy XML parser. Please note that the code imports classes from the `org.apache.poi.xssf`, the package used to access the newer Excel format. For the older format (pre-2007), we would have imported classes from the `org.apache.poi.xssf` package.

The script creates an `XSSFWorkbook` instance from the `Workbook1.xlsx` file and iterates on all the sheets found in the document. For each sheet, we use two nested closures (one for the rows and one for the current row's cells) to traverse the cells that have content and print the value on the console.

See also

▸   The *Simplifying dependency management with Grape* recipe in *Chapter 2, Using Groovy Ecosystem*

▸   `http://poi.apache.org/`

Extracting data from a PDF

The ubiquity of PDF files is due to the ability of almost every PC, Mac, and smart device to open and process this format. Electronic documents are often exchanged as PDF because they cannot be easily altered and are, by default, read-only.

Many organizations use PDF files to distribute reports, bank statements, and invoices. Being able to read such documents and extract the information they provide it's an invaluable tool in the belt of a Groovy programmer.

This recipe focuses on mining information from a PDF file.

Getting ready

As for ZIP files (see the *Reading data from a ZIP file* recipe), Groovy doesn't have any class to deal with PDF files. Java too doesn't offer any built-in feature to read or write PDFs. Therefore, we are left to resorting to a third-party library. A Google search for Java read PDF yields numerous results with links to various libraries.

In this recipe, we will use **iText**, the most popular PDF library for the Java ecosystem. iText is a very powerful library for generating PDF files, but it also has a very simple API for mining the text inside the PDF file.

For demonstration purposes, we are going to use a PDF version of *Chapter 1*, *Getting Started with Groovy* of this book (a version of the file is attached to the code distribution) located in the `groovy2cookbook_chapter1.pdf` file:

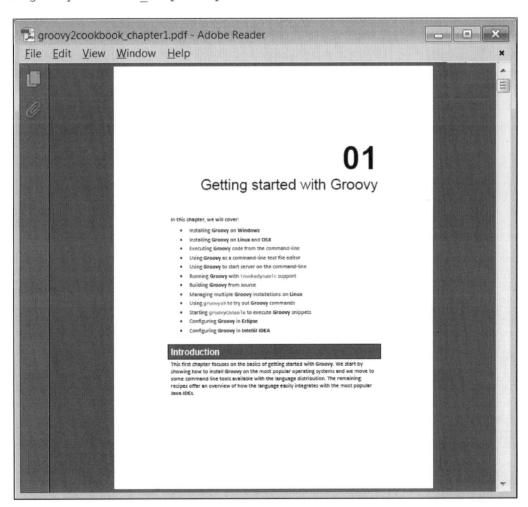

How to do it...

The Groovy code that follows shows you how to open a PDF file and dump the contents of the pages of a PDF file in the console.

1. First of all, we need to `@Grab` the iText library and declare all imported classes that we are going to make use of:

    ```
    @Grab('com.itextpdf:itextpdf:5.3.2')
    import com.itextpdf.text.pdf.parser.*
    import com.itextpdf.text.pdf.*
    ```

2. After that, we can construct objects that help to achieve our final target:

    ```
    def pdf = new PdfReader('groovy2cookbook_chapter1.pdf')
    def maxPages = pdf.numberOfPages + 1
    def parser = new PdfTextExtractor()
    ```

3. And now, all that is left is to iterate through all the pages and extract the text:

    ```
    (1..<maxPages).each { pageNumber ->
      println parser.getTextFromPage(pdf, pageNumber)
    }
    ```

4. Output should be as follows:

    ```
    01
    Getting started with Groovy
    In this chapter, we will cover:
    ? Installing Groovy on Windows
    ? Installing Groovy on Linux and OSX
    ...
    ```

How it works...

The previous script does some interesting stuff. First, we use Grape (see the *Simplifying dependency management with Grape* recipe in *Chapter 2, Using Groovy Ecosystem*) to fetch the latest version of iText from a Maven repository (v5.3.2), through the `Grab` annotation. Then an instance of the `com.itextpdf.text.pdf.PdfReader` class is created for reading the PDF document. `PdfReader` can be constructed with different arguments, but we chose `String` for simplicity. After instantiating `PdfReader`, we get the number of pages of the PDF file we intend to analyze. Again, to get the number of pages, it's a simple call to the `getNumberOfPages` method of `PdfReader`.

Finally, we loop through all the pages and, for each page, we call `getTextFromPage` from the `com.itextpdf.text.pdf.parser.PdfTextExtractor` class. The method returns the text found in the page which is printed on the console.

There's more...

Extracting text from a PDF file is relatively easy in Groovy (and Java), but interpreting the structure of a PDF file can be a very daunting task as PDF files have a layout-oriented structure rather than a content-oriented one. If you have to cope with PDF documents that have a nonstandard structure (for example, columns or tables), you may want to write your own strategy for text extraction. The `getTextFromPage` method of the `PdfTextExtractor` class accepts instances of the `TextExtractionStrategy` interface.

iText has some implementations of the interface, such as `SimpleTextExtractionStrategy`, which stores all the snippets in the order they occur in the stream; but it is smart enough to detect which text portions should be combined into a single word or separated with a space character.

There is also a `LocationTextExtractionStrategy` interface that allows you to extract text only from certain area of a PDF file. The next script is a modified version of the previous one and shows you how to use `LocationTextExtractionStrategy` combined with `FilteredTextRenderListener`. We define a small rectangular area from which the text is extracted. In this case, it's the area of the chapter's title. The part of the code that does the text extraction changes as we are passing the strategy to the `getTextFromPage` method and we only execute for the first page:

```
@Grab('com.itextpdf:itextpdf:5.3.2')
import com.itextpdf.text.pdf.parser.*
import com.itextpdf.text.pdf.*
import com.itextpdf.text.Rectangle
def rect = new Rectangle(0, 550, 1000, 800)
def pdf = new PdfReader('groovy2cookbook_chapter1.pdf')
def parser = new PdfTextExtractor()
def strategy = new FilteredTextRenderListener(
  new LocationTextExtractionStrategy(),
  new RegionTextRenderFilter(rect))
println parser.getTextFromPage(pdf, 1, strategy)
```

The output should be as follows:

```
01
Getting started with Groovy
```

Another thing that you may face when parsing the PDF files is dealing with non-English texts. iText does a good job extracting text data for you, but in order to get proper result you need to know which encoding was used in the PDF file for the text you want to extract. For example, for saving Russian text encoded with the KOI8-R charset, you can use the following snippet:

```
new File('output.txt').withWriter('KOI8-R') { writer ->
  (1..<maxPages).each {
    writer << parser.getTextFromPage(pdf, it)
  }
}
```

This code saves the extracted text into the `output.txt` file using the specified encoding.

See also

▸ `http://itextpdf.com/`

5

Working with XML in Groovy

In this chapter, we will cover the following recipes:

- ▶ Reading XML using XmlSlurper
- ▶ Reading XML using XmlParser
- ▶ Reading XML content with namespaces
- ▶ Searching in XML with GPath
- ▶ Searching in XML with XPath
- ▶ Constructing XML content
- ▶ Modifying XML content
- ▶ Sorting XML nodes
- ▶ Serializing Groovy Beans to XML

Introduction

Dealing with XML in Java is notoriously a tedious business. The Java architects traded flexibility for simplicity, and the Java XML APIs are considered among the lower peaks of the language. Fortunately, Groovy offers a marvelous alternative for reading and producing XML. It's so good that once you experience Groovy's native parsers and emitters, you'll wonder why you used anything else.

This chapter is divided into recipes that deal with reading XML and producing XML. The two Groovy parsers, XmlParser and XmlSlurper, are discussed in detail as well as the two XML producers, MarkupBuilder and StreamingMarkupBuilder. We also touch on advanced topics such as the serialization of Java and Groovy objects to XML, and element tree navigation with XPath and GPath.

Reading XML using XmlSlurper

The **eXtensible Markup Language** or simply XML is the standard data format for exchanging information among computer systems. The first two recipes of this chapter show how to parse XML using Groovy. There are two parsers available in the groovy.util package, XmlParser and XmlSlurper. They both expose similar API; but there are use cases for when it is more appropriate to use one or the other. In this recipe, we look at how to read XML with XmlSlurper and its main peculiarities.

Getting ready

For the examples in the rest of this recipe, we will work with an XML document (shown in the following code) containing a list of works from William Shakespeare. The document is named shakespeare.xml:

```xml
<?xml version="1.0" ?>
<bib:bibliography xmlns:bib="http://bibliography.org"
  xmlns:lit="http://literature.org">
<bib:author>William Shakespeare</bib:author>
  <lit:play>
    <lit:year>1589</lit:year>
    <lit:title>The Two Gentlemen of Verona.</lit:title>
  </lit:play>
  <lit:play>
    <lit:year>1594</lit:year>
    <lit:title>Love's Labour's Lost.</lit:title>
  </lit:play>
  <lit:play>
    <lit:year>1594</lit:year>
    <lit:title>Romeo and Juliet.</lit:title>
  </lit:play>
  <lit:play>
    <lit:year>1595</lit:year>
    <lit:title>A Midsummer-Night's Dream.</lit:title>
  </lit:play>
</bib:bibliography>
```

How to do it...

Let's go through the process of parsing the previously mentioned XML file:

1. One way to read XML data using `XmlSlurper` is to create an instance of the class and pass a `java.io.File` object, which references the file we want to read, into the `parse` method:

    ```
    def xmlSource = new File('shakespeare.xml')
    def bibliography = new XmlSlurper().parse(xmlSource)
    ```

2. The `parse` method returns an implementation of `groovy.util.slurpersupport.GPathResult`, which can be used to navigate the XML element tree. For example, the following code will print the text representation of the author element:

    ```
    println bibliography.author
    ```

3. Deeper elements and element collections can also be referenced with the help of the `"."` operator. Also, a set of finder and iterator methods are available to build complex search expressions:

    ```
    bibliography.play
            .findAll { it.year.toInteger() > 1592 }
            .each { println it.title }
    ```

    The expressions that are used to navigate (and eventually also modify) the XML tree are referred to as GPath expressions. More examples of those expressions can be found in the *Searching in XML with GPath* recipe.

4. The output of the script should be as follows:

    ```
    William Shakespeare
    Love's Labour's Lost.
    Romeo and Juliet.
    A Midsummer-Night's Dream.
    ```

How it works...

The previous example selects all the plays written after `1592` and prints their titles.

Groovy's `XmlSlurper` resides in the `groovy.util` package, which is imported automatically by Groovy. That's why we do not need an `import` statement for that class.

`XmlSlurper` is a SAX-based parser; it loads the full document in memory, but it doesn't require extra memory to process the document using GPath. GPath expressions are lazily evaluated and no extra objects are created when evaluating the expression. `XmlSlurper` is also `null`-safe: when accessing an attribute that doesn't exist, it returns an empty string; the same goes for a non-existing node.

As a rule of thumb, you want to use `XmlSlurper` when you intend to process only a small part of the document; while it is more efficient to use `XmlParser` when you have to process the whole XML.

See also

> ▸ *Reading XML using XmlParser*

> ▸ *Searching in XML with GPath*

> ▸ `http://groovy.codehaus.org/api/groovy/util/XmlSlurper.html`

> ▸ `http://groovy.codehaus.org/api/groovy/util/slurpersupport/`
>   `GPathResult.html`

> ▸ `http://groovy.codehaus.org/Processing+XML`

Reading XML using XmlParser

In the previous recipe, *Reading XML using XmlSlurper*, we learned how to read an XML document using the `XmlSlurper` provided by Groovy. Now it's time to look at the other parser available in Groovy, `groovy.util.XmlParser`. Its internal implementation differs from `groovy.util.XmlSlurper`, but it exposes a very similar API when it comes to document parsing, navigation, and modification.

In this recipe, we will cover the essential usage scenarios for the `XmlParser` class and its differences from `XmlSlurper`.

How to do it...

Let's use the same `shakespeare.xml` file we used in the *Reading XML using XmlSlurper* recipe.

1. Reading XML data is very similar to `XmlSlurper`. You need to create an instance of `XmlParser` and pass a file reference to its `parse` method as shown:

   ```
   def xmlSource = new File('shakespeare.xml')
   def bibliography = new XmlParser().parse(xmlSource)
   ```

2. As with `XmlSlurper`, GPath expressions (see the *Searching in XML with GPath* recipe for more advanced examples) are also possible with `XmlParser`. For example, the code to print the titles of all plays written after `1592` would be as follows:

```
println bibliography.'bib:author'.text()

bibliography.'lit:play'
        .findAll { it.'lit:year'
                        .text().toInteger() > 1592 }
        .each { println it.'lit:title'.text() }
```

3. The output of the script will be the same as in the previous recipe:

```
William Shakespeare
Love's Labour's Lost.
Romeo and Juliet.
A Midsummer-Night's Dream.
```

How it works...

Navigating XML data with `XmlParser` is slightly different from `XmlSlurper`. In order to find an element, you need to use its **fully qualified name** (**FQN**) including the exact prefix. Since, in our XML example, we use the `bib:` prefix for the author element, we need to refer to author's data as `bib:author` (or as `*:author` to be more independent).

If our XML example didn't contain a FQN, then we could have referred to them in a very similar way as we did for `XmlSlurper`, for example, `bibliography.author`.

In step 2, you may have noticed that we have used the `text` method to get the textual representation of the `author` element. That's because `XmlParser` returns instances of `groovy.util.Node`, whose `toString` method does not return the element's textual content by default. There is also the `attribute` method that accepts a name and returns the given attribute. If you ask for an attribute that doesn't exist, `attribute` returns null (this is the opposite behavior of `XmlSlurper` that returns an empty string).

The main difference between `XmlParser` and `XmlSlurper` is that the first uses the `groovy.util.Node` type and its GPath expressions result in lists of nodes, which are easily manipulable using our knowledge of lists and collections. Compared to `XmlSlurper`, `XmlParser` consumes more memory because it has to create an intermediate data structure to represent the node tree, but it makes XML tree queries a bit faster. So, it's up to developers to decide which implementation better suits their needs.

See also

▶ *Reading XML using XmlSlurper*

▶ *Searching in XML with GPath*

▶ `http://groovy.codehaus.org/api/groovy/util/XmlParser.html`

▶ `http://groovy.codehaus.org/api/groovy/util/Node.html`

▶ `http://groovy.codehaus.org/api/groovy/util/NodeList.html`

▶ `http://groovy.codehaus.org/GPath`

Reading XML content with namespaces

XML namespaces, in a way, are similar to Java packages because they allow creating an additional context for grouping a set of elements. We already noted some differences in namespace handling for the `XmlParser` and `XmlSlurper` classes in the *Reading XML using XmlParser* and *Reading XML using XmlSlurper* recipes.

In this recipe, we dig a bit deeper into the details of XML namespace support in Groovy.

Getting ready

Let's use the same `shakespeare.xml` file we used for the *Reading XML using XmlParser* and *Reading XML using XmlSlurper* recipes.

How to do it...

`XmlParser` requires you to specify an element name exactly as it appears in the parsed XML, including the name of the prefix used in the actual XML content. This makes the code fragile because the namespace prefixes have to match.

1. In order to make code that is based on `XmlParser` more reliable in respect to namespaces, we can resort to the `groovy.xml.Namespace` class as shown in the following code:

```
import groovy.xml.Namespace

def xmlSource = new File('shakespeare.xml')
def bibliography = new XmlParser().parse(xmlSource)

def bib = new Namespace('http://bibliography.org', 'bib')
def lit = new Namespace('http://literature.org', 'lit')

println bibliography[bib.author].text()
println bibliography[lit.play].findAll {
  it[lit.year].text().toInteger() > 1592
}.size()
```

2. `XmlSlurper` has a similar API for declaring the prefixes and namespaces required to navigate the nodes, shown in the following code:

```
def xmlSource = new File('shakespeare.xml')
def bibliography = new XmlSlurper().parse(xmlSource)

bibliography.declareNamespace(
   bib: 'http://bibliography.org',
   lit: 'http://literature.org')

println bibliography.'bib:author'
println bibliography.'lit:play'.findAll {
   it.'lit:year'.toInteger() > 1592
}.size()
```

3. The output of both scripts is indistinguishable:

```
William Shakespare

3
```

How it works...

Both of the previous code snippets extract the author's name and the number of plays written after `1592` from our reference bibliography data XML document.

In the case of `XmlParser`, we declare two instances of the `groovy.xml.Namespace` class. When we fetch a property (for example, `bibliography[bib.author]`) from the `Namespace` object, this is really what happens:

▶ The `bib.author` expression returns a value of `javax.xml.namespace.QName` type.

▶ The array reference `bibliography[bib.author]` is translated by Groovy into a call to the `getAt` method of the `groovy.util.Node` class. This method accepts a `QName` as an argument and returns a node if the `QName` is found, as shown next:

```
QName ns = bib.author
Node n = bibliography.getAt(ns)
```

In the case of `XmlSlurper`, the `groovy.util.slurpersupport.GPathResult` class instance (returned by the `parse` method) has an additional method to declare namespaces called, not surprisingly, `declareNamespace`.

Please note that unlike `XmlParser`, the `XmlSlurper` implementation (or more specifically `GPathResult`) does not force you to depend on namespaces or prefixes at all. You can refer to elements and attributes using their local names, and only resort to using namespace prefixes if there are same local names under different namespaces.

If you try to use a fully qualified name (for example. `bib:author`) before declaring the namespace within an `XmlSlurper` instance, you'll get no result back. Also, namespace prefixes defined by `declareNamespace` do not have to match prefixes appearing in the actual XML file.

The `declareNamespace` method takes a map of prefixes and namespaces. When those are defined, you can use them to reference elements using their fully qualified names.

There's more...

If you plan to switch between `XmlParser` and `XmlSlurper` implementations and you need to parse XML that uses namespaces, then the safest approach is to use the `*:` prefix for element or attribute queries. For example:

```
println bibliography.'*:author'.text()
```

See also

- *Reading XML using XmlParser*
- *Reading XML using XmlSlurper*
- *Searching in XML with GPath*
- http://groovy.codehaus.org/api/groovy/util/XmlParser.html
- http://groovy.codehaus.org/api/groovy/util/XmlSlurper.html
- http://groovy.codehaus.org/api/groovy/util/Node.html
- http://groovy.codehaus.org/api/groovy/xml/Namespace.html

Searching in XML with GPath

When using `XmlSlurper` or `XmlParser` with Groovy (see the *Reading XML using XmlSlurper* and *Reading XML using XmlParser* recipes), the returned parsed result can be queried using GPath. GPath is a way to navigate nested data structures in Groovy. Sometimes GPath is called an expression language integrated into Groovy; but, in fact, GPath does not have a separate compiler or interpreter, it's just the way Groovy language and core classes are designed to make data structure navigation and modification concise and easy-to-read.

GPath, in certain ways, is similar to XPath (`http://www.w3.org/TR/xpath/`) that is used for querying XML data. The main difference is that it uses dots instead of slashes to navigate the XML hierarchy and it can be used for navigating the hierarchy of objects (**Plain Old Java Objects** (**POJOs**) and **Plain Old Groovy Objects** (**POGOs**) respectively).

The GPath syntax closely resembles **E4X** (**ECMAScript for XML**), which is an ECMAScript extension for accessing XML content.

This recipe will show how to parse an XML document and query its values and attributes through GPath.

Getting ready

As usual, we start by defining an XML snippet to test out our XML recipe. In this recipe, we deal with movies. *IMDB (Internet Movie Database)* at `http://www.imdb.com` is the *de facto* standard for everything you want to know around the cinema universe. IMDB stores information about pretty much every movie ever made, along with actors and production data. IMDB is also a good citizen of the Internet and exposes API to retrieve the same data available on the site in XML. The API is not really documented, so we decide to roll out our own XML format based on the data we fetch from IMDB. Let's print the information about some movies having the word `groovy` in the title (admittedly not many!).

```
def groovyMoviez = '''<?xml version="1.0" ?>
  <movie-result>
    <movie id="tt0116288">
      <title>Groovy Days</title>
      <year>1996</year>
      <director>Peter Bay</director>
      <country>Denmark</country>
      <stars>
        Ken Vedsegaard,
        Sofie Gråbøl,
```

```
        Martin Brygmann</stars>
   </movie>
   <movie id="tt1189088">
     <title>Cool and Groovy</title>
     <year>1956</year>
     <director>Will Cowan</director>
     <country>USA</country>
     <stars>Anita Day,
        Buddy De Franco and
        Buddy DeFranco Quartet</stars>
   </movie>
   <movie id="tt1492859">
     <title>Groovy: The Colors of Pacita Abad</title>
     <year>2005</year>
     <director>Milo Sogueco</director>
     <country>Philippines</country>
     <stars/>
   </movie>
  </movie-result>
'''
```

How to do it...

Let's see how we can navigate the previous XML with GPath.

1. The first step is to process the XML using `XmlSlurper` so that we can access the GPath API:

   ```
   def results = new XmlSlurper().parseText(groovyMoviez)
   ```

2. The rest is just Groovy's magic. The XML structure is magically converted into a navigable object structure based on the tags and attribute of the XML document:

   ```
   for (flick in results.movie) {
     println "Movie with id ${flick.@id} " +
       "is directed by ${flick.director}"
   }
   ```

3. The code snippet yields the following output:

   ```
   Movie with id tt0116288 is directed by Peter Bay
   Movie with id tt1189088 is directed by Will Cowan
   Movie with id tt1492859 is directed by Milo Sogueco
   ```

   The code becomes extremely fluent and *ceremony-free*, just code and data.

4. Want to see something more awesome? Check out what we can do with the Groovy's *spread-dot* operator (* .):

```
results.movie*.title.each { println "- ${it}" }
results.movie.findAll {
   it.year.toInteger() > 1990
}*.title.each {
   println "title: ${it}"
}
```

5. The output will be as follows:

```
title: Groovy Days

title: Groovy: The Colors of Pacita Abad
```

6. Searching inside the XML document for specific content is also pretty simple:

```
results.movie.findAll {
   it.director.text().contains('Milo')
}.each {
   println "- ${it.title}"
}
```

The findAll method is applied to the movie node and the closure passed to the findAll method checks for the presence of the word Milo in the director tag.

7. Should you need to search across all the nodes of the document (as opposed to a specific set of children, such as movie), it is possible to use the depthFirst method (or its shortcut **) on the root node:

```
results.'**'.findAll {
   it.director.text().contains('Milo')
}.each {
   println "- ${it.title}"
}
```

8. The output will be as follows:

```
- Groovy: The Colors of Pacita Abad
```

How it works...

In the first step, we create a parser, an XmlSlurper in this case.

 Please note how this time, we use the parseText method to read a string containing a valid XML document.

Step 2 shows how we can easily access the attributes and values of a `movie`, while iterating on the `results`.

Groovy cannot possibly know anything in advance about the elements and attributes that are available in the XML document. It happily compiles anyway. That's one capability that distinguishes a dynamic language.

Step 4 introduces the spread-dot operator: a shortcut to the `collect` method of a collection. The result is a new collection containing the outcome of the operation applied to each member of the original collection.

There's more...

To iterate over collections and transform each element of the collection in Groovy, the `collect` method can be used. The transformation is defined as a closure passed to the method:

```
assert [0,2,4,6] == (0..3).collect { it * 2 }
```

By using a spread-dot operator, we can rewrite the previous snippet as follows:

```
assert [0,2,4,6] == (0..3)*.multiply(2)
```

In the context of a GPath query for XML, the spread-dot accesses the properties of each node returned from the `findAll` method, movies produced after the year 1990.

See also

- ▸ *Reading XML using XmlParser*
- ▸ *Reading XML using XmlSlurper*
- ▸ `http://groovy.codehaus.org/GPath`
- ▸ `http://groovy.codehaus.org/api/groovy/util/slurpersupport/GPathResult.html`

Searching in XML with XPath

XPath is a W3C-standard query language for selecting nodes from an XML document. That is somewhat equivalent to SQL for databases or regular expressions for text. XPath is a very powerful query language, and it's beyond the scope of this book to delve into the extended XPath capabilities. This recipe will show some basic queries to select nodes and groups of nodes.

Getting ready

Let's start as usual by defining an XML document that we can use for selecting nodes:

```
def todos = '''
<?xml version="1.0" ?>
<todos>
  <task created="2012-09-24" owner="max">
    <title>Buy Milk</title>
    <priority>3</priority>
    <location>WalMart</location>
    <due>2012-09-25</due>
    <alarm-type>sms</alarm-type>
    <alert-before>1H</alert-before>
  </task>
  <task created="2012-09-27" owner="lana">
    <title>Pay the rent</title>
    <priority>1</priority>
    <location>Computer</location>
    <due>2012-09-30</due>
    <alarm-type>email</alarm-type>
    <alert-before>1D</alert-before>
  </task>
  <task created="2012-09-21" owner="rick">
    <title>Take out the trash</title>
    <priority>3</priority>
    <location>Home</location>
    <due>2012-09-22</due>
    <alarm-type>none</alarm-type>
    <alert-before/>
  </task>
</todos>
'''
```

The previous snippet represents the data for an application for personal task management; there aren't enough of those these days! Surely no self-respecting to-do application comes without a powerful filtering feature, such as finding all due tasks, or showing only the task that I can execute in a specific place.

How to do it...

Let's go into the details of this recipe.

1. Before we can fire our XPath queries, the document has to be parsed using the Java DOM API:

```
import javax.xml.parsers.DocumentBuilderFactory
import javax.xml.xpath.*

def inputStream = new ByteArrayInputStream(todos.bytes)
def myTodos = DocumentBuilderFactory.
                    newInstance().
                    newDocumentBuilder().
                    parse(inputStream).
                    documentElement
```

2. Once the XML document is parsed, we can create an instance of the XPath engine:

```
def xpath = XPathFactory.
                    newInstance().
                    newXPath()
```

3. Now we are ready to run some queries on our task list. The simplest thing to do is to print all the task names:

```
def nodes = xpath.evaluate(
                    '//task',
                    myTodos,
                    XPathConstants.NODESET
                )

nodes.each {
    println xpath.evaluate('title/text()', it)
}
```

4. The output yielded is as follows:

Buy Milk
Pay the rent
Take out the trash

5. OK, now that we've got the API basics out of the way, it's time for more complex queries. The next example shows how to print the titles in a more Groovy way:

```
xpath.evaluate(
            '//task/title/text()',
            myTodos,
            XPathConstants.NODESET
        ).each { println it.nodeValue }
```

Note that we are using the API `getNodeValue()` method to extract the content of the node.

6. What about fetching only tasks with a low priority (that is 2, 3, 4, and so on)?

```
xpath.evaluate(
        '//task[priority>1]/title/text()',
        myTodos,
        XPathConstants.NODESET
    ).each { println it.nodeValue }
```

7. The output yielded is as follows:

Buy Milk

Take out the trash

8. Naturally, it is also possible to filter by node attribute. For instance, to fetch all tasks assigned to `lana`:

```
xpath.evaluate(
        "//task[@owner='lana']/title/text()",
        myTodos,
        XPathConstants.NODESET
    ).each { println it.nodeValue }
```

9. The output yielded is as follows:

Pay the rent

10. Finally, we are going to retrieve nodes based on the actual content. Let's build a slightly more complex query that retrieves tasks based on the content of the `location` and `alarm-type` tag:

```
xpath.evaluate(
        '//task[location="Computer" and ' +
        'contains(alarm-type, "email")]/' +
        'title/text()',
        myTodos,
        XPathConstants.NODESET
    ).each { println it.nodeValue }
```

11. The output yielded is as follows:

Pay the rent

12. The previous snippet uses the XPath's `contains` keyword to probe for a string match in a specific tag. We can also use the same keyword to search on all tags:

```
xpath.evaluate(
        "//*[contains(.,'WalMart')]/title/text()",
        myTodos,
        XPathConstants.NODESET
    ).each { println it.nodeValue }
```

13. The output yielded is as follows:

Buy milk

How it works...

In order to use XPath, we need to build a Java DOM parser. Neither `XmlParser` nor `XmlSlurper` offer XPath querying capabilities, so we have to resort to building a parser using the not-so-elegant Java API. In step 1, we create a new instance of `DocumentBuilderFactory` from which we create a `DocumentBuilder`. The default factory implementation defined by this plugin mechanism is `com.sun.org.apache.xerces.internal.jaxp.DocumentBuilderFactoryImpl`. The factory is used to produce a builder which parses the document.

The `evaluate` function used to run the XPath queries takes the following three parameters:

▸ The actual XPath query string (in step 3, we use `//task` to select all the nodes named `task`)

▸ The document

▸ The desired return type

In step 3, the return type is a `NodeList`, a list implementation on which Groovy can easily iterate on. When the return type is not specified the default return type is a String.

There's more...

What if you need to find all the tasks due today in your task list?

XPath 1.0 (the default implementation bundled with the JDK 6 and 7, dating back to 1999) doesn't support date functions, and you are left to rather ugly string comparison tricks.

The more recent specification of XPath, v2.0, supports date functions and a plethora of new extremely powerful features. Luckily third-party libraries supporting XPath 2.0 are available and can be readily used with Groovy. One of these libraries is Saxon 9, which supports XSLT 2.0, XQuery 1.0, and XPath 2.0 at the basic level of conformance defined by W3C.

In this example, we are going to build a query that filters out the task due today. The XML data defined at the beginning of this recipe is used also in this snippet:

```groovy
@Grab('net.sf.saxon:Saxon-HE:9.4')
@GrabExclude('xml-apis:xml-apis')
import javax.xml.parsers.DocumentBuilderFactory
import javax.xml.xpath.*
import net.sf.saxon.lib.NamespaceConstant

def today = '2012-09-21'

def todos = '''
<?xml version="1.0" ?>
<todos>
   ...
</todos>
'''

def inputStream = new ByteArrayInputStream(todos.bytes)
def myTodos     = DocumentBuilderFactory.
                     newInstance().
                     newDocumentBuilder().
                     parse(inputStream).
                     documentElement

// Set the SAXON XPath implementation
// by setting a System property
System.setProperty(
   'javax.xml.xpath.XPathFactory:' +
   NamespaceConstant.OBJECT_MODEL_SAXON,
   'net.sf.saxon.xpath.XPathFactoryImpl'
)

// Create the XPath 2.0 engine
def xpathSaxon = XPathFactory.
                   newInstance(
                      XPathConstants.DOM_OBJECT_MODEL
                   ).newXPath()

// Print out all task names
// expiring on 22, September 2012
xpathSaxon.evaluate(
            '//task[xs:date(due) = ' +
            'xs:date("2012-09-22")]/title/text()',
```

```
            myTodos,
            XPathConstants.NODESET
        ).each { println it.nodeValue }

// Bonus: print out all tasks
// for which the due date falls in September
xpathSaxon.evaluate(
            '//task[month-from-date(due)=9]/title/text()',
            myTodos,
            XPathConstants.NODESET
        ).each { println it.nodeValue }
```

See also

More information about the XPath query language can be found at
`http://www.w3.org/TR/xpath`. Also, the following links may be useful for further reading:

- ▶ `http://www.w3.org/TR/xpath20/`
- ▶ `http://saxon.sourceforge.net/`

Constructing XML content

The previous *Reading XML using XmlSlurper*, *Reading XML using XmlParser*, and *Searching in XML with GPath* recipes have been useful to learn the ingredients and the techniques for consuming and querying XML documents. In this recipe, we will cover how to produce XML using Groovy's `MarkupBuilder`.

How to do it...

Let's create a bibliography XML similar to the one we used in the *Reading XML using XmlSlurper* recipe.

1. In order to start using `MarkupBuilder`, you first need to import it since it's not available by default:

    ```
    import groovy.xml.MarkupBuilder
    ```

2. Then you need to create a writer object that will be responsible for the final output of the XML content. For the sake of simplicity let's use:

    ```
    java.io.StringWriter:
    def writer = new StringWriter()
    ```

3. Finally, we need to create an instance of `MarkupBuilder` and pass the writer object to it:

    ```
    def xml = new MarkupBuilder(writer)
    ```

4. At this point, we are ready to create some XML:

    ```
    xml.bibliography {
        author('William Shakespeare')
        play {
            year('1595')
            title('A Midsummer-Night\'s Dream.')
        }
    }
    ```

5. And now, by printing our writer object:

    ```
    println writer
    ```

    We'll get the following output:

    ```
    <bibliography>
        <author>William Shakespeare</author>
        <play>
            <year>1595</year>
            <title>A Midsummer-Night's Dream.</title>
        </play>
    </bibliography>
    ```

How it works...

The previous XML construction code is a set of nested dynamic method calls that are mapped directly to XML element names. String parameter passed to those methods defines the content of the element (for example, `author('William Shakespeare')`).

All the magic happens behind the scenes with the help of Groovy's **Meta Object Protocol** (**MOP**), which is heavily used by `MarkupBuilder` (and in general, any other builder class within Groovy, see the *Defining data structures as code in Groovy* recipe in *Chapter 3, Using Groovy Language Features*). Every object in Groovy extends from `groovy.lang.GroovyObject`, which offers two methods: `invokeMethod` and `getProperty`. Those methods are overridden by `MarkupBuilder` to handle dynamic method names that are translated into an XML tree.

It is possible to construct any kind of markup with this approach including HTML/XHTML.

There's more...

Another way to create XML content is by using the `groovy.xml.` `StreamingMarkupBuilder` class. Its API is similar, but a bit more complex than the `MarkupBuilder` API. On the other hand, it offers better memory management and allows creating large XML files with minimal memory footprint:

```
import groovy.xml.StreamingMarkupBuilder
def builder = new StreamingMarkupBuilder()
def bibliography = builder.bind {
  bibliography {
    author('William Shakespeare')
    play {
      year('1595')
      title('A Midsummer-Night's Dream.')
    }
  }
}
println bibliography
```

The previous code snippet achieves a similar result to the initial example.

In general, `MarkupBuilder` to `StreamingMarkupBuilder` is the same as `XmlParser` (see the *Reading XML using XmlParser* recipe) is to `XmlSlurper` (see the *Reading XML using XmlSlurper* recipe). There are three main differences between `MarkupBuilder` and `StreamingMarkupBuilder`:

- `StreamingMarkupBuilder` doesn't output the XML until a writer is explicitly passed, while `MarkupBuilder,` by default, outputs to `System.out`.

- `MarkupBuilder` processes the XML generation synchronously while `StreamingMarkupBuilder` generates the XML only when is passed to a Writer. It is possible, for instance, to define a number of closures containing snippets of XML and generate the markup only when needed.

- `MarkupBuilder` formats the output for increased readability whereas `StreamingMarkupBuilder` does not.

See also

- *Reading XML using XmlSlurper*
- *Reading XML using XmlParser*
- `http://groovy.codehaus.org/Creating+XML+using+Groovy%27s+Marku pBuilder`
- `http://groovy.codehaus.org/api/groovy/xml/MarkupBuilder.html`

> ▶ `http://groovy.codehaus.org/gapi/groovy/xml/`
> `StreamingMarkupBuilder.html`

Modifying XML content

In this recipe, we will learn how to update and delete nodes of a parsed XML document using the `XmlParser`.

Getting ready

Let's start by parsing the following XML with the `XmlParser` (see the *Reading XML using XmlParser* recipe):

```
def carXml = '''
<?xml version="1.0" ?>
<cool-cars>
  <car manufacturer="Ferrari">
    <model>430 Scuderia</model>
  </car>
  <car manufacturer="Porsche">
    <model>911</model>
  </car>
  <car manufacturer="Lotus">
    <model>Elan</model>
  </car>
  <car manufacturer="Pagani">
    <model>Huayra</model>
  </car>
</cool-cars>
'''

def coolCars = new XmlParser().parseText(carXml)
```

How to do it...

The simplest way to change the value of a node is to reference it using the position of the node itself.

1. For instance, if we want to change the model of the Lotus brand to Elise, we can reference the model node as showed in the example:

   ```
   coolCars.car[2].model[0].value = 'Elise'
   ```

2. Alternatively, it is possible to find a node by its contents and alter it:

```
coolCars.find {
   it.@manufacturer == 'Ferrari'
}.model[0].value = 'Testarossa'
```

Instead of referencing the node by its position, we use the `find` method to reference the attribute of the node.

3. What about modifying an attribute of a node?

```
coolCars.car[1].@manufacturer = 'Ford'
```

4. Finally, to delete nodes, you can use a very similar approach:

```
coolCars.remove(coolCars.car[3])
coolCars.remove(coolCars.car[1])
```

or even better:

```
coolCars.findAll { it.@manufacturer.startsWith('P') }
        .each    { coolCars.remove(it) }
```

This previous example deletes every car's manufacturer, whose name starts with the letter P.

5. Now we can print the result:

```
new XmlNodePrinter().print(coolCars)
```

6. The output will be as follows:

```
<cool-cars>
  <car manufacturer="Ferrari">
    <model>
       Testarossa
    </model>
  </car>
  <car manufacturer="Lotus">
    <model>
       Elise
    </model>
  </car>
</cool-cars>
```

How it works...

Thanks to Groovy's dynamic typing and metaprogramming capabilities, we can access the members of our document directly by name, as shown in several other recipes from this chapter: *Reading XML using XmlSlurper*, *Searching in XML with GPath*, and *Constructing XML content*.

In most cases, we operate directly on the `groovy.util.Node` classes or collections of nodes. The full power of the Groovy Collection API can be applied easily to navigate and modify the document tree.

In the previous code, we also made use of the `.@` operator, which gives access to an attribute of an XML element.

In the last step, we print out the resulting in-memory node tree to the standard output with the help of the `XmlNodePrinter` class. This class pretty prints a `groovy.util.Node` including all children in XML format.

See also

▶ `http://groovy.codehaus.org/api/groovy/util/Node.html`

▶ `http://groovy.codehaus.org/api/groovy/util/XmlNodePrinter.html`

Sorting XML nodes

Sometimes it is important to preserve XML data in certain order. Ordered data is easier to read and search, and some computer systems may require data they consume to be sorted. One of the most basic requirements that arise when dealing with XML is being able to sort nodes either by node value or attribute value. In this recipe, we are going to go through a couple of ways of achieving this with Groovy.

How to do it...

For this recipe, we will reuse the same XML document defined in the *Searching in XML with GPath* recipe.

1. The *grooviest* way to sort nodes is to replace the entire element tree with a sorted one:

```
import groovy.xml.XmlUtil
def groovyMoviez = '''
<?xml version="1.0" encoding="UTF-8"?>
...
'''
def movieList = new XmlParser().parseText(groovyMoviez)
movieList.value = movieList.movie.sort {
                    it.title.text()
                }
println XmlUtil.serialize(movieList)
```

2. This will yield:

```
<?xml version="1.0" encoding="UTF-8"?>
<movie-result>
  <movie>
    <title>Cool and Groovy</title>
    ...
  </movie>
  <movie>
    <title>Groovy Days</title>
    ...
  </movie>
  <movie>
    <title>Groovy: The Colors of Pacita Abad</title>
    ...
  </movie>
</movie-result>
```

How it works...

In step 1, we call the dynamic method, `movie`, which returns a `NodeList` (see the *Searching in XML with GPath* recipe). To sort the elements of the `NodeList`, we invoke the `sort` method. The `groovy.util.NodeList` super type is, in fact, an `ArrayList` and benefits of the multitude of great features that come with Groovy collections. The closure passed to the `sort` method defines the expression used to sort elements of the collection. In this case, we used movie titles, which are sorted in lexicographical order. If we need to sort movie collection in a descending order, then we can either reverse a collection:

```
movieList.value = movieList.movie.sort {
  it.title.text()
}.reverse()
```

Or pass a more verbose closure that operates on two compared elements, to the `sort` method:

```
movieList.value = movieList.movie.sort { a, b ->
  b.title.text() > a.title.text()
}
```

At the end of the script, we use the `groovy.xml.XmlUtil` class, which is a handy utility that Groovy provides for serializing XML node trees. Another alternative to serializing XML is the `XmlNodePrinter` class, which we touch in the *Modifying XML content* recipe. In fact, `XmlUtil` is using `XmlNodePrinter` under the hood.

There's more...

We can also create more complex sort expressions, such as:

```
movieList.value = movieList.movie.sort { a, b ->
    a.year.text().toInteger() <=> b.year.text().toInteger() ?:
    a.country.text() <=> b.country.text()
}
```

In this example, the *Elvis* operator (`?:`) is used, which is a handy shortcut for a ternary operator. First we compare movie release years, and if they match, we sort based on country name. The *spaceship* operator (`<=>`) it's just a shortcut for the `compareTo` function. It returns -1 when the left side is smaller than the right side, 1 if the left side is greater, and 0 if they are equal.

 Please note that, in the case of the `year` element, the value is converted to an integer value for the sorting algorithm to work correctly.

For the sake of completeness, we will also demonstrate how to sort an XML tree using XSLT. This approach is not exactly easy on the eye, but can be used also as a general way to use XSLT transformations with Groovy.

The first step is to declare an XSLT transformation set. The sorting is applied to the `title` tag:

```
def sortXSLT = '''<?xml version="1.0" encoding="ISO-8859-1"?>
<xsl:stylesheet version="1.0"
xmlns:xsl="http://www.w3.org/1999/XSL/Transform">
<xsl:template match="@* | node()">
    <xsl:copy>
        <xsl:apply-templates select="@* | node()">
            <xsl:sort select="title"/>
        </xsl:apply-templates>
    </xsl:copy>
</xsl:template>
</xsl:stylesheet>'''
```

Next, you need to add a bunch of imports to your code:

```
import javax.xml.transform.TransformerFactory
import javax.xml.transform.stream.StreamResult
import javax.xml.transform.stream.StreamSource
```

Finally, here is the code to run the transformation on the original XML document:

```
def factory = TransformerFactory.newInstance()
def xsltSource = new StreamSource(new StringReader(sortXSLT))
def transformer = factory.newTransformer(xsltSource)
def source = new StreamSource(new StringReader(groovyMoviez))
def result = new StreamResult(new StringWriter())
transformer.transform(source, result)
println result.writer.toString()
```

See also

▸ *Searching in XML with GPath*

▸ *Constructing XML content*

▸ *Modifying XML content*

▸ `http://groovy.codehaus.org/Operators`

▸ `http://groovy.codehaus.org/api/groovy/xml/XmlUtil.html`

▸ `http://groovy.codehaus.org/api/groovy/util/XmlNodePrinter.html`

▸ `http://www.w3.org/TR/xslt20/`

Serializing Groovy Beans to XML

In this recipe, we are going to learn how to serialize a Groovy Bean into XML and back. Groovy Beans are discussed in detail in the *Writing less verbose Java Beans with Groovy Beans* recipe from *Chapter 3, Using Groovy Language Features*. The steps from this recipe can be applied either to POJO or POGO.

Getting ready

Groovy doesn't have a default XML object serializer. The `groovy.xml.MarkupBuilder` is an excellent tool for generating XML in a fluent way but doesn't offer any simple mechanism to create an XML document out of bean properties.

There is, on the other hand, a large offer of third-party Java libraries for XML serialization. In this recipe, we are going to look at XStream (`http://xstream.codehaus.org/`). XStream is a very popular library, with frequent releases and a dead-simple API. Did we mention XStream is also fast and has a ridiculously low memory footprint?

How to do it...

The following steps offer an insight into how to achieve our task:

1. Before we can use XStream, we need to fetch the dependency using Grape and import it:

```
@Grab('com.thoughtworks.xstream:xstream:1.4.3')
import com.thoughtworks.xstream.*
import com.thoughtworks.xstream.io.xml.*
```

2. Then we continue by creating a couple of Groovy Beans representing a customer:

```
import groovy.transform.TupleConstructor
@TupleConstructor
class Customer {
    Long id
    String name
    String lastName
    Address businessAddress
}
@TupleConstructor
class Address {
    String street
    String postcode
    String city
    String country
}
```

The `@TupleConstructor` annotation is mentioned in the *Writing less verbose Java Beans with Groovy Beans* from *Chapter 3, Using Groovy Language Features*.

3. Finally, let's get down to business and serialize our customer:

```
def xstream = new XStream()
def john = new Customer(
            100,
            'John',
            'Red',
            new Address(
                'Ocean Drive 101',
                '33139',
                'Miami',
                'US'
            )
        )
def xmlCustomer = xstream.toXML(john)
println xmlCustomer
```

4. The generated XML looks as follows:

```
<Customer>
  <id>100</id>
  <name>John</name>
  <lastName>Red</lastName>
  <businessAddress>
    <street>Ocean Drive 101</street>
    <postcode>33139</postcode>
    <city>Miami</city>
    <country>US</country>
  </businessAddress>
</Customer>
```

Very cool indeed.

5. To convert the XML back into a bean, it's straightforward as well:

```
def xstream = new XStream(new DomDriver())
Customer johnred = xstream.fromXML(xmlCustomer)
println johnred.id
println johnred.businessAddress.postcode
```

6. The final lines will print:

```
100
33139
```

How it works...

Whenever XStream encounters an object that needs to be converted to/from XML, it delegates to a suitable converter implementation associated with the class of that object.

XStream comes bundled with many converters for common types, including primitives, string, collections, arrays, null, date, etc. XStream also has a default converter that is used when no other converters match a type. This uses reflection to automatically generate the XML for all the fields in an object.

If an object is composed of other objects, the converter may delegate to other converters.

There's more...

With XStream, it is also possible to drive the way the XML gets generated through aliases. There are different types of aliasing that can be applied to the serialization engine.

- ▶ **Class aliasing**: The name of the root element of the serialized class can be changed by applying an alias at the class level:

```
xstream.alias('Person', Customer)
```

The serialization process generates the following XML:

```
<Person>
  <id>100</id>
  <name>John</name>
  ...
</Person>
```

- ▶ **Field aliasing**: The name of the bean field can also be modified when it gets serialized:

```
xstream.aliasField('customer-id', Customer, 'id')
```

This changes the element name id into customer-id:

```
<Customer>
  <customer-id>100</customer-id>
  ...
</Customer>
```

- ▶ **Attribute aliasing**: In case you need to convert a bean field into an XML attribute, XStream gets you covered. Let's say that we want to make the id field an attribute of the <Person> element. It couldn't be easier:

```
xstream.useAttributeFor(Customer, 'id')
```

The resulting serialized XML looks like:

```
<Person id="100">
  <name>John</name>
</Person>
```

See also

The documentation for XStream is extremely good, and if you want to use this tool to its full potential, it is recommended to spend some time reading the manual at http://xstream.codehaus.org/.

6
Working with JSON in Groovy

In this chapter, we will cover:

- ▶ Parsing JSON messages with JsonSlurper
- ▶ Constructing JSON messages with JsonBuilder
- ▶ Modifying JSON messages
- ▶ Validating JSON messages
- ▶ Converting JSON message to XML
- ▶ Converting JSON message to Groovy Bean
- ▶ Using JSON to configure your scripts

Introduction

JSON (JavaScript Object Notation) (http://www.json.org/) is a data interchange format, similar in scope to XML or CSV. It uses a very lightweight serialization form and works very well for exchanging data between a web client (a browser) and a remote server, but it is not limited to only that.

JSON is also a subset of the object literal notation of JavaScript. Being a subset of JavaScript implies that a JSON payload can be processed by the language natively. This is the main reason why JSON has become such a popular format for transferring serialized data between a remote API (often a RESTful API) and a JavaScript client.

But JSON is also very lightweight—especially if we compare it to the very chatty XML, the dethroned king of serialization—making it a suitable candidate for a general purpose data processing format (if you can live with some of its limitations such as the lack of namespace or poor complex data types support).

This chapter's recipes introduce the reader to Groovy native support for reading and producing JSON. We also look at some more advanced recipes such as conversion from and to XML and Groovy Beans.

Parsing JSON messages with JsonSlurper

The first thing you probably want to do with the JSON data is to parse it. JSON support was introduced in Groovy 1.8. The class for consuming JSON is named JsonSlurper and it behaves similarly to the XmlSlurper, presented in the *Reading XML using XmlSlurper* recipe in *Chapter 5, Working with XML in Groovy*.

This recipe introduces the reader to `JsonSlurper` and shows how to parse a JSON file and how to navigate the data structure created by `JsonSlurper`.

Getting ready

Let's assume we have a `ui.json` file which stores a definition of the UI layout for some JavaScript framework:

```
{
  "items":[
  {
    "type":"chart",
    "height":270,
    "width":319,
    "animate":true,
    "insetPadding":20,
    "axes":[
    {
      "type":"Time",
      "fields":[ "x" ],
      "position":"left",
      "title":"Time"
    },
    {
      "type":"Numeric",
      "fields":[ "y" ],
      "position":"bottom",
      "title":"Profit in EUR"
```

```
        }
        ],
        "series":[
        {
            "type":"bar",
            "label":{
                "display":"insideEnd",
                "field":"y",
                "color":"#333",
                "text-anchor":"middle"
            },
            "axis":"bottom",
            "xField":"x",
            "yField":[ "y" ]
        }
        ]
    }
    ]
}
```

How to do it...

The JSON data can be easily parsed with the help of the `groovy.json.JsonSlurper` class.

1. The `groovy.json` package is not included in the list of packages imported by default. For this reason, you need to explicitly import `JsonSlurper`:

```
import groovy.json.JsonSlurper
def reader = new FileReader('ui.json')
def ui = new JsonSlurper().parse(reader)
```

The `parse` method of `JsonSlurper` accepts a `File` or a `Reader` object. It is also possible to pass a `String` to `JsonSlurper` by invoking the `parseText` method.

2. After the JSON payload is successfully parsed, you can easily navigate through the resulting object using the familiar GPath-like expressions and closures:

```
ui.items.each { println it.type }

println ui.items[0]
    .axes
    .find {
        it.fields.contains('y')
    }.title
```

3. The complete output of the script looks like:

```
chart
Profit in EUR
```

How it works...

The first line in step 2 iterates through all the elements in the items node, which is a top-level collection in our JSON object and it prints the value of the `type` attribute of each of those objects. Since we have only one object in that collection it only prints `chart` in return.

The second line uses a slightly more complex expression. The expression's goal is simply to find the title used by the `y` axis.

The expression selects the first element of the items collection and subsequently gets the axes collection. It then searches the axes collection for the first element of the nested fields collection having the y value. Finally, it returns the title of the found element.

Unlike `XmlSlurper`, which uses an intermediate set of classes to present the XML tree, `JsonSlurper` transforms a JSON message to a nested combination of `Maps` and `Lists`.

For example, to show the actual classes used behind the scenes, we can fire up the following code:

```
println ui.getClass()
println ui.items.getClass()
```

It will print out the following class names:

```
class java.util.HashMap
class java.util.ArrayList
```

Knowing that the structure created by `JsonSlurper` is backed by Groovy's Collections, you can easily leverage all the `Collection` extension methods (such as `each`, `find`, and `collect`) available in Groovy to build expressions that search and modify your JSON objects.

There's more...

`JsonSlurper` is rather well-suited for most parsing needs. On the other hand, there are plenty of libraries available in the Java/Groovy ecosystem, which offer similar functionality:

▶ Google GSON: `http://code.google.com/p/google-gson/`

▶ JSONLib: `http://json-lib.sourceforge.net/`

▶ Jackson: `http://jackson.codehaus.org/`

▶ JSON.simple: `http://code.google.com/p/json-simple/`

See also

▸ *Constructing JSON messages with JsonBuilder*

▸ The *Reading XML using XmlSlurper* recipe in *Chapter 5, Working with XML in Groovy*

▸ `http://www.json.org/`

▸ `http://groovy.codehaus.org/gapi/groovy/json/JsonSlurper.html`

Constructing JSON messages with JsonBuilder

This recipe provides an overview of another class introduced in Groovy 1.8, which helps to construct JSON messages, the `JsonBuilder`.

This class works like any other builder class in Groovy (see the *Defining data structures as code in Groovy* recipe from *Chapter 3, Using Groovy Language Features*). A data structure based on `Lists` and `Maps` is defined, and JSON is split out when the string representation is requested.

How to do it...

The following steps will show some examples of using `JsonBuilder`.

1. Let's start right away with a simple script that builds the representation of a fictional customer:

```
import groovy.json.JsonBuilder

def builder = new JsonBuilder()
builder.customer {
  name 'John'
  lastName 'Appleseed'
  address {
    streetName 'Gordon street'
    city 'Philadelphia'
    houseNumber 20
  }
}
println builder.toPrettyString()
```

2. The output of the previous script yields:

```
{
  "customer": {
  "name": "John",
  "lastName": "Appleseed",
  "address": {
    "streetName": "Gordon street",
    "city": "Philadelphia",
    "houseNumber": 20
    }
  }
}
```

3. Here is a slightly more complex example of `JsonBuilder` usage, used to build the definition of a chart widget:

```
def chart = [
  items: [
    type: 'chart',
    height: 200,
    width: 300,
    axes: [
      {
        type 'Time'
        fields ([ 'x' ])
        position 'left'
        title 'Time'
      },
      {
        type 'Numeric'
        fields ( [ 'y' ] )
        position  'bottom'
        title 'Profit in EUR'
      }
    ]
  ]
]

def builder = new JsonBuilder(chart)
println builder.toPrettyString()

The output of the previous statement is:
{
  "items": [
    {
```

```
    "type": "chart",
    "height": 200,
    "width": 300,
    "axes": [
      {
        "type": "Time",
        "fields": [ "x" ],
        "position": "left",
        "title": "Time"
      },
      {
        "type": "Numeric",
        "fields": [ "y" ],
        "position": "bottom",
        "title": "Profit in EUR"
      }
    ]
  }
 ]
}
```

How it works...

JsonBuilder can produce JSON-formatted output from Maps, Lists, and Java Beans (see the *Converting JSON message to Groovy Bean* recipe). The output is stored in memory, and it can be written to a stream or processed further. If we want to directly stream (instead of storing it in memory) the data as it's created, we can use StreamingJsonBuilder instead of the JsonBuilder.

In the example at step 1, we create an instance of the JsonBuilder class and we simply define the key/value pairs that contain the data structure we wish to create. The approach is very similar to any other builder, such as MarkupBuilder (see the *Constructing XML content* recipe in *Chapter 5, Working with XML in Groovy*).

In the second example, the builder is directly created by passing a variable containing a Map. The Map's keys are Strings as defined by the JSON standard, but the assigned values can be one of the following types:

- ▶ One of the simple data type (for example, Boolean and String) permitted by JSON
- ▶ Another Map
- ▶ Collection of the above
- ▶ A closure or a collection of closures

To demonstrate the flexibility of `JsonBuilder` in our example, we used different types, including closures.

See also

▸ *Parsing JSON messages with JsonSlurper*

▸ The *Constructing XML content* recipe in *Chapter 5, Working with XML in Groovy*

▸ `http://groovy.codehaus.org/gapi/groovy/json/JsonBuilder.html`

Modifying JSON messages

After we've got acquainted with a way to read existing JSON messages (see the *Parsing JSON messages with JsonSlurper* recipe) and create our own (see *Constructing JSON messages with JsonBuilder* recipe), we need to have the ability to modify the messages that flow through our system.

This recipe will show how straightforward it is to alter the content of a JSON document in Groovy.

How to do it...

Let's use the same JSON data located in the `ui.json` file that we used in the *Parsing JSON messages with JsonSlurper* recipe.

1. First of all we need to load and parse the JSON file:

```
import groovy.json.*

def reader = new FileReader('ui.json')
def ui = new JsonSlurper().parse(reader)
```

Since the data is actually just a nested structure, which consists of Maps, Lists and primitive data types, we can use the same API we would use for collections to navigate and change JSON data.

2. Consider the following snippet of code, which changes and removes some bits of the original JSON message:

```
ui.items[0].type = 'panel'
ui.items[0].title = 'Main Window'
ui.items[0].remove('axes')
ui.items[0].remove('series')
```

3. The next step is to save the modified message. There is the `groovy.json.JsonOutput` class, which is designed specifically for that purpose. By using the static `toJson` and `prettyPrint` methods we can get an indented text version of the modified message:

```
println JsonOutput.prettyPrint(JsonOutput.toJson(ui))
```

4. Our initial modifications will lead to the following output:

```
{
    "items": [
        {
            "title": "Main Window",
            "animate": true,
            "height": 270,
            "width": 319,
            "insetPadding": 20,
            "type": "panel"
        }
    ]
}
```

How it works...

As we are operating on a `Map`, the code above does not do anything else but adding and removing `Map` entries.

The `toJson` method returns a `String` with a compact version of the JSON data. The `prettyPrint` method adds additional indentation spaces to any given JSON string.

See also

▸ *Parsing JSON messages with JsonSlurper*

▸ `http://groovy.codehaus.org/gapi/groovy/json/JsonSlurper.html`

▸ `http://groovy.codehaus.org/gapi/groovy/json/JsonOutput.html`

Validating JSON messages

JSON is replacing XML for many applications, but one of the features that XML is exceptionally good for is the ability to validate XML content against a DTD or an XML Schema.

Due to the lightweight nature of JSON, it is quite simple to construct invalid or incomplete messages. That's why the necessity of JSON validation will arise quite soon if you plan to develop high-quality and error-free applications.

This recipe will list some ways to validate your JSON input with the help of Groovy.

Getting ready

For this recipe, we are going to use a simple JSON document representing a vehicle and some of its core attributes. Let's define a `vehicle.json` file containing a JSON representation of a car:

```
{
  "brand": "Mazda",
  "model": "5",
  "fuel": "PETROL",
  "releaseYear": 2007,
  "transmission": {
    "gears": "5",
    "type": "MANUAL"
  }
}
```

How to do it...

Since JSON messages are represented by `Maps` and `Lists`, you can just use the Groovy operators and collection methods—or simple GPath expressions—to navigate and express the validation rules over a parsed JSON message. More information about GPath can be found in the *Searching in XML with GPath* recipe in *Chapter 5, Working with XML in Groovy*.

1. We begin by parsing our document in the same way we did it in previous recipes (for example, *Parsing JSON messages with JsonSlurper*):

   ```
   import groovy.json.*

   def reader = new FileReader('vehicle.json')
   def vehicle = new JsonSlurper().parse(reader)
   ```

2. Now we can define the following validation functions in our script:

   ```
   def isValidTransmission(vehicle) {
     vehicle?.transmission?.type in
       [ 'MANUAL', 'AUTOMATIC' ] &&
       vehicle?.transmission?.gears > 3
   }
   ```

```
def isValidFuel(vehicle) {
  vehicle?.fuel in
    [ 'DIESEL', 'PETROL', 'GAS', 'ELECTRIC']
}

def hasWheels(vehicle) {
  vehicle?.wheels?.size() > 0
}
```

3. Calling the validation methods as:

```
println 'Vehicle has valid transmission data: ' +
  isValidTransmission(vehicle)

println 'Vehicle has valid fuel:          ' +

  isValidFuel(vehicle)
println 'Vehicle has wheels:              ' +

  hasWheels(vehicle)
```

4. The previous script yields the following output:

```
Vehicle has valid transmission data: true
Vehicle has valid fuel:              true
Vehicle has wheels:                  false
```

How it works...

The previous code makes use of several very useful Groovy operators, which make Boolean expressions look very short.

One of them is the safe navigation operator ?., which stops evaluating the Boolean expression and returns `null` immediately if left operand is null. That means no ugly nested `if` statements and no unexpected `NullPointerExceptions`, because the expression is not evaluated further and because `null` will yield `false` in Boolean context.

So, for example, `vehicle?.transmission?.gears > 3` will return false if `vehicle` or `transmission` are null, or if `transmission` is not null, but there are no `gears` and so on.

There's more...

Another approach would be to use **JSON Schema**. It is an emerging standard that is created by the JSON community and it is essentially targeted to offer a similar functionality to what XML Schema provides for XML.

JSON Schema, in the same fashion as XML Schema, can be expressed in JSON itself. To give you an idea of how it looks, for our vehicle data we can define the following schema in a file:

```
{
    "$schema": "http://json-schema.org/draft-03/schema#",
    "description" : "Vehicle data schema",
    "type" : "object",
    "properties" : {
      "brand" : {
        "type" : "string",
        "required" : true
      },
      "model" : {
        "type" : "string",
        "required" : true
      },
      "fuel" : {
        "type" : "string",
        "enum" : ["DIESEL", "PETROL", "GAS", "ELECTRIC"]
      },
      "releaseYear" : {
        "type" : "integer"
      },
      "transmission" : {
        "type" : "object",
          "properties" : {
            "gears": {
              "type" : "integer"
            },
            "type": {
              "type" : "string",
              "enum" : ["MANUAL", "AUTOMATIC"]
            }
          }
      }
    }
}
```

Basically, a JSON Schema defines a JSON object structure with the help of standard property names and conventions, for example, the `type` attribute defines the type (for example, String, integer, date, object, array, and so on) of the structure appearing on the same level in JSON message, properties attribute contains a collection of nested property definitions, which also describe type, name and restrictions like enum or required of the property value.

 Please note that the JSON Schema is still a moving target: the example above uses the slightly older draft 3 format. A newer version, named `draft 4`, is available.

Currently there aren't many implementations of the JSON Schema in Java/Groovy. For this example, we are going to use an implementation called `json-schema-validator`.

```
@Grab('com.github.fge:json-schema-validator:2.0.1')
import com.github.fge.jsonschema.main.JsonSchemaFactory
import com.github.fge.jsonschema.report.ProcessingReport
import com.github.fge.jsonschema.util.JsonLoader
import com.github.fge.jsonschema.main.JsonSchema

def factory = JsonSchemaFactory.byDefault()

def schemaFile = new File('vehicle_schema.json')
def metadata = JsonLoader.fromFile(schemaFile)
def data = JsonLoader.fromFile(new File('vehicle.json'))

def schema = factory.getJsonSchema(metadata)

def report = schema.validate(data)

def success = report.isSuccess()
println("Validation ${success ? 'succeeded' : 'failed'}")

if (!success) {
   println('---- BEGIN REPORT ----')
   report.each { message -> println message }
   println('---- END REPORT ----')
}
```

First of all, we `Grab`-ed the dependency for `json-schema-validator` and imported several required classes. The `json-schema-validator` library internally uses the `JsonNode` data structure to keep the JSON data. For this reason, we need to rely on `JsonLoader` to load the JSON files.

Noticeably, data and schema are loaded in the same way. After constructing a `JsonSchema` object using `JsonSchemaFactory`, we finally can validate the data. The last code lines just call the validation routine and print out validation messages, if any.

The script reports one error (the following output is formatted for readability):

```
Validation failed
---- BEGIN REPORT ----
{
 level="error",
 schema={
   "loadingURI":"#",
   "pointer":"/properties/transmission/properties/gears"
 },
 instance={"pointer":"/transmission/gears"},
 domain="validation",
 keyword="type",
 message="instance type does not match any
          allowed primitive type",
 expected=["integer"],
 found="string"
}
---- END REPORT ----
```

The error reported by the validator is related to `/transmission/gears`: the JSON validation code expects an Integer, but the JSON document provides a `String`:

```
    {
      ...
      "transmission": {
        "gears": "5",
        "type": "MANUAL"
      }
      ...
    }
```

JSON Schema provides a more generic approach to validation error handling compared to the custom Groovy code.

See also

- ▶ *Parsing JSON messages with JsonSlurper*
- ▶ `http://groovy.codehaus.org/Operators`
- ▶ `http://docs.codehaus.org/display/GROOVY/Groovy+Truth`
- ▶ `http://json-schema.org/`
- ▶ `https://github.com/fge/json-schema-validator`
- ▶ `https://github.com/EqualExperts/json-schema-validator`

Converting JSON message to XML

JSON and XML are the *de facto* data interchange standard formats used by industry applications. The two formats share many similarities, but have different goals in their design. JSON is designed to be a data exchange language, which is human readable and easy for computers to parse and use. XML also shares the readability goal, but suffers from a higher degree of verbosity and complexity.

Nevertheless, the two formats are here to stay, and a case for converting from one format to the other is recurring in the IT industry.

This recipe shows how to convert a JSON document into XML using a Groovy only solution as well as introducing a less "groovier" solution in the There's more... section.

Getting ready

The JSON document to convert is the `ui.json` file that we already encountered in the *Parsing JSON messages with JsonSlurper* recipe.

How to do it...

The conversion is based on `groovy.xml.MarkupBuilder`, which allows full control on the final output but makes the code more verbose because we have to explicitly specify all the transformation rules.

1. In a script copy the following code, making sure that the `ui.json` file is in the same folder as the Groovy script:

```
import groovy.json.JsonSlurper
import groovy.xml.MarkupBuilder

def reader = new FileReader('ui.json')
```

```
def ui = new JsonSlurper().parse(reader)

def writer = new StringWriter()
def xml = new MarkupBuilder(writer)
```

2. Now you can use the builder to pass data from the parsed message:

```
xml.items {
  ui.items.each { widget ->
    item(type: widget.type,
    height: widget.height,
    width: widget.width) {
      axes {
        widget.axes.each { widgetAxis ->
          axis(type: widgetAxis.type,
          name: widgetAxis.title)
        }
      }
    }
  }
}

println writer.toString()
```

3. The output of the code is as follows:

```
<items>
  <item type='chart' height='270' width='319'>
    <axes>
      <axis type='Time' name='Time' />
      <axis type='Numeric' name='Profit in EUR' />
    </axes>
  </item>
</items>
```

How it works...

The code in step 2 is really a testament to the sheer efficiency of builders (see the *Defining data structures as code in Groovy* recipe in *Chapter 3, Using Groovy Language Features*). The variable xml is used to construct the XML element names and attributes that are extracted, via dynamic methods, from the ui variable, created by the MarkupBuilder. More information on MarkupBuilder can be found in the *Constructing XML content* recipe in *Chapter 5, Working with XML in Groovy*.

To avoid confusing the Groovy compiler, when we are inside the iterator closures (for example, `widget.axes.each { widgetAxis -> ...`) we have to use variable names that are different from the XML element names (for example, `axis(type: widgetAxis.type ...`).

There's more...

The second approach mentioned in this recipe's introduction is to use a third-party library, such as JSON-lib to perform the transformation with little coding. The following code makes use of the `XMLSerializer` class to transform the JSON data to XML.

```
@Grapes([
  @Grab(group='net.sf.json-lib',
    module='json-lib',
    version='2.3',
    classifier='jdk15'),
  @Grab('xom:xom:1.2.5')
])
import net.sf.json.JSONObject
import net.sf.json.xml.XMLSerializer

def object = JSONObject.fromObject(new File('ui.json').text)

println new XMLSerializer().write(object)
```

Here we trade lines of code for lack of control above the produced XML, that is not quite as readable as the Groovy only example:

```
<?xml version="1.0" encoding="UTF-8"?>
<o>
  <items class="array">
    <e class="object">
      <animate type="boolean">true</animate>
      <axes class="array">
        <e class="object">
          <fields class="array">
            <e type="string">x</e>
          </fields>
          <position type="string">left</position>
          <title type="string">Time</title>
          <type type="string">Time</type>
        </e>
        ...
```

```
        </axes>
        ...
      </e>
      ...
    </items>
  </o>
```

The output can still be tweaked by setting different options of the XmlSerializer class, but you would not be able to fully control the complete structure of the output. The technique outlined here may be established for very complex JSON documents, which would require a non-trivial amount of code to perform the conversion to XML. An additional approach could be to apply XSLT transformation to the result produced by the XmlSerializer, but describing the process goes beyond the scope of this recipe.

See also

 ▸ *Constructing JSON messages with JsonBuilder*

 ▸ The *Constructing XML content* recipe in *Chapter 5, Working with XML in Groovy*

 ▸ http://json-lib.sourceforge.net/

 ▸ http://json-lib.sourceforge.net/apidocs/jdk15/net/sf/json/xml/ XMLSerializer.html

 ▸ http://groovy.codehaus.org/gapi/groovy/json/JsonBuilder.html

 ▸ http://groovy.codehaus.org/api/groovy/xml/MarkupBuilder.html

Converting JSON message to Groovy Bean

The power of the Java/Groovy type system, reflection API, and other goodies may be very handy if you need to make more type-safe code.

JSON by definition is not doing any type checking, but it is possible to map the JSON data to the Java/Groovy objects to present data inside your application and get access to type information. And that's what we will demonstrate in this recipe.

Getting ready

First of all let's define a Groovy Bean (POGO) class, which holds data representing some vehicle information:

```
package org.groovy.cookbook

import groovy.transform.ToString

@ToString
```

```
class Vehicle {

    static enum FuelType { DIESEL, PETROL, GAS, ELECTRIC }
    static enum TransmissionType { MANUAL, AUTOMATIC }

    @ToString
    static class Transmission {
        long gears
        TransmissionType type
    }

    String brand
    String model
    FuelType fuel
    Long releaseYear
    Transmission transmission

}
```

As you can notice it's nothing, but a set of fields of simple types, enumerations, and a nested class, which again consists of simple type fields. In order for that class to be available for the conversion script, let's place it into a `vehicle.groovy` file and compile it with the `groovyc` command:

`groovyc vehicle.groovy`

The JSON document to which we want to map the class is the one defined in the recipe, *Validating JSON messages*. Create a `vehicle.json` file in the same directory as the `vehicle.groovy`.

To simplify the mapping, we used the same property names in both, JSON message and the `Vehicle` class.

How to do it...

Create a new Groovy script, `convert.groovy`, making sure that it's located in the same folder as the JSON file.

1. Add the following code to the script:

   ```
   import groovy.json.JsonSlurper
   import org.groovy.cookbook.Vehicle

   def reader = new FileReader('vehicle.json')
   def jsonVehicle = new JsonSlurper().parse(reader)

   def vehicle = new Vehicle (
       brand: jsonVehicle.brand,
   ```

```
    model: jsonVehicle.model,
    transmission: new Vehicle.Transmission(
      gears: jsonVehicle.transmission.gears,
      type: jsonVehicle.transmission.type),
    releaseYear: jsonVehicle.releaseYear,
    fuel: jsonVehicle.fuel)

  println vehicle
```

2. Run the script in a usual way:

    groovy convert.groovy

3. The `println` command outputs:

    org.groovy.cookbook.Vehicle(Mazda, 5, PETROL, 2007,

    org.groovy.cookbook.Vehicle$Transmission(5, MANUAL))

How it works...

Groovy performs some of the data type mapping automatically for us; making the conversion code simpler. For example, `jsonVehicle.fuel` is actually a `String`, but it is transformed to `FuelType` enumeration automatically since the values are matching. Also, `jsonVehicle.transmission.gears` is a `String` in our original JSON message (because it is included in the double quotes), but it is still safely converted to a long field in the `Transmission` object.

Thanks to the `@ToString` annotation, the `Vehicle` class shows all its internal data upon printing by the last line of the script.

There's more...

Writing the conversion code for every possible type you may need, is time consuming. Fortunately, existing third-party libraries come to the rescue. In the following sections, we will show how Groovy Bean conversion can be achieved with the JSON-lib, Jackson and GSON libraries. Please note that for the next examples to work the `Vehicle` class is imported, therefore, it must be extracted to a `Vehicle.groovy` class and added to the classpath when running the code.

▶ JSON-lib can be used in the following way:

```
@Grapes([
  @Grab(group='net.sf.json-lib',
    module='json-lib',
    version='2.3',
    classifier='jdk15'),
  @Grab('xom:xom:1.2.5')
])
```

```
import net.sf.json.JSONObject
import org.groovy.cookbook.Vehicle

def file = new File('vehicle.json')
def jsonObject = JSONObject.fromObject(file.text)

println JSONObject.toBean(jsonObject, Vehicle)
```

▶ Jackson can be used in the following way:

```
@Grab('com.fasterxml.jackson.core:jackson-databind:2.1.0')
import com.fasterxml.jackson.databind.ObjectMapper
import org.groovy.cookbook.Vehicle

def mapper = new ObjectMapper()
def file = new File('vehicle.json')

println mapper.readValue(file, Vehicle)
```

▶ GSON can be used in the following way:

```
@Grab('com.google.code.gson:gson:2.2.2')
import com.google.gson.Gson

import org.groovy.cookbook.Vehicle

def gson = new Gson()
def reader = new FileReader('vehicle.json')

println gson.fromJson(reader, Vehicle)
```

All of those frameworks produce similar results, and they can be further tweaked for more complex data conversion requirements.

See also

▶ *Parsing JSON messages with JsonSlurper*

▶ `http://json-lib.sourceforge.net/`

▶ `http://code.google.com/p/google-gson/`

▶ `http://wiki.fasterxml.com/JacksonHome`

Using JSON to configure your scripts

The target of this recipe is to show how to use JSON as a format for configuring a Groovy application.

The requirements for a configuration file format are:

- ▶ Simple
- ▶ Human-readable
- ▶ Cross-platform
- ▶ Multi-language support
- ▶ Unicode support

JSON fully satisfies the above requirements, thus making a great candidate for configuring an application.

Getting ready

For this recipe, we work on a fictional application that maintains a connection to multiple databases. Each database has a number of parameters to configure such as host, port, credentials, and connection pool initial size.

The following is a sample JSON based configuration file for our application:

```
{
  "configuration":{
    "database":[
      {
        "name":"database1",
        "host":"10.20.30.40",
        "port":"4930",
        "user":"user-alpha",
        "password":"secret",
        "pool-initial-size":"10",
        "pool-max-size":"10"
      },
      {
        "name":"database2",
        "host":"192.168.10.30",
        "port":"5001",
        "user":"user-beta",
        "password":"secret",
        "pool-initial-size":"5",
```

```
        "pool-max-size":"30"
      }
    ]
  }
}
```

It takes very little code (compared to Java) to build a simple configuration handler in Groovy.

How to do it...

Let's start by copying the JSON configuration displayed above to a file named db-config. json. For the sake of conciseness, let's keep all the code in one single Groovy script: create a new file named configurator.groovy.

1. Add the following class to the file: it will hold the configuration data for each database.

    ```groovy
    import groovy.json.*
    import groovy.transform.TupleConstructor

    @TupleConstructor
    class Database {
        String name
        String host
        Integer port
        String user
        String password
        Integer initPool
        Integer maxPool
    }
    ```

    This is a terse Groovy Bean (see the *Writing less verbose Java Beans with Groovy Beans* recipe in *Chapter 3, Using Groovy Language Features*) with a bunch of attributes which are mapped 1-1 to the configuration data.

2. What follows is the configuration handling class. Copy the code after the Database class definition:

    ```groovy
    class AppConfig {

        def databases = []

        AppConfig(conf) {
            if (conf) {
                conf.configuration
                .database.each {
                    databases << new Database(
                        it.name,
    ```

```
                    it.host,
                    it.port.toInteger(),
                    it.user,
                    it.password,
                    it.'pool-initial-size'.toInteger(),
                    it.'pool-max-size'.toInteger())
              }
          }
      }

      def getDatabaseConfig = { name ->
        databases.find { it.name == name }
      }

  }
```

3. Finally, let's put our class to work by parsing the configuration file and calling the newly defined class:

```
def reader = new FileReader('db-config.json')
def conf = new JsonSlurper().parse(reader)
def dbConfig = new AppConfig(conf)
// Execute application logic
println dbConfig.getDatabaseConfig('database2').host
println dbConfig.getDatabaseConfig('database1').user
...
```

4. Our configurable script will output the following lines in this case:

```
192.168.10.30
user-alpha
```

How it works...

The `AppConfig` class takes `java.util.HashMap` as constructor parameter, which is the outcome of a parsed JSON payload using `JsonSlurper`.

For each database found in the data structure, a new `Database` object is built and added to the list of databases to configure. The `Database` object doesn't force us to specify the constructor argument name, because the POGO class is annotated with `@TupleConstructor`.

The `getDatabaseConfig` closure elegantly returns the database configuration object that matches the given name of the database to configure.

If found, the database properties are accessible as Groovy Bean getters.

There's more...

Another popular format similar to JSON for dealing with the configuration data is YAML.

YAML is a lightweight data serialization format designed with readability in mind and with support for hierarchical data structures. **YAML** stands for **YAML Ain't Markup Language**. It is easier on the eyes than JSON and sports a simple typing system.

Additionally, YAML can be considered a superset of JSON. That means, a valid JSON file is also a valid YAML file (but not vice versa).

The ultimate goal of YAML is to be very comfortable on the eyes. The following is an example of YAML formatted data.

```
firstname: Mike
lastname: Ross
position: CFO
```

Groovy doesn't have any native YAML parser. So, the most convenient approach is to use a third-party Java library, such as JYaml.

```
@Grab('org.jyaml:jyaml:1.3')
import org.ho.yaml.Yaml

yamlData = '''
   firstname: Mike
   lastname: Ross
   position: CFO
''
'
class Staff {
   def firstname, lastname, position
}

Staff s = Yaml.loadType(yamlData, Staff)

println s.firstname
println s.position
```

The script will print:

Mike

CFO

This solution doesn't use any Groovy specific feature, but it nevertheless represents a good compromise if YAML is among the requirements of your application.

Another alternative to configure your scripts is to use Groovy's native `ConfigSlurper` class, which is capable of consuming configuration data defined in the form of Groovy scripts.

See also

- *Parsing JSON messages with JsonSlurper*
- `http://jyaml.sourceforge.net/`
- `http://groovy.codehaus.org/gapi/groovy/util/ConfigSlurper.html`

7
Working with Databases in Groovy

In this chapter, we will cover:

- ▸ Creating a database table
- ▸ Connecting to an SQL database
- ▸ Querying an SQL database
- ▸ Modifying data in an SQL database
- ▸ Calling a stored procedure
- ▸ Reading BLOB/CLOB from a database
- ▸ Building a simple ORM framework
- ▸ Using Groovy to access Redis
- ▸ Using Groovy to access MongoDB
- ▸ Using Groovy to access Apache Cassandra

Introduction

The group of recipes presented in this chapter deals with data persistence, either through a relational SQL database or a NoSQL database.

The first recipe describes how to access and modify data stored in a relational database, such as Oracle or MySQL. Groovy makes accessing data using the SQL language a very elegant affair, compared to the clunky Java's JDBC APIs.

The last three recipes show how to use Groovy with the emerging NoSQL databases, such as Redis, MongoDB, and Cassandra. Each of those recipes contains the steps to connect, persist, and retrieve data with one of the three key/value stores.

Creating a database table

As a starting point for this chapter about database access and SQL, we look at how to create a database schema using Groovy. The database model outlined in this recipe will serve as a reference for the rest of this chapter.

The **Data Definition Language** (**DDL**) is an essential part of the SQL standard. Through its syntax, it allows defining database objects. These database objects include schemas, tables, views, sequences, catalogs, indexes, and aliases.

Groovy doesn't come with any specific support for this portion of the SQL language. Nevertheless, we can leverage Groovy's conciseness to simplify the database creation operations.

Getting ready

The following image contains a diagram depicting the tables of the schema we will create in this recipe:

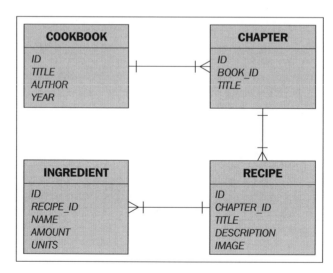

As you can notice, the model represents a cookbook which consists of a set of chapters with cooking recipes. Each recipe has a title, detailed description, image of the desired result, and a list of ingredients required to implement it.

The database that we are going to use all along is HyperSQL 2.3.0 (**HSQLDB**) in-memory database. HSQLDB is a very popular database written in Java that is very often used for unit testing and creation of application prototypes—thanks to its lightweight nature.

How to do it...

In order to get started, create a new Groovy script named DBUtil.groovy that will contain some routines that will be used throughout this chapter:

1. Add the following code to the script:

```
@GrabConfig(systemClassLoader=true)
@Grab('org.hsqldb:hsqldb:2.3.0')
import org.hsqldb.Server

class DBUtil {

  static dbSettings = [
    url: 'jdbc:hsqldb:hsql://localhost/cookingdb',
    driver: 'org.hsqldb.jdbcDriver',
    user: 'sa',
    password: ''
  ]

  static startServer() {
    Server server = new Server()
    def logFile = new File('db.log')
    server.setLogWriter(new PrintWriter(logFile))
    server.with {
      setDatabaseName(0, 'cookingdb')
      setDatabasePath(0, 'mem:cookingdb')
      start()
    }
    server
  }

}
```

2. In a second script, createDb.groovy, add the following import statements for the DBUtil class and Groovy's SQL utilities to be visible:

```
import static DBUtil.*
import groovy.sql.Sql
```

3. We need to define a list of DDL statements we want to run in order to create the database schema. Let's use just a list of strings for that purpose:

```
def ddls = [

    '''
    CREATE TABLE COOKBOOK(
        ID INTEGER PRIMARY KEY,
        TITLE VARCHAR(100),
        AUTHOR VARCHAR(100),
        YEAR INTEGER)
    ''',

    '''
    CREATE TABLE CHAPTER(
        ID INTEGER PRIMARY KEY,
        BOOK_ID INTEGER,
        TITLE VARCHAR(100))
    ''',

    '''
    CREATE TABLE RECIPE(
        ID INTEGER PRIMARY KEY,
        CHAPTER_ID INTEGER,
        TITLE VARCHAR(100),
        DESCRIPTION CLOB,
        IMAGE BLOB)
    ''',

    '''
    CREATE TABLE INGREDIENT(
        ID INTEGER PRIMARY KEY,
        RECIPE_ID INTEGER,
        NAME VARCHAR(100),
        AMOUNT DOUBLE,
        UNITS VARCHAR(20))
    '''
]
```

4. Complete the second script with the following code that executes all the previous SQL statements through a `groovy.sql.Sql` instance in a loop:

```
startServer()

Sql sql = Sql.newInstance(dbSettings)
ddls.each { ddl ->
    sql.execute(ddl)
}
println 'Schema created successfully'
```

5. Assuming that both scripts are in the same folder, launch the `createDb.groovy` script passing the folder path (or `"."` if it's a current directory), where both scripts reside to the `-cp` parameter:

```
groovy -cp . createDb.groovy
```

6. The script should print the following line:

```
Schema created successfully
```

The script process will continue to run since the database server thread is still active. You can reuse that to connect to the database and perform queries for later recipes (see the *Connecting to an SQL database* and *Querying an SQL database* recipes).

How it works...

In this first recipe, we have covered quite a lot of ground and some explanation is due. The first script contains a utility class to start the HyperSQL server. The database is started with a name (`cookingdb`) and the path is set to use memory as storage. This means that when we kill the database process, all the data is lost.

Most of the recipes in this chapter can be run against any relational database. After all this is what SQL is about, a vendor-independent language to query data provided that the proper JDBC drivers are available in the classpath.

This is exactly what the `@Grab` annotation is there for. It fetches the HyperSQL database drivers as well as the server libraries. This is actually an exception, because, in most database scenarios (MySQL, Oracle, etc.) you'd fetch the drivers only and not a full database engine implementation! The `@Grab` annotation is accompanied by a second annotation:

```
@GrabConfig(systemClassLoader=true)
```

This annotation is forcing Grape to place the dependencies in the system class loader. By default, the dependencies are available in the same class loader as our Groovy script or application. But sometimes this is not enough; a typical case is exactly our case, a database driver which is required to be in the system classpath for the `java.sql.DriverManager` class to access it.

The `DBUtil` class also contains the database connection settings that we need to access the in-memory database: one those are defined as a Map and contain the standard information required to connect to any relational database, such as the driver or the server host. You will need to adjust all the parameters to `newInstance` to connect to your database, especially username and password.

The second script, in which the database tables are actually created, is very simple but contains a key class that we will see over and over in the rest of this chapter's recipes, `groovy.sql.Sql` (see the *Connecting to an SQL database* and the *Querying an SQL database* recipes).

This class does all the connectivity heavy lifting: it connects to the database specified in the dbSettings variable (note that the newInstance method of the Sql class accepts also a plain string) and returns an object that is ready to be used to fire queries to the database to which we are connected to.

Once we get a valid connection, the code simply iterates over the list of SQL statements defined in the ddls variable, and runs them through the execute method of the Sql class.

See also

- ► *Connecting to an SQL database*
- ► *Querying an SQL database*
- ► http://hsqldb.org/
- ► http://groovy.codehaus.org/api/groovy/sql/Sql.html

Connecting to an SQL database

This recipe is about the various approaches we can use to connect to a database using Groovy and the groovy.sql.Sql class that we briefly encountered in the *Creating a database table* recipe.

Getting ready

As mentioned in the first recipe of this chapter, we are going to reuse the DBUtil class, which contains some helper methods to simplify our work with the database. Create a new Groovy script and add the following import statements before adding the code presented in the next section:

```
@Grab('commons-dbcp:commons-dbcp:1.4')
import static DBUtil.*
import groovy.sql.Sql
import org.apache.commons.dbcp.BasicDataSource
```

Do not forget to start the HyperSQL server by calling startServer. As shown in the *Creating a database table* recipe, pass the -cp argument to the groovy command with the path to the folder with the DBUtil.groovy script in order to execute the script containing the steps of this recipe.

How to do it...

The simplest way to connect to a running instance of a database is by calling the `newInstance` method on the `groovy.sql.Sql` class.

1. The `newInstance` method is written as follows:

    ```
    Sql sql = Sql.newInstance(
        'jdbc:hsqldb:hsql://localhost/cookingdb',
        'sa',
        '',
        'org.hsqldb.jdbcDriver'
        )
    println 'connected with connection data: ok'
    ```

2. If we want to reuse an existing connection (normally when using a connection pool), then we can simply pass it to the class constructor:

    ```
    Sql reusedConnection = new Sql(sql.createConnection())
    println 'connected with reused connection: ok'
    ```

3. A third way to connect to a database using the Groovy provided `Sql` class is by passing a `javax.sql.DataSource` instance to the constructor:

    ```
    @Grab('commons-dbcp:commons-dbcp:1.4')
    import org.apache.commons.dbcp.BasicDataSource
    def ds = new BasicDataSource()
    ds.with {
        driverClassName = 'org.hsqldb.jdbcDriver'
        password = ''
        username = 'sa'
        url = 'jdbc:hsqldb:hsql://localhost/cookingdb'
    }
    Sql sql3 = new Sql(ds)
    println 'connected with datasource: ok'
    ```

4. Finally, we need to clean up:

    ```
    reusedConnection.close()
    ```

How it works...

Internally `groovy.sql.Sql` uses the JDBC driver infrastructure to connect to the database and eventually make the SQL calls. The required database driver has to be added to the classpath either with the help of `@Grab` annotation, which will load any required dependency from the central dependency repository (`http://repo1.maven.org/`), or in case the driver is not available on a public server, you can use any other standard Java way to add the driver's JAR to the classpath.

For example, in order to connect to a MySQL database you need to use the following `@Grab` annotation:

```
@Grab('mysql:mysql-connector-java:5.1.21')
import com.mysql.jdbc.Driver
```

The `newInstance` method creates a new connection every time it is invoked, so it should be used with caution as you may end up exhausting the database resources. In the *Creating a database table* recipe, we saw how to call `newInstace` with a Map. In step 1 of this recipe, we use the standard constructor which accepts four arguments: database connection URL, username, password, and driver class name. In step 2, we pass a `java.sql.Connection` to the `groovy.sql.Sql` constructor.

This method of establishing a connection is normally used in conjunction with a connection pool that manages the connections for us, decreasing dramatically the time it takes to open a new connection. It is the caller's responsibility to close the connection after the `Sql` instance has been used. The preferred approach is to call the `close` method which will close the connection, but also free any cached resources (see step 4).

The `Sql` class exposes a constructor that also accepts a `javax.sql.Datasource` object, as shown in step 3. Datasource objects are normally retrieved via a JNDI invocation from an application server such as Tomcat, Oracle Weblogic, or IBM Websphere. A Datasource object is an abstraction that avoids manually specifying the connection properties in the code. It renders hard coding the driver name or JDBC URL obsolete, making the software more portable.

Moreover, storing the Datasource on an application server increases the maintainability of the software: changes to the database (for example, a new IP address) do not impact the deployed applications but only the server configuration. Lastly, Datasource normally provides connection pooling and transactional services.

In step 3, we create a BasicDataSource object from the time-honored Apache Commons DBCP project. When using JNDI, we would write code similar to the following snippet:

```
def ctx = new InitialContext()
def ds = (DataSource) ctx.lookup('jdbc/bookDB')
```

When using the constructor that accepts a Datasource, each operation will use a connection from the Datasource pool and close it when the operation is completed putting it back into the pool.

See also

▶ *Querying an SQL database*

▶ *Modifying data in an SQL database*

▶ `http://www.oracle.com/technetwork/java/javase/jdbc/index.html`

- `http://groovy.codehaus.org/api/groovy/sql/Sql.html`
- `https://commons.apache.org/proper/commons-dbcp/`

Querying an SQL database

Usually data is more often read than it is written, and performing data queries is the most important task done by database-driven applications. The standard JDBC API is rather verbose and adds a lot of boilerplate code around actual queries. Groovy provides more elegance to the querying code by simplifying access and mapping logic.

This recipe contains a highlight of some of the methods you can use to query a database using Groovy.

Getting ready

As for the previous recipes from this chapter, we will use the DBUtil class defined in the *Creating a database table* recipe as well as the same database structure.

Considering that this recipe is about querying data, we need to populate our database first. The database population code is quite verbose, so we leave it out of this recipe and we ask the reader to refer to the accompanying code for this chapter. The DBUtil.groovy available in the download section has been refactored with two new methods:

- `createSchema`: It triggers the same code we wrote for the *Creating a database table* recipe
- `populate`: It inserts some rows into the tables

How to do it...

The following steps will let us dive into SQL queries with the help of Groovy.

1. Let's start by creating a new Groovy script file (`queryDb.groovy`) where we import the DBUtil module and we initialize the database:

   ```
   import static DBUtil.*
   import groovy.sql.Sql

   def server = startServer()
   createSchema()
   populate()
   ```

2. Create the Sql class instance and initialize it with the default database connection settings:

   ```
   def sql = Sql.newInstance(dbSettings)
   ```

3. Write your first query:

```
sql.eachRow('SELECT * FROM COOKBOOK') { cookbook ->
    printf '%-20s%s\n',
            cookbook.id,
            cookbook[1]
}
```

4. Clean up and *kill* the server:

```
sql.close()
server.stop()
```

5. By running this script, the output should look as follows:

```
> groovy -cp /path/to/script/folder queryDb.groovy
schema created successfully
Database populated: ok
1                       30-minute-meals
2                       Ministry of food
```

6. Immediately after the first one, try another query, where we pass arguments to the SQL query:

```
println ': using named arguments'
sql.eachRow('SELECT * FROM COOKBOOK ' +
        'WHERE id = :id ',
        [id:2]) { cookbook ->

    printf '%s|%s|%s\n',
        cookbook.id,
        cookbook.author,
        cookbook.title

}
```

7. Running the script again yields the following output:

```
: using named arguments
2|Jamie Oliver|Ministry of food
```

8. You can also limit the result set by specifying the maximum number of rows and the number of the "page" (offset) to return:

```
println ': using offset'
sql.eachRow(
    'SELECT * FROM COOKBOOK',
    1, 5) { cookbook ->
```

```
    printf '%s|%s|%s\n',
      cookbook.id,
      cookbook.author,
      cookbook.title

}
```

9. The `query` method grants you direct access to the `java.sql ResultSet` object, should you need to interact with it:

```
println ': using ResultSet'
sql.query('SELECT * FROM COOKBOOK') { rs ->
  while (rs.next()) {
    println rs.getString('title')
  }
}
```

10. If we want to process all the rows but don't want to use an iterator, we can use the `rows` method on the `Sql` instance. It returns an instance of the `ArrayList` class containing the result data, as shown here:

```
println ': using rows method'
List allCookbooks = sql.rows('SELECT * FROM COOKBOOK')
assert allCookbooks.size() == 2
println allCookbooks[0]?.title
```

11. If you only need the first record of the result set or your query is meant to return only one result, then you can use the `firstRow` method:

```
def firstCookbook = sql.firstRow('SELECT * FROM COOKBOOK')
println firstCookbook?.title
```

How it works...

The `groovy.sql.Sql` class has three main methods to query the database:

▶ `eachRow`

▶ `rows`

▶ `query`

Each method has several overloaded versions (eachRow, for instance, has 20 overloaded methods) that can be used to tweak the way the results are fetched and presented. eachRow, in its simplest form, requires an SQL statement and a closure to process each row of data. In step 3, we can see an example: eachRow executes SQL's SELECT query on the COOKBOOK table and processes all its rows. We then iterate (as the name each indicates) over each row and print the result. But what is the actual object we are iterating on. Let's look at the code once again:

```
sql.eachRow('SELECT * FROM COOKBOOK') { cookbook ->
  printf '%-20s%s\n',
    cookbook.id,
    cookbook[1]
}
```

The cookbook variable is used as if it was an object: note how we call the method id on it. At the same time, we treat it as a List, by referencing a column by index. So what is it? It's an object of type groovy.sql.GroovyResultSet which wraps the underlying java.sql. ResultSet. The property invocation (id) is intercepted and mapped to the column name, if the two match. Similarly, referencing the column name by index achieves the same result (starting from zero, allowing negative indexes that count from the end).

The various rows method available in the Sql class have all the same outcome: they return the result set as a List, allowing a developer to leverage the rich Groovy Collection API, with methods such as find, findAll, grep, any, and every.

The query method (step 9) trades some convenience for a higher degree of customization in the iteration process. The method produces a java.sql.ResultSet and has the usual quirks associated with this rather old Java class. The method next must be called to move the cursor to the next row, you need to call type-specific getters (getString, getDate, and so on) and indexes start at one instead of zero. The query method still hides some of the ceremoniousness related to resource management by automatically opening/closing the connection and the statement.

There's more...

If you are doing many similar queries within the same code block you can cache prepared SQL statement objects with the help of the cacheStatements method, which accepts a Closure as its only parameter. The Closure may contain other groovy.sql.Sql calls:

```
sql.cacheStatements {
  sql.eachRow('SELECT * FROM RECIPE ' +
    ' WHERE COOKBOOK_ID = 1') { recipe ->
  sql.eachRow('SELECT COUNT(*) FROM INGREDIENTS ' +
    'WHERE recipe_id = ?', [recipe.id]) {
    ...
    }
  }
}
```

As you can notice we do a nested SQL query, which will benefit from being prepared and cached for performance reasons.

See also

- ▶ `http://groovy.codehaus.org/api/groovy/sql/Sql.html`
- ▶ `http://groovy.codehaus.org/api/groovy/sql/DataSet.html`
- ▶ `http://groovy.codehaus.org/api/groovy/sql/GroovyRowResult.html`

Modifying data in an SQL database

The logical step after querying a database (see the *Querying an SQL database* recipe) is writing data to it. This recipe shows how a few lines of Groovy and very little boilerplate is needed to do the job of modifying data in a database table.

Getting ready

This recipe also uses the same table structure and the way to start a database server defined in the *Creating a database table* recipe.

How to do it...

As usual, create a new Groovy script named `modifyDb.groovy`. As for the previous recipes, in this case we also need to import the `DBUtil` class.

1. Add the following code to the newly created script:

   ```
   import static DBUtil.*
   import groovy.sql.Sql

   def server = startServer()
   createSchema()
   ```

2. The next logical step is to define the initial data to write to the database. Add the following code to the script, a variable containing a list of Maps with the data to persist:

   ```
   def cookbooks = [
     [ id: 1,
       title: '30-minute-meals',
       author: 'Jamie Oliver',
       year: 2010],
     [ id: 2,
       title: 'Ministry of food',
   ```

```
      author: 'Jamie Oliver',
      year: 2005],
    [ id: 3,
      title: 'Vegan food',
      author: 'Mr. Spock',
      year: 2105]
  ]
```

3. It's all we need to insert data into the COOKBOOK table, by iterating on the list and passing each entry to the execute method:

```
def sql = Sql.newInstance(dbSettings)
cookbooks.each { cookbook ->
  sql.execute(
    'INSERT INTO COOKBOOK ' +
    'VALUES(:id, :title, :author, :year)',
    cookbook
  )
}
```

4. We can verify that the data was correctly inserted by triggering an SQL query and asserting that data is indeed there:

```
assert 3 == sql.rows('SELECT * FROM COOKBOOK').size()
```

5. In order to modify one or more columns of a row, the execute method is again the method to call, this time in conjunction with the UPDATE statement.

```
sql.execute(
  'UPDATE COOKBOOK ' +
  'SET title = :title ' +
  'WHERE ID = :id',
  [title: '15-minutes meals', id: 1]
)
```

Also in this case, a Map containing the values to alter is passed to the execute method. This method can also be invoked with a single string, as follows:

```
sql.execute(
  'UPDATE COOKBOOK ' +
  'SET title = "15-minutes meal" ' +
  'WHERE ID = 1'
)
```

6. Let's check again that our update query has worked as intended:

```
assert '15-minutes meals' ==
  sql.rows('SELECT * FROM COOKBOOK ' +
    'WHERE ID = 1')[0].title
```

7. Deleting one or more rows is as simple. The following statement deletes the row having the ID with value 3.

```
sql.execute(
   'DELETE from COOKBOOK WHERE ID = :id',
   [id: 3]
)
assert 2 == sql.rows('SELECT * FROM COOKBOOK').size()
```

How it works...

The `execute` method of the `Sql` class does most of the work for you when it comes to executing SQL queries: it gets a connection, builds and configures the SQL statement, fires it, logs any error, and eventually closes the resources, even if an exception is thrown. The method returns a boolean, which is true if the first result is a `java.sql.ResultSet` object; false if it is an update count or there are no results.

In step 3, we can observe how to execute a simple INSERT statement. What if the INSERT statement is executed on a row with an autogenerated identifier? How do we get the value of the primary key for the newly inserted row?

The `groovy.sql.Sql` has a handy `executeInsert` method, which behaves exactly as the execute one, but returns a list of the autogenerated column values for each inserted row. The generated key values are array based. For example, to access the second autogenerated column value of the third row, use keys[3][1]:

```
def insertedIds = db.executeInsert(
    'insert into customers ' +
    'values(null, "John", "Doe" )'
    )
assert 9000 == insertedIds[0][0]
```

There's more...

In many cases, updating a database should happen in the context of a transaction. For instance, we may want to execute an INSERT and an UPDATE within a transaction, so that if the second UPDATE statement fails, also the first INSERT is rolled back.

Groovy's `groovy.sql.Sql` has a method, which does exactly that, and it's named, not surprisingly, `withTransaction`. The method accepts a Closure containing the statements to execute.

```
sql.withTransaction {

    sql.executeInsert(
        'INSERT INTO COOKBOOK ' +
        'VALUES(:id, :title, :author, :year)',
        [id: 99, title: 'Food for robots',
        author: 'Hal Ninethousand', year: 2001]
    )

    sql.executeInsert(
        'INSERT INTO COOKBOOK ' +
        'VALUES(:id, :title, :author, :year)',
        [id: 100, title: '0 Carb Meals',
        author: 'Harry Slim', year: 1987]
    )

}
```

Should any of the operations inside the `withTransaction` block fail, the whole block is rolled back, if the underlying database supports transactions.

Another useful feature of the `groovy.sql.Sql` class introduced in Groovy 1.7 is the `withBatch` method, which executes a group of SQL statements in a batch. This method is very useful, when for example, we need to read data from a file and persist it in a database:

```
def updateCounts =
    sql.withBatch(20, 'INSERT into COOKBOOK ' +
        'values (?, ?, ?,?)') { ps ->

    ps.addBatch(
        10,
        'In Defense of Food: An Eater\'s Manifesto',
        'Michael Pokkan',
        2009)

    ps.addBatch(
        12,
        'Now....you\'re cooking! Comfort Food Classics',
        'Joan Donogh',
        2011)

    ps.addBatch(
```

```
14,
'50 Superfoods Recipes',
'Rebecca Fallon',
2012)

...

}
```

The previous example shows `withBatch` used with a batch size value of 20. For each 20 `INSERT`s, the JDBC's `executeBatch` will be automatically called. Also in this case, the `withBatch` operation works only if the database driver supports it.

See also

▶ http://groovy.codehaus.org/api/groovy/sql/Sql.html

Calling a stored procedure

Stored procedure implementation in most SQL database servers is vendor-specific. JDBC offers a generic way for calling those and Groovy's `Sql` class helps to simplify that task.

This recipe will demonstrate how to utilize the `Sql` class to make stored procedure calls.

Getting ready

Let's use the same cookbook database, created and populated, like in the *Querying an SQL database* recipe:

```
import static DBUtil.*
import groovy.sql.Sql

def server = startServer()
createSchema()
populate()
```

Let's also assume we have defined a stored procedure with the following structure:

```
CREATE PROCEDURE INGREDIENT_USAGE(
    OUT INGREDIENTS_RATE INTEGER,
    IN INGREDIENT_NAME VARCHAR(100))
READS SQL DATA
BEGIN ATOMIC
  SELECT COUNT(*)
```

```
      INTO INGREDIENTS_RATE
      FROM INGREDIENT
     WHERE NAME LIKE '%' || INGREDIENT_NAME || '%';
END
```

The `INGREDIENT_USAGE` procedure declares one `IN` parameter and one `OUT` parameter. The input parameter determines what kind of ingredient we are searching for, and the output parameter returns the number of times that ingredient appears in our recipes.

You can use the same approach we used for other DDL statements in the *Creating a database table* recipe to append a new stored procedure definition to the database schema.

How to do it...

The following simple steps demonstrate how we can accomplish our recipe's goal:

1. In order to call a stored procedure you need to create a list of parameter types and values first:

   ```
   def params = [ Sql.INTEGER, 'sugar' ]
   ```

2. Then by using the `call` method and JDBC syntax we can invoke the desired procedure in the database:

   ```
   def sql = Sql.newInstance(dbSettings)
   sql.call(
     '{ CALL INGREDIENT_USAGE(:rate, :pattern) }',
     params) { rate ->
     println "Sugar usage: $rate"
   }
   ```

3. The script should print something similar to:

   ```
   Sugar usage: 2
   ```

How it works...

We have specified two values in the list passed to the `call` method. The first value is the type of the `OUT` parameter that we expect to receive, and the second one is the value for the `IN` parameter that we pass to the procedure. `Sql.DOUBLE` is a constant (of `groovy.sql.OutParameter` type) defined in the `groovy.sql.Sql` class. There is a constant for every standard JDBC type.

`OUT` parameter values received back from the procedure are passed to the closure given to the `call` method as a second parameter. Inside that closure, you are free to manipulate received values, for example, by printing them.

There's more...

If a stored procedure contains several OUT, IN, or even INOUT parameters, then invoking that does not look much more complex. Let's assume we have the following stored procedure signature:

```
CREATE PROCEDURE INGREDIENT_USAGE2(
    IN COOKBOOK_ID INTEGER,
    OUT INGREDIENTS_RATE INTEGER,
    INOUT INGREDIENT_NAME VARCHAR(100))
READS SQL DATA
BEGIN ATOMIC
    ...
END
```

Calling that procedure will look as follows:

```
def params = [1, Sql.INTEGER, Sql.inout(Sql.VARCHAR('sugar'))]

sql.call(
  '{ CALL INGREDIENT_USAGE2(:cookbook_id, :rate, :pattern)}',
  params) { rate, pattern ->
  println rate
  println pattern
}
```

The difference from our original snippet is that we pass the INOUT parameter with the help of the Sql.inout(Sql.VARCHAR('sugar')) construct and that final closure runs over two output parameters, rate and pattern.

See also

- ▶ *Creating a database table*
- ▶ *Querying an SQL database*
- ▶ http://docs.oracle.com/javase/tutorial/jdbc/basics/storedprocedures.html
- ▶ http://groovy.codehaus.org/api/groovy/sql/Sql.html
- ▶ http://groovy.codehaus.org/api/groovy/sql/InParameter.html
- ▶ http://groovy.codehaus.org/api/groovy/sql/OutParameter.html
- ▶ http://groovy.codehaus.org/api/groovy/sql/InOutParameter.html

Reading BLOB/CLOB from a database

Large binary object types are meant to store data, which is otherwise not splittable into relational tables and columns, or which is easier to store in a binary form for application-specific or performance needs. Groovy does not offer any special methods for handling SQL's large binary objects, but, on the other hand, this recipe will show how to apply Groovy's I/O API extensions to make the code more readable.

Getting ready

Let's again use the database model we created in the *Creating a database table* recipe. In the RECIPE table, we have the DESCRIPTION column of CLOB type and the IMAGE column of BLOB type.

How to do it...

To read the data, we can just use the same query methods we used in the *Querying an SQL database* recipe:

```
sql.eachRow('SELECT * FROM RECIPE') { recipe ->

    println recipe.description.characterStream.text

    def recipeImage = new File("recipe-${recipe.id}.jpg")
    recipeImage.delete()
    recipeImage << recipe.image.binaryStream

}
```

How it works...

The types of recipe.description and recipe.image fields are java.jdbc.Clob and java.jdbc.Blob respectively. Those are standard JDBC types used to handle large binary data. By using instances of those types, you can create an InputStream to get the actual data from the database. And that's what happens in the previous code snippet. The only difference between the fields is that they serve different stream types. We just make use of Clob.getCharacterStream and Blob.getBinaryStream methods.

Thanks to the Groovy extensions of standard Java API, we can transform an InputStream directly into String with the help of the getText method (or simply text). We can as well send another stream directly to a file with the help of the leftShift method (or simply << operator) available in java.io.File extension.

There's more...

You can also write BLOB/CLOB data into the database with simple insert statements.
Let's assume we have the following recipe information stored in a Map:

```
def recipe = [
   id: 1000, chapter_id: 100, title: 'steak indian-style',
   description: '''\
TO START Get all your ingredients and equipment ready.
Put a griddle pan on a high heat...
''',
   image: Sql.BLOB(new File('steak.jpg').bytes)
]
```

As you can see we defined the CLOB data of description field as simple string and wrapped
the binary image file data into a `groovy.sql.InParameter` instance with the help of `Sql.`
`BLOB` method. Now you can just call the `execute` method to insert data as we did in the
Modifying data in an SQL database recipe:

```
sql.execute(
   'INSERT INTO RECIPE ' +
   'VALUES(:id, :chapter_id, :title, :description, :image)',
   recipe
)
```

It is important to consider if the data persisted using a BLOB is small enough to comply
with your memory usage requirements. If the size of the BLOB is large then you risk getting a
dreaded OutOfMemoryException. To avoid any memory related issue, you have to use plain
old JDBC API and stream data into the database.

Also, if CLOB/BLOB support in your database driver is not optimal you need to consider using
native support. For example, the Oracle JDBC driver is widely known to require handling of
BLOB/CLOB in a native way that is bypassing generic JDBC classes and interfaces, using
classes of your driver implementation directly.

See also

▶ *Creating a database table*

▶ *Querying an SQL database*

▶ `http://docs.oracle.com/javase/6/docs/api/java/sql/Blob.html`

▶ `http://docs.oracle.com/javase/6/docs/api/java/sql/Clob.html`

▶ `http://groovy.codehaus.org/groovy-jdk/java/io/File.html`

▶ `http://groovy.codehaus.org/groovy-jdk/java/io/InputStream.html`

Building a simple ORM framework

The `groovy.sql.Sql` class meets the needs of querying and modifying data stored in a relational database. Still, as the name implies, this class requires knowledge of the SQL language and has a strong relationship with the verbosity of the Java's JDBC API.

Wouldn't be great if we could access and insert data into a database table without writing a single line of SQL? The `groovy.sql.DataSet` class can make that happen.

In this recipe, we are going to cover a simple approach to building a database mapping solution using Groovy facilities.

Getting ready

For this recipe, we are going to create a new table, named EMPLOYEE. Create a new script, named `orm.groovy` and add the following code:

```
import static DBUtil.*
import groovy.sql.Sql
import groovy.sql.DataSet

class Person {
    Integer id
    String name
    String lastName
    Integer age
    Integer department
}

def server = startServer()
def sql = Sql.newInstance(dbSettings)

sql.execute('''CREATE TABLE EMPLOYEE (
    ID INTEGER PRIMARY KEY,
    NAME VARCHAR(100),
    LASTNAME VARCHAR(100),
    AGE INTEGER,
    DEPARTMENT INTEGER)''')
```

Similarly to the other recipes in this chapter, we make use of the DBUtil class. Therefore, the script must be invoked by specifying the location of `DBUtil.groovy` in the classpath, as follows:

```
groovy -cp /path/to/script/folder orm.groovy
```

The script also contains the definition of the class `Person` that we will map to the
`EMPLOYEE` table.

How to do it...

Let's start adding some code after the table creation statement:

1. This is how to insert data into a table without (explicitly) issuing an SQL statement:

    ```
    def persons = new DataSet(sql, 'EMPLOYEE')
    person.add(name: 'John',
        lastname: 'Willis',
        id: 1,
        age: 40,
        DEPARTMENT: 100)
    person.add(name: 'Alfred',
        lastname: 'Morris',
        id: 2,
        age: 50,
        DEPARTMENT: 101)
    person.add(name: 'Mickey',
            lastname: 'Rourke',
            id: 3,
            age: 30,
            DEPARTMENT: 101)
    person.add(name: 'Santo',
            lastname: 'Mongo',
            id: 4,
            age: 45,
            DEPARTMENT: 101)
    ```

2. This is how to fetch the data from the database using Dataset:

    ```
    persons.each {
       println "employee ${it.id} - ${it.name} ${it.lastname}"
    }
    ```

    This will yield something similar to the following:

    console   employee 1 - John Willis   employee 2 - Alfred Morris

How it works...

The `DataSet` represents a list, in which each element is a map of key/value pairs, matching
the corresponding table row. Row data can be easily accessed through property names.
The name of the property is case-insensitive, but must match the original column name.

The `DataSet` class issues the relevant SQL statements only when the `each` method
is invoked.

Here is an example of using the `DataSet` class with some WHERE conditions:

```
persons.findAll { it.age > 45 }.each {
  println it
}
```

The output may be as follows:

```
>[ID:2, NAME:Alfred, LASTNAME:Morris, AGE:50, DEPARTMENT:101]
>[ID:4, NAME:Santo, LASTNAME:Mongo, AGE:45, DEPARTMENT:101]
```

In this case, the `findAll` produces an SQL statement that reflects the expression within the closure. This generated statement is encapsulated in the returned `persons` data set.

There's more...

Filters inside the `Dataset` can be combined to create more powerful query conditions:

```
persons.findAll { it.department == 101 && it.age < 50 }
        .sort { it.lastname }
        .each {
      println it
}
```

The output may be as follows:

```
>[ID:4, NAME:Santo, LASTNAME:Mongo, AGE:45, DEPARTMENT:101]
>[ID:3, NAME:Mickey, LASTNAME:Rourke, AGE:30, DEPARTMENT:101]
```

Did you spot the `sort`? As for any other collection in Groovy you can indeed sort the result.

See also

▶   http://groovy.codehaus.org/api/groovy/sql/DataSet.html

Using Groovy to access Redis

Redis is an open source data structure server with an in-memory data set. It is called a data structure server, and not simply a key/value store, because Redis implements data structures allowing keys to contain binary safe strings, hashes, sets and sorted sets, as well as lists. This combination of flexibility and speed makes Redis the ideal tool for many applications.

Redis has incredible performance, due to the in-memory data set, but it is still possible to persist the data either by saving a snapshot of the data set to disk once in a while or appending each command to a log.

Redis also supports trivial-to-setup master/slave replication, with very fast non-blocking synchronization, auto reconnection on network split and so forth.

Redis first started in early 2009 as a key value store developed by Salvatore Sanfilippo in order to improve the performance of his own LLOOGG, an analytics product. Redis grew in popularity after getting support from people and companies in the developer world and has since been supported by VMWare, who hired Salvatore and Pieter Noordhuis to work full-time on the project.

This recipe will present a way of accessing a Redis data store with the help of existing libraries and Groovy.

Getting ready

In this recipe, we are going to take a look at the most common commands and data structures available in Redis.

Redis is easy to install. The recommended way to install Redis is by compiling the sources, as it doesn't have any external dependencies. Redis sources can be downloaded from the official website (`http://redis.io`) or directly from GitHub (`https://github.com/antirez/redis`). Build instructions can be found at the Redis quick start page (`http://redis.io/topics/quickstart`).

Alternatively, you can download the binaries (including Windows binaries) directly from the Redis download page (`http://redis.io/download`).

This recipe assumes that you have an instance of Redis 2.6 or higher, up and running on your development machine.

The Redis communication protocol is quite simple. A client needs to open a TCP/IP connection to the server and issue a Redis command terminated by \r\n (CR LF).

The general form is as follows:

```
*<number of arguments> CR LF
$<number of bytes of argument 1> CR LF
<argument data> CR LF
..
$<number of bytes of argument N> CR LF
<argument data> CR LF
```

Dealing with Redis at such a low level is not ideal. In order to simplify working with the commands, several clients have been implemented in the last years for almost every possible language.

There is no _pure_ Groovy client at the moment, but there are several Java clients available. The one we are going to use in this recipe is Jedis, developed by Jonathan Leibiusky and considered the standard Java client for Redis.

Jedis can be downloaded directly from the project's GitHub page (`https://github.com/xetorthio/jedis`) or referenced as dependency with Grape.

For a complete list of Redis clients, please, refer to the official client page on the Redis website (`http://redis.io/clients`).

How to do it...

Let's see how we can access a Redis instance.

1. As usual while dealing with external libraries in Groovy, the first step is to declare the Jedis dependency via Grape:

    ```
    @Grab('redis.clients:jedis:2.1.0')
    import redis.clients.jedis.*
    ```

2. The Jedis API is essentially a mirror of the Redis commands (`http://redis.io/commands`). It is exposed by the `Jedis` class, which can be instantiated by passing the host of the Redis server:

    ```
    def jedis = new Jedis('localhost')
    ```

    Jedis connects to the Redis default port, 6379. Should Redis run on a nonstandard port, you can pass the port value too:

    ```
    def jedis = new Jedis('localhost', 9000)
    ```

3. When the client is successfully connected, it's possible to issue the commands to store and retrieve the values:

    ```
    jedis.set('foo', 'bar')
    String value = jedis.get('foo')
    assert value == 'bar'
    ```

4. To increment a value fire this snippet:

    ```
    jedis.set('counter', '1')
    jedis.incr('counter')
    jedis.incr('counter')
    assert jedis.get('counter') == '3'
    ```

5. To set expiration period for a key you call the `expire` method passing the key and the number of seconds for the key to live:

    ```
    jedis.set('short lived', '10')
    jedis.expire('short lived', 3)
    Thread.sleep(3000)
    assert jedis.exists('short lived') == false
    ```

6. One of the appealing features of Redis is the presence of proper data structures inside the key store, such as lists, sets, hashes, and sorted sets. Lists are used to store an (ordered) collection of items:

```
jedis.rpush('myList', 'a', 'b', 'c')
assert 3 == jedis.llen('myList')
assert '1' == jedis.lrange('myList', 0,0)[0]

jedis.lpush('myList', '3', '2', '1')
assert 6 == jedis.llen('myList')
```

7. Stacks and queues can be very easily modeled with lists, using the rpop method, which gets and removes the last element of a list:

```
jedis.del('myQueue')
jedis.lpush('myQueue', 'new york')
jedis.lpush('myQueue', 'dallas')
jedis.lpush('myQueue', 'tulsa')

assert 'new york' == jedis.rpop('myQueue')
assert 'dallas' == jedis.rpop('myQueue')
assert 'tulsa' == jedis.rpop('myQueue')
```

How it works...

Each method call of the Jedis API is translated into an actual Redis command. For example, the INCR command, called in the step 4, atomically increments an integer value. It is important to note that this is a string operation, because Redis does not have a dedicated integer type. The EXPIRE command, used in step 5, defines the amount of seconds a key is allowed to "live" before it expires.

Other commands that we demonstrated in the previous examples do the following:

▶ The RPUSH command appends values at the start of a list.

▶ The LRANGE command returns the specified elements from a list.

▶ The LPUSH command appends values at the end of a list.

▶ The RPOP command returns and removes the last value from a list.

There's more...

One of the reasons Redis is a very popular caching solution for large web applications is the presence of hashes. A hash is essentially a map storing string fields and string values: the perfect data type for storing objects.

So, let's start by creating a simple User bean.

```
class User {
   Long userid
   String username
   String password
}
```

The `User` bean is a typical domain object that we want to store in Redis. Groovy has a very handy method exposed on the `Object` class, `getProperties`, which returns a `Map` of the object's properties. The key/value structure is exactly what we need to store the domain object in Redis.

```
User u = new User()
u.userid = 2001
u.username = 'john'
u.password = '12345'
```

After creating an instance of the `User` class, we proceed to store it in Redis by calling the `HMSET` command.

```
jedis.hmset(
   "user:$u.userid",
   u.properties.findAll {
      !['class', 'userid'].contains(it.key)
   }.collectEntries { k,v ->
      [k, v.toString()]
   }
)
```

The `hmset` method accepts a `String` (the key) and a `Map`, which contains the key/values we want to store. Logically, the key of the map is the primary key of the User, so we set it as user: `$u.userid`.

The `getProperties` method returns in the `Map` also the actual class of the object on which we call the method on (in our case, `User`). We don't need to store it, so we filter it out along with the `userid` key, which would be redundant.

Finally, the `collectEntries` method, invoked on the filtered `Map` returns a new `Map` where all the keys are `Strings`, as this is the only data type Redis (and Jedis) accepts.

By calling the `HGETALL` command:

```
println jedis.hgetAll("user:$u.userid")
```

We get the following output:

```
> [username:john, password:12345]
```

One more Redis aspect we are going to touch is atomic operations. Redis doesn't support transactions in the same way as a relational database does (no rollbacks), but it is still possible to execute a number of commands atomically. Enter the MULTI and EXEC commands. The MULTI command marks the beginning of a transaction, in which the following commands are queued and executed atomically.

This is how a MULTI command works when executed in the Redis **CLI (Command Line Interface)**:

```
> MULTI
OK
> INCR foo
QUEUED
> INCR bar
QUEUED
> EXEC
```

Jedis does support the MULTI command, and we can actually implement it in a more Groovy way.

The following atomic method allows executing a group of commands inside the MULTI/EXEC transaction.

```
jedis = new Jedis('localhost')
def atomic(Closure c) {
  def results = null
  try {
    def tx = jedis.multi()
    c.delegate = tx
    c.call()
    results = tx.exec()
  } catch(e) {
    tx.discard()
  }
  results
}
```

The Jedis multi method returns a `Transaction` object on which the commands have to be executed. This is an example of the actual Java code:

```
Transaction t = jedis.multi();
t.set("foo", "bar");
Response<String> result1 = t.get("foo");
```

Thanks to Groovy closures and the `Closure`'s delegate property we can invoke the atomic function as follows:

```
def res = atomic {
   incr ('foo')
   incr ('bar')
}
println jedis.get('foo')
assert '1' == jedis.get('bar')
assert res == [1, 1]
```

The two `INCR` commands are executed atomically, and the `res` variable contains the result of last command.

See also

 ▶   `http://redis.io`
 ▶   `http://redis.io/topics/quickstart`
 ▶   `https://github.com/xetorthio/jedis`
 ▶   `http://www.grails.org/plugin/redis`

Using Groovy to access MongoDB

MongoDB (`http://www.mongodb.org`) is a document-oriented database written in C++ with RDBMS-like features such as indexing and replication. It is developed and supported by 10gen.

MongoDB is very popular mainly for its simplicity: documents are created as JSON-like records (key/value pairs with a rich data type model) and the interface is simple enough to be used directly from JavaScript. It has been designed for scalability in mind. Its document-oriented data model allows it to automatically split up data across multiple servers, letting developers focus on application logic instead of scaling up the data store.

Other very useful features of MongoDB are built-in support for Map/Reduce-style aggregation and geospatial indexes.

This recipe will show you how to execute CRUD-like operations on a MongoDB instance and how to search for data.

Getting ready

MongoDB installation is quite simple, especially if you are on Linux or OS X, where you can use a package manager such as Yum or Homebrew. Detailed installation instructions are available for every operating system on the MongoDB website (`http://docs.mongodb.org/manual/installation`).

Before we get into the details of this recipe, we will give a quick crash course on the main MongoDB's entities.

MongoDB has databases, collections, and documents. MongoDB stores a database in its own file. A database has specific permissions and can be conceptually mapped to a relational database.

A collection is a group of documents stored in a database. A collection has no schema, meaning that each document in a collection is free to have any kind of structure (it is recommended to keep similar documents in the same collection).

Finally, the document is an ordered set of key/value pairs. Each programming language has a data structure to represent a key/pair values, such as maps or dictionaries.

This is a Javascript representation of a MongoDB document.

```
{ "name": "Oscar", "lastName": "Wilde" }
```

The Java driver (`https://github.com/mongodb/mongo-java-driver/downloads`) is the oldest MongoDB driver. It is very stable and a popular choice for enterprise developers. The driver is enough to get started, but as it often happens with Java libraries, it is very verbose. The verbosity is quite evident when building documents to be sent to the server.

Fortunately, there is a Groovy wrapper for the MongoDB Java driver, named GMongo, developed and actively maintained by Paulo Poiati (`http://blog.paulopoiati.com/`). The wrapper is maintained at the same pace as the main Java driver, making it an excellent option for Groovy developers.

How to do it...

Ensure that your MongoDB instance is running; the server usually listens for connections on port 27017.

1. As usual, it is necessary to import the third-party library that will be used throughout this recipe, GMongo.

```
@Grab('com.gmongo:gmongo:1.2')
import com.gmongo.GMongo
```

2. Then, the GMongo class instance is created to access the database `groovy-book`. The `getDB` method does actually create a database, if that does not exist.

```
def mongo = new GMongo()
def db = mongo.getDB('groovy-book')
```

3. Now, let's insert some documents into a collection named `todos`.

```
db.todos.insert([name: 'buy milk'])
db.todos.insert(name: 'pay rent')
db.todos << [name: 'read document']
```

The previous snippet inserts three to-do documents into MongoDB. You can notice that the syntax for inserting data is slightly different in each statement. In the first two cases we are actually calling the same method; Groovy allows omitting square brackets ([]) when the method's only parameter is a Map. The last statement is making use of the `leftShift` method, which under the hood results in the same call to the `insert` method.

4. So, you can now select a document from the collection using for example the `findOne` method:

```
println db.todos.findOne()
```

The output will be as follows:

```
> [_id:50b299e81a88da0e521db954, name:buy milk]
```

How it works...

The `findOne` method with no arguments returns the first document in the collection. MongoDB automatically adds an id, named `ObjectID`, to a new document. The `ObjectID` is a 12-byte value consisting of a 4-byte timestamp (seconds since epoch), a 3-byte machine id, a 2-byte process id, and a 3-byte counter.

`findOne` can be also used with an argument, very much like an SQL SELECT statement.

```
println db.todos.findOne(name: 'pay rent')
```

The output will be as follows:

```
> [_id:50b29b091a88d361473e6b46, name:pay rent]
```

The `find` method allows searching for documents using regular expressions. Groovy supports regular expressions natively with the help of the ~ operator, which creates a compiled `Pattern` object from the given string:

```
db.todos.find([name: ~/^pay/]).each {
    println it
}
```

The output will be as follows:

```
> [_id:50b29b091a88d361473e6b46, name:pay rent]
```

Updating documents is also as easy as inserting them. A MongoDB collection is schemaless, so each document can have its own *shape*.

```
db.todos.update(
   name: 'pay rent',
   [$set: [name: 'pay December rent']]
)
assert db.todos.count(
   name: 'pay December rent') == 1
```

The `update` method changes the value of the name field using the `$set` operator. This operator appends the new field or fields to the document or replaces the existing value of the field(s) in case they are already present in the document.

```
db.todos.update(name: 'pay December rent', [$set:[priority:1]])
```

The second update example adds a new attribute to the document, the priority field. Please note that the value of priority is an Integer and not a String. MongoDB supports several data types internally through the BSON format, which includes dates and binary.

Another way to update a document is the following:

```
def todo = db.todos.findOne(name: 'buy milk')
todo.priority = 2
db.todos.save todo
println todo
```

The output will be as follows:

```
> [_id:50b2a3aa1a8848c02c604025, name:buy milk, priority:2]
```

The syntax to remove documents is very similar to the one for updating.

```
db.todos.insert([name: 'call John', priority: 2])
assert db.todos.count(priority: 2) == 2

db.todos.remove(priority: 2, name: 'call John')
assert db.todos.count(priority: 2) == 1
```

There's more...

Similar to the *Using Groovy to access Redis* recipe, we are going to show a simple way to store Groovy objects (POGO) to MongoDB. Let's define a `Todo` class and instantiate it:

```
class Todo {
    def name
    def priority
    def context
}

def td = new Todo(name: 'open account',
    priority: 1,
    context: 'finance')
```

Now, the `getProperties` method in Groovy returns a `Map` of the object's properties, including some properties we don't want to store in MongoDB, such as `class` or `metaClass`.

```
db.todos << td.properties.findAll {
  !['class', 'metaClass'].contains(it.key)
}
println db.todos.findOne(name:'open account')
```

The output will be as follows:

```
> [_id:50b2a8b21a8820042e85bc6b, context:finance,
   priority:1, name:open account]
```

In the previous snippets, the `properties` method is invoked on the `Todo` instance and some properties are filtered out. The resulting `Map` is simply added to the `todos` collection.

See also

 ▶ http://www.mongodb.org/
 ▶ https://github.com/poiati/gmongo
 ▶ http://blog.paulopoiati.com/

Using Groovy to access Apache Cassandra

The **Apache Cassandra** project was started at Facebook in 2007 to offer users a better experience when searching their inbox. The challenges that Facebook engineers had to face was mostly related to massive amount of data, very high throughput, and scalability at a mind-blowing rate.

Cassandra is a distributed column-oriented database designed to manage humongous amounts of structured data in a decentralized, highly scalable way. The absence of a single point of failure makes Cassandra highly available and fault tolerant.

While Cassandra resembles a traditional database and shares some design strategies, it does not support a full relational data model. On the contrary, the Cassandra's data model is flexible, because each row can contain a variable number of columns.

In this recipe, we will go through different aspects of connecting and querying a Cassandra database.

Getting ready

For this recipe, we assume that the reader has already some familiarity with the Cassandra core concepts and data model (columns, super columns, column family, and keyspaces). Installing Cassandra is straightforward.

The only requirement for running Cassandra is a Java 1.6 JVM. Just download the distribution from the product website (`http://cassandra.apache.org/download/`), unzip it, and run the `bin/cassandra` or `bin/cassandra.bat` executable to start a single node.

Before we start, we have to create a couple of entities in Cassandra, a *Keyspace* and a *Column Family*. Fire up the CQLSH console located in the bin folder and type:

```
create keyspace hr with strategy_class='SimpleStrategy'
and strategy_options:replication_factor=1;
use hr;
create columnfamily employee (empid int primary key);
```

These commands create a Keyspace named `hr` and a column family named `employee`. The column family has one field only, which is also a primary key (of type `int`).

How to do it...

There are several client strategies to interact with Cassandra. In this recipe, we are going to use the open source library Hector, which is a well-established high level Java client.

The Hector APIs are not very fluent, and it takes a lot of boilerplate code to insert or manipulate data with it.

Why not create a simpler, more fluent wrapper on top of the Hector API using Groovy?

```groovy
@Grab('org.hectorclient:hector-core:1.1-2')
@GrabExclude('org.apache.httpcomponents:httpcore')
import me.prettyprint.hector.api.Cluster
import me.prettyprint.hector.api.factory.HFactory
import me.prettyprint.hector.api.Keyspace
import me.prettyprint.cassandra.serializers.*
import me.prettyprint.hector.api.Serializer
import me.prettyprint.hector.api.mutation.Mutator
import me.prettyprint.hector.api.ddl.*
import me.prettyprint.hector.api.beans.ColumnSlice

class Gassandra {

    def cluster
    def keyspace
    def colFamily
    Serializer serializer
    def stringSerializer = StringSerializer.get()

    private Gassandra (Keyspace keyspace) {
      this.keyspace = keyspace
    }

    Gassandra() {}

    void connect(clusterName, host, port) {
      cluster = HFactory.
        getOrCreateCluster(
        clusterName,
        "$host:$port"
        )
    }

    List<KeyspaceDefinition> getKeyspaces() {
      cluster.describeKeyspaces()
    }

    Gassandra withKeyspace(keyspaceName) {
      keyspace = HFactory.
        createKeyspace(
          keyspaceName,
          cluster
```

```
      )
    new Gassandra(keyspace)
}

Gassandra withColumnFamily(columnFamily, Serializer c) {
    colFamily =  columnFamily
    serializer = c
    this
}

Gassandra insert(key, columnName, value) {
    def mutator = HFactory.
        createMutator(
          keyspace,
          serializer
        )
    def column  = HFactory.
        createStringColumn(
          columnName,
          value
        )
    mutator.insert(key, colFamily, column)
    this
}

Gassandra insert(key, Map args) {
    def mutator = HFactory.
        createMutator(
          keyspace,
          serializer
        )
    args.each {
      mutator.insert(
        key,
        colFamily,
        HFactory.
          createStringColumn(
            it.key,
            it.value
          )
      )
    }
    this
}
```

```
            ColumnSlice findByKey(key)  {
               def sliceQuery = HFactory.
                  createSliceQuery(
                     keyspace,
                     serializer,
                     stringSerializer,
                     stringSerializer
                  )
               sliceQuery.
                  setColumnFamily(colFamily).
                  setKey(key).
                  setRange('', '', false, 100).
                  execute().
                  get()
            }
         }
```

How it works...

The `Gassandra` class exposes a very simple, fluent interface that leverages the dynamic nature of Groovy. The class imports the Hector API and allows writing code as follows:

```
def g = new Gassandra()
g.connect('test', 'localhost', '9160')

def employee = g
    .withKeyspace('hr')
    .withColumnFamily('employee', IntegerSerializer.get())
employee.insert(5005, 'name', 'Zoe')
employee.insert(5005, 'lastName', 'Ross')
employee.insert(5005, 'age', '31')
```

The `withKeySpace` and `withColumnFamily` methods are written in a fluent style, so that we can pass the relevant information to Hector. Note that the `withColumnFamily` requires a *Serializer* type to specify the type of the primary key.

The `insert` method accepts a *Map* as well, so that the previous code can be rewritten as:

```
employee.insert('5005',
    ['name': 'Zoe',
    'lastName': 'Ross',
    'age': '31'
    ])
```

To find a row by primary key, there is a `findByKey` method that returns a `me.prettyprint.hector.api.beans.ColumnSlice` object.

```
println employee.findByKey(5005)
```

The previous statement will output:

```
ColumnSlice([HColumn(age=31),
    HColumn(lastName=Ross),
    HColumn(name=Zoe)])
```

The `Gassandra` class lacks many basic methods to update or delete rows and other advanced query features. We leave them to the reader as an exercise.

See also

▶ `http://cassandra.apache.org/`

▶ `http://hector-client.github.com/hector/build/html/index.html`

8
Working with Web Services in Groovy

In this chapter, we will cover:

- ▶ Downloading content from the Internet
- ▶ Executing an HTTP GET request
- ▶ Executing an HTTP POST request
- ▶ Constructing and modifying complex URLs
- ▶ Issuing a REST request and parsing a response
- ▶ Issuing a SOAP request and parsing a response
- ▶ Consuming RSS and Atom feeds
- ▶ Using basic authentication for web service security
- ▶ Using OAuth for web service security

Introduction

The recipes collected in this chapter deal with the so called programmable web.

Today's applications consume data from a multitude of external sources. These sources are often accessed through HTTP and one of the two main methods for exchanging data over the web, SOAP and REST.

The first recipes describe how to execute simple calls to external web services through HTTP POST and GET request methods, as well as construct complex URLs. The next recipes of the chapter delve into SOAP and REST: how to make a request and parse the result using Groovy. We continue with the RSS and Atom formats and how to consume them. The last recipe covers the basic authentication mechanism and how to interact with the OAuth protocol - the dominant open authorization standard.

Downloading content from the Internet

The title of this recipe may not seem related to web services at a first glance, but since most of the available services are actually based on **Hyper Text Transfer Protocol** (**HTTP**) as well as most of the content on the Internet, it is worth starting with getting a basic understanding of simple HTTP operations before diving into the more complex world of web services.

How to do it...

For downloading HTTP-based content, we don't need any special libraries or stratagem. All that is needed are the standard Java classes—File and URL—and their Groovy extensions:

1. We first start with defining our target and source files:

```
def outputFile = new File('image.png')
def baseUrl = 'http://groovy.codehaus.org'
def imagePath = '/images/groovy-logo-medium.png'
def url = new URL("${baseUrl}${imagePath}")
```

2. Then, just in case, the outputFile already exists, we need to delete it to avoid appending content:

```
outputFile.delete()
```

3. The last step is to stream the URL's content into the outputFile:

```
url.withInputStream { inputStream ->
  outputFile << inputStream
}
```

How it works...

The withInputStream method is a Groovy extension added to the URL class. We already presented many extension methods that Groovy appends to the standard JDK classes in previous chapters (for example, the *Using Java Classes from Groovy* recipe in *Chapter 2, Using Groovy Ecosystem*), and we showed the way to write your own extensions in the *Adding a functionality to the existing Java/Groovy classes* recipe in *Chapter 3, Using Groovy Language Features*. More information on extended functionality, which exists in Groovy for the java. net.URL class, can be found at http://groovy.codehaus.org/groovy-jdk/java/net/URL.html.

Basically, the `withInputStream` method takes care of flushing and closing the stream automatically, and gives access to the `java.io.InputStream` instance, which contains the binary data retrieved from a remote resource over the HTTP protocol. More information on manipulating files and input streams can be found in *Chapter 4, Working with Files in Groovy*.

Under the hood, the `URL` class performs an HTTP GET request for the resource specified by the URL. A lengthier description on how to construct complex GET requests can be found in the *Executing an HTTP GET request* recipe.

With this new knowledge about the basics of executing an HTTP GET request described in this recipe, you can use many REST-based APIs in a read-only mode as well as download WSDL and XSD for the SOAP-based web services.

There's more...

If the content to download is textual, we can use a more concise way to fetch it with the help of the `getText` method available on the `URL` class:

```
def outputFile = new File('groovy.html')
def baseUrl = 'http://groovy.codehaus.org'
def url = new URL(baseUrl)

// Saving textual content.
outputFile.text = url.text
```

See also

▶ http://groovy.codehaus.org/groovy-jdk/java/net/URL.html

▶ *Executing an HTTP GET request*

▶ *Chapter 4, Working with Files in Groovy*

Executing an HTTP GET request

In the previous recipe, *Downloading content from the Internet*, we described a simple way of getting binary/textual content from a URL. In this recipe, we will present a method to execute HTTP GET requests with more control over the returned data.

How to do it...

As a starting point, we will use again the same URL class encountered in the previous recipe. This time we'll explore the openConnection method of the URL class in order to have more options for understanding the intricacies of the response returned by the remote server:

1. We can make the code which retrieves the remote content more reliable by checking the response code as follows:

```
def url = new URL('http://groovy.codehaus.org/')
def connection = url.openConnection()
connection.requestMethod = 'GET'
if (connection.responseCode == 200) {
  println connection.content.text
  println connection.contentType
  println connection.lastModified
  connection.headerFields.each { println "> ${it}"}
} else {
  println 'An error occurred: ' +
          connection.responseCode + ' ' +
          connection.responseMessage
}
```

2. The code will print something similar to the following output:

```
<!DOCTYPE html>

<html>

    ...

</html>

text/html; charset=UTF-8

0

> null=[HTTP/1.1 200 OK]

> Date=[Tue, 03 Sep 2013 13:03:13 GMT]

> Content-Length=[39028]

> Connection=[close]

> Content-Type=[text/html; charset=UTF-8]

> Server=[Resin/3.0.14]
```

How it works...

The `java.net.URLConnection` object, returned by the `openConnection` method, is convenient for getting hold of the additional response data such as, `responseCode`, `contentType`, or `response headers`.

As you can notice, we set the `requestMethod` property on the connection object to `GET` value; but, in fact, it's not needed, because it is a default value anyway.

`responseCode` is the *Status Code Definition* returned from the web server. For instance, a 404 status code, informs the client that the requested resource doesn't exist.

The connection object has the `getContent` method, which is declared to return `java.lang.Object` by the JDK API. The mechanism used by JDK to handle specific content types is out of scope of this recipe. However, the `getContent` method typically returns an implementation of the `InputStream` interface. That's why it is safe to retrieve the `text` property, which is made available by Groovy on all classes that implement the `InputStream` functionality.

There's more...

An HTTP `GET` request often requires additional parameters needed by the server or remote application. These parameters are propagated inside the URL through a query string:

```
http://groovy.codehaus.org/Project+Information?print=1
```

The previous URL passes to the server the following key/value information: `print=1`, which is used to retrieve the Groovy project information page in printer-friendly format. In Groovy, the plain procedure to add a query string to a URL is just to use a string object. For example:

```
println ('http://groovy.codehaus.org/' +
         'Project+Information?print=1').toURL().text
```

Query strings can be way lengthier than a single key/value entry. A `Map` is the perfect data structure for representing the query string data. Let us see how a `Map` can be converted into a query string:

```
def baseUrl =
    'http://docs.codehaus.org/pages/editpage.action?'

def params = [spaceKey: 'GROOVY',
              title: 'Project+Information']

def query = params.collect { k,v ->
  "$k=${URLEncoder.encode(v)}"
}.join('&')

println "${baseUrl}${query}"
```

The code yields the following output:

```
> http://docs.codehaus.org/pages/editpage.action?spaceKey=GROOVY&title=Pr
oject+Information
```

The code snippet that transforms a `Map` into a query uses the `collect` method of the `Map`. It iterates through the `Map` entries and executes a simple transformation closure returning a List. The closure simply encodes each parameter value using the `java.net.URLEncoder` class and adds the `=` sign between a parameter name and its content. Finally, the `join` method is applied to the resulting collection to concatenate all entries into a single string using `&` symbol.

See also

▸ *Downloading content from the Internet*

▸ *Constructing and modifying complex URLs*

▸ *Executing an HTTP POST request*

▸ `http://docs.oracle.com/javase/6/docs/api/java/net/`
`URLConnection.html`

▸ `http://docs.oracle.com/javase/6/docs/api/java/net/URLEncoder.`
`html`

Executing an HTTP POST request

In this recipe, we demonstrate how to POST data to a remote HTTP server using Groovy. The POST request method is often used to upload a file or submit a web form to a server. This method sits at the opposite end of the spectrum of the HTTP GET method, used to retrieve information from the server.

How to do it...

The code required to execute a POST request with Groovy is fairly similar to the one discussed in the previous recipe, *Executing an HTTP GET request*, except that it's more convoluted:

1. The sending of a POST request is expressed in the following way:

```
def baseUrl = new URL('http://api.duckduckgo.com')
def queryString = 'q=groovy&format=json&pretty=1'
def connection = baseUrl.openConnection()
connection.with {
  doOutput = true
  requestMethod = 'POST'
```

```
      outputStream.withWriter { writer ->
        writer << queryString
      }
      println content.text
   }
```

2. The printed results will look similar to the following code snippet:

```
{
    "Definition" :
     "groovy definition: marvelous, wonderful, excellent.",
    "DefinitionSource" : "Merriam-Webster",
    "Heading" : "Groovy",
    "AbstractSource" : "Wikipedia",
    "Image" : "",
    "RelatedTopics" : [
       ...
    ]
    ...
}
```

How it works...

The first few lines of the script open a connection to an API provided by the `DuckDuckGo` search engine, which is an alternative privacy-oriented search service.

To reduce code verbosity we use Groovy's `with` method, which basically allows us to suppress references to the connection variable and call its methods and properties directly within a closure passed to the Groovy's `with` method.

Before making a request, we set several connection properties such as `requestMethod` to indicate that we actually want to fire a `POST` request. Finally, the code creates a writer object to append to the stream containing the data that will be posted to the remote connection. The response is read by using the text property of the `InputStream` method returned by the content property (see the *Executing an HTTP GET request* recipe).

There's more...

Another way to `POST` data to a web server is to use the `HTTPBuilder` third-party library (`http://groovy.codehaus.org/modules/http-builder/doc/index.html`). The project is discussed in more details in the *Issuing a REST request and parsing a response* recipe.

As we are working with an external dependency, we use Grape to fetch the `HTTPBuilder` library:

```
@Grab(
  group='org.codehaus.groovy.modules.http-builder',
  module='http-builder',
  version='0.6'
)
import groovyx.net.http.*

def baseUrl = 'http://api.duckduckgo.com'
def queryString = 'q=groovy&format=json&pretty=1'
def http = new HTTPBuilder(baseUrl)
http.request(Method.POST) {
  send ContentType.URLENC, queryString
  response.success = { response, reader ->
    println response.statusLine
    println reader.text
  }
  response.failure = { response ->
    println response.statusLine
  }
}
```

The result of the posted data is handled in the `response.success` closure. We also handle failures (for example, 404 or 500 status codes) in the failure closure. The `response` variable holds the response metadata such as the status code and the headers. The `reader` object is used to get access to the remote data stream. Since the reader implements a `java.io.Reader` interface, we can use the text property provided by Groovy to fully-fetch response content and print it to the standard output.

See also

- ▶ `http://groovy.codehaus.org/modules/http-builder`
- ▶ The *Simplifying dependency management with Grape* recipe in *Chapter 2, Using Groovy Ecosystem*
- ▶ *Constructing and modifying complex URLs*
- ▶ *Executing an HTTP GET request*

Constructing and modifying complex URLs

At the heart of any HTTP request, there is a **Universal Resource Locator** (**URL**) or a more generic **Universal Resource Identifier** (**URI**) which identifies the target of the operation we need to perform.

We have seen in the previous recipes (for example, the *Downloading content from the Internet* recipe) that it's very hard to avoid dealing with URLs when interacting with the HTTP protocol. In this recipe, we are going to present a more structured approach to constructing and modifying complex URLs with the help of an additional Groovy library.

How to do it...

If you have worked with Java's URL class before, you know that the only way to construct instances of that class is to provide a full URL to the constructor, which will return an immutable (non-changeable) object.

Groovy's core does not add any special support for URL manipulation apart from what Java already offers, but there is an officially supported HttpBuilder module that is hosted on Groovy's website (http://groovy.codehaus.org/modules/http-builder) and that can be used to make more accessible URL creation and modification:

1. First of all, we need to @Grab that module and import the URIBuilder class, which will help us with our task:

```
@Grab(
    group='org.codehaus.groovy.modules.http-builder',
    module='http-builder',
    version='0.6'
)
import groovyx.net.http.URIBuilder
```

2. At this point, we can create a URIBuilder instance and pass baseUri to that:

```
def baseUri =
        'http://groovy.services.com/service1/operation2'
def uri = new URIBuilder(baseUri)
```

3. Now, we can modify any URI's component with simple property assignments, as follows:

```
uri.with {
    scheme = 'https'
    host = 'localhost'
    port = 8080
```

```
    fragment = 'some_anchor'
    path = 'some_folder/some_page.html'
    query = [param1: 2, param2: 'x']
}
```

4. With the information passed to `URIBuilder`, we can create `URI`, `URL`, or `String` instances at any point:

```
uri.toURI()
uri.toURL()
uri.toString()
```

How it works...

Internally the `URIBuilder` class stores all URI components such as, scheme (`http://` and `https://`), user information (`username:password`), host, port, path, and fragment separately. This allows creating new URLs incrementally and changing existing URLs without a need to write custom string parsing/concatenating logic.

See also

▶   `http://groovy.codehaus.org/modules/http-builder/doc/uribuilder.html`

▶   `http://groovy.codehaus.org/modules/http-builder/apidocs/groovyx/net/http/URIBuilder.html`

Other implementations of URI builder functionality can be found in JAX-WS API and Apache's HttpClient available in the following link:

▶   `http://hc.apache.org/httpcomponents-client-ga/httpclient/apidocs/org/apache/http/client/utils/URIBuilder.html`

▶   `http://docs.oracle.com/javaee/6/api/javax/ws/rs/core/UriBuilder.html`

Issuing a REST request and parsing a response

A proper introduction to REST is out of scope for this recipe. Countless materials describing the REST architectural style are available both online and offline. Wikipedia's entry on *Representational State Transfer* at `http://en.wikipedia.org/wiki/Representational_State_Transfer` provides a compact description of REST's main concepts, its limits, and the guiding principles to design RESTful applications. A more tongue-in-cheek introduction to REST can be found on Ryan Tomayko's website at `http://tomayko.com/writings/rest-to-my-wife`.

There are several ways to execute a REST request using Groovy. In this recipe, we are going to show how to execute a `GET` operation against a RESTful resource using `RESTClient` from the `HTTPBuilder` project (`http://groovy.codehaus.org/modules/http-builder/doc/index.html`). HTTPBuilder is a wrapper for Apache `HttpClient`, with some Groovy syntactical sugar thrown on top.

Getting ready

For this recipe, we will use the RESTful API exposed by the *Bing Map Service* (`http://www.bing.com/maps/`). The API allows performing tasks such as, creating a static map with pushpins, geocoding an address, retrieving imagery metadata, or creating a route.

In order to access the service, an authentication key must be obtained through a simple registration process (see `https://www.bingmapsportal.com`). The key has to be passed with each REST request.

How to do it...

The following steps will use the Location API, through which we will find latitude and longitude coordinates for a specific location:

1. The first step is to create a class. The class has a method, which accepts the information to query the map service with:

```
@Grab(
    group='org.codehaus.groovy.modules.http-builder',
    module='http-builder',
    version='0.6'
)
import static groovyx.net.http.ContentType.JSON
import static groovyx.net.http.ContentType.XML
import groovyx.net.http.RESTClient

class LocationFinder {

    static final KEY = '...'
    static final URL = 'http://dev.virtualearth.net'
    static final BASE_PATH = '/REST/v1/Locations/'

    def printCityCoordinates(countryCode, city) {

        def mapClient = new RESTClient(URL)
        def path = "${countryCode}/${city}"
        def response = mapClient.get(
```

```
                                     path: "${BASE_PATH}${path}",
                                     query: [key: KEY]
                          )

                assert response.status == 200
                assert response.contentType == JSON.toString()

                println response.
                          data.
                          resourceSets.
                          resources.
                          point.
                          coordinates


        }
}
```

2. We can use the class in the following way:

```
LocationFinder map = new LocationFinder()
map.printCityCoordinates('fr', 'paris')
map.printCityCoordinates('uk', 'london')
```

3. The code will output the coordinates for Paris and London:

```
[[[48.856929779052734, 2.3412001132965088]]]
[[[51.506320953369141, -0.12714000046253204]]]
```

How it works...

The RESTClient class greatly simplifies dealing with REST resources. It leverages the automatic content type parsing and encoding, which essentially parses the response for us and converts it into the proper type. The get method accepts a Map of arguments, including the actual path to the resource, the request content type, query, and headers. For a full list of arguments, refer to the Javadoc at http://groovy.codehaus.org/modules/http-builder/apidocs/groovyx/net/http/HTTPBuilder.RequestConfigDelegate.html#setPropertiesFromMap(java.util.Map).

In the previous example, the response is automatically parsed and transformed into a nested data structure, which makes dealing with the response values a very simple affair.

By default, all request methods return an `HttpResponseDecorator` instance, which provides convenient access to the response headers and the parsed response body. The response body is parsed based on the content type. HTTPBuilder's default response handlers function in the same way: the response data is parsed (or buffered in the case of a binary or text response) and returned from the request method. The response either carries no data, or it is expected to be parsable and transformed into some object, which is always accessible through the `getData()` method.

The actual data returned by the service looks like the following code snippet:

```
{
    "authenticationResultCode": "ValidCredentials",
    "brandLogoUri": "...",
    "copyright": "...",
    "resourceSets": [
        {
            "estimatedTotal": 1,
            "resources": [
                {
                    "name": "Paris, Paris, France",
                    "point": {
                        "type": "Point",
                        "coordinates": [
                            48.856929779053,
                            2.3412001132965
                        ]
                    },
                    ...
                }
            ]
        }
    ],
    "statusCode": 200,
    "statusDescription": "OK",
    "traceId": "..."
}
```

See also

- ► http://groovy.codehaus.org/modules/http-builder/doc/rest.html
- ► http://msdn.microsoft.com/en-us/library/ff701713.aspx
- ► https://www.bingmapsportal.com

Issuing a SOAP request and parsing a response

SOAP stands for a **Simple Object Access Protocol**. And, indeed, the protocol is very simple and extensible, since it only defines the container parts of the message being transferred, such as, body, header, and fault. But it does not strictly define format or validation rules for the content of the message apart from requesting the message to be XML-compatible.

Also, SOAP has several low-level protocol bindings such as, SOAP-over-HTTP, SOAP-over-SMTP, and SOAP-over-JMS. HTTP binding is the most popular choice for SOAP-based web services.

Usually, a SOAP web service is associated with a **Web Service Definition Language** (**WSDL**) and probably a set of **XML Schema Definition** (**XSD**) that more precisely define the contents of the service operation requests and responses. But strictly speaking those are not required by the SOAP standard, even though they definitely help to understand the service input and output formats.

There is also a family of WS-* (WS-I, WS-Policy, WS-Addressing, WS-Security, and so on) standards that define different aspects of web service authentication, authorization, interoperability, notification, validation, and so on, which can enrich a SOAP message with additional headers, structures, and faults.

There are plenty of libraries available out there to support different WS-* and X-* flavors, but there is no single answer (at least in the open source world) to all of them.

In essence, any SOAP request is an HTTP `POST` request containing a SOAP Envelope with message data and headers.

In this recipe, we will focus on constructing simple SOAP requests at the HTTP protocol level using the `HTTPBuilder` library that we just encountered in the previous recipe, *Issuing a REST request and parsing a response*.

Getting ready

For testing purposes, we will use SOAP web services hosted at `http://www.holidaywebservice.com`. We will try to call the `GetMothersDay` operation on the `USHolidayDates` service. The following XML snippet is the SOAP request we will send to the service:

```
<?xml version="1.0" encoding="UTF-8"?>
<soap-env:Envelope
 xmlns:soap-env='http://schemas.xmlsoap.org/soap/envelope/'>
  <soap-env:Header/>
  <soap-env:Body>
    <GetMothersDay
```

```
   xmlns='http://www.27seconds.com/Holidays/US/Dates/'>
     <year>2013</year>
   </GetMothersDay>
  </soap-env:Body>
</soap-env:Envelope>
```

As you can guess, it tries to retrieve a date of the Mother's Day for 2013.

How to do it...

Let's perform the following steps to construct our SOAP client for the holiday web service:

1. First of all we need to `@Grab` and import the required classes as shown in the following code snippet:

```
@Grab(
  group='org.codehaus.groovy.modules.http-builder',
  module='http-builder',
  version='0.6'
)
import static groovyx.net.http.Method.*
import static groovyx.net.http.ContentType.*
import groovyx.net.http.HTTPBuilder
```

2. Then we need to create an instance of `HTTPBuilder` and point to our web service:

```
def baseUrl = 'http://www.holidaywebservice.com/' +
                'Holidays/US/Dates/USHolidayDates.asmx'
def client = new HTTPBuilder(baseUrl)
```

3. Now, we need to define several namespace variables to refer to during the XML building stage:

```
def holidayBase = 'http://www.27seconds.com/Holidays'
def holidayNS = "$holidayBase/US/Dates/"
def soapAction = "$holidayBase/US/Dates/GetMothersDay"
def soapNS = 'http://schemas.xmlsoap.org/soap/envelope/'
```

4. At this point, we are ready to POST a SOAP request to the service:

```
def response = client.request( POST, XML ) {
  headers = [
    'Content-Type': 'text/xml; charset=UTF-8',
    'SOAPAction': soapAction
  ]
  body = {
    mkp.pi(xml:'version="1.0" encoding="UTF-8"')
    'soap-env:Envelope'('xmlns:soap-env': soapNS) {
```

```
'soap-env:Header'()
'soap-env:Body' {
  GetMothersDay('xmlns': holidayNS) {
    year(2013)
  }
}
```
```
        }
      }
    }
  }
}
```

5. Now, we are ready to process the response, for example, by printing the following code line:

```
println response
```

How it works...

As you can guess, `HTTPBuilder` just makes a `POST` request. We also give a hint to `HTTPBuilder` that we are going to send XML data to the service. When that hint is given, the body parameter is processed with the help of `StreamingMarkupBuilder` (see the *Constructing XML content* recipe in *Chapter 5, Working with XML in Groovy*) and encoded.

Since the service, which we are trying to connect to, is based on SOAP 1.1, we need to add a special `SOAPAction` header (in SOAP 1.2 that header is no longer needed). Also, the `Content-Type` header is mandatory, because otherwise the web service will not recognize the type of content we are trying to submit.

The response object is of the `GPathResult` type, which can be navigated, searched, and printed in the same way as any other XML structure in Groovy with the help of the `GPath` expressions. For more information on XML processing, refer to *Chapter 5, Working with XML in Groovy*.

There's more...

On the Groovy's website, you can find references to two other SOAP supporting libraries: `GroovySOAP` and `GroovyWS`. Both of them are considered deprecated in favor of the `groovy-wslite` library (https://github.com/jwagenleitner/groovy-wslite) developed by *John Wagenleitner*. The library has a terrific support for SOAP features and is a bit less verbose than plain `HTTPBuilder`.

The following script makes use of `groovy-wslite` and does exactly the same as the script described previously:

```
@Grab('com.github.groovy-wslite:groovy-wslite:0.8.0')
import wslite.soap.*

def baseUrl = 'http://www.holidaywebservice.com/' +
              'Holidays/US/Dates/USHolidayDates.asmx'

def client = new SOAPClient(baseUrl)

def holidayBase = 'http://www.27seconds.com/Holidays'
def holidayNS = "$holidayBase/US/Dates/"
def soapAction = "$holidayBase/US/Dates/GetMothersDay"

def response = client.send(SOAPAction: soapAction) {
  body {
    GetMothersDay('xmlns': holidayNS) {
      year(2013)
    }
  }
}

println response.GetMothersDayResponse
```

See also

▶ http://groovy.codehaus.org/modules/http-builder/

▶ https://github.com/jwagenleitner/groovy-wslite

▶ http://groovy.codehaus.org/GroovyWS

▶ http://groovy.codehaus.org/Groovy+SOAP

Consuming RSS and Atom feeds

RSS feeds and **Atom** feeds are a standardized way to distribute headlines and updates from websites and blogs. Both RSS and Atom feeds are XML documents. RSS is older but widely popular, while Atom is newer and has several advantages over RSS, chiefly the namespace support.

For the main differences between Atom and RSS, check the Wikipedia entry about RSS: `http://en.wikipedia.org/wiki/RSS`. Both formats are largely supported, and often blogs and sites output headline feeds in RSS and Atom at the same time.

In this recipe, we are going to cover the basics of RSS and Atom feed parsing with Groovy.

Getting ready

As RSS and Atom feeds are XML based, it's easy to parse them using one of the several tools offered by Groovy (see the *Reading XML using XmlParser* recipe in *Chapter 5, Working with XML in Groovy*).

We will show how to detect if a feed is RSS or Atom and parse it accordingly.

How to do it...

We will create a `FeedParser` class which will contain the code to open a URL of a feed (RSS or Atom), parse it, and return a list of the `FeedEntry` objects populated with the content of the feed entries:

1. Let's define the classes in a separate script file as follows:

```
class FeedParser {

  def readFeed(url) {
    def xmlFeed = new XmlParser(false, true).parse(url)
    def feedList = []
    if (isAtom(xmlFeed)) {
      (0..< xmlFeed.entry.size()).each {
        def entry = xmlFeed.entry.get(it)
          feedList << new AtomFeedEntry(
                        entry.title.text(),
                        entry.author.text(),
                        entry.link.text(),
                        entry.published.text()
                      )
      }
    } else {
      (0..< xmlFeed.channel.item.size()).each {
        def item = xmlFeed.channel.item.get(it)
        RSSFeedEntry feed = new RSSFeedEntry(
                              item.title.text(),
                              item.link.text(),
```

```
                            item.description.text(),
                            item.pubDate.text()
                         )
        feedList << feed
      }
    }
    feedList
  }

  def isAtom(Node node) {
    def rootElementName = node.name()
    if (rootElementName instanceof groovy.xml.QName) {
      return (rootElementName.localPart == 'feed') &&
             (rootElementName.namespaceURI ==
               'http://www.w3.org/2005/Atom')
    }
    false
  }

}

abstract class FeedEntry {

}

@groovy.transform.Canonical
class RSSFeedEntry extends FeedEntry {
  String title
  String link
  String desc
  String pubDate
}

@groovy.transform.Canonical
class AtomFeedEntry extends FeedEntry {
  String title
  String author
  String link
  String pubDate
}
```

2. The `FeedParser` class can be simply called within the same script file; for example, to print all the titles of the posts from the blog *Lambda the Ultimate*, which can be found at `http://lambda-the-ultimate.org/`:

```
def parser = new FeedParser()
def feedUrl = 'http://lambda-the-ultimate.org/rss.xml'
def feed = parser.readFeed(feedUrl)

feed.each {
  println "${it.title}"
}
```

3. After execution, the code should print a list of latest titles as shown in the following output:

```
Dynamic Region Inference

Dependently-Typed Metaprogramming (in Agda)

...

It's Alive! Continuous Feedback in UI Programming

Feed size: 15
```

How it works...

The `FeedParser` class opens the XML stream (an HTTP URI), and after detecting if the feed is Atom-based or RSS-based, it processes each entry by creating an instance of the `FeedEntry` class, which contains headline data.

There's more...

Another approach to consume feeds using Groovy is using the Rome library. Rome is a venerable framework, which has been around for quite a long time, and it's the default library for consuming and producing RSS or Atom feeds in Java.

```
@Grab('org.rometools:rome-fetcher:1.2')
import org.rometools.fetcher.impl.HttpURLFeedFetcher

def feedFetcher = new HttpURLFeedFetcher()
def feedUrl = 'http://lambda-the-ultimate.org/rss.xml'
def feed = feedFetcher.retrieveFeed(feedUrl.toURL())

feed.entries.each {
  println "${it.title}"
}

println "Feed size: ${feed.entries?.size()}"
```

The code is way more compact than the custom solution we presented in the beginning. Rome handles the differences between feed types (it also supports less common formats).

See also

- ▶ http://rometools.org/
- ▶ http://en.wikipedia.org/wiki/RSS
- ▶ The *Reading XML using XmlParser* recipe in *Chapter 5, Working with XML in Groovy*

Using basic authentication for web service security

Basic authentication is one of the simplest and thus the least secure authentication mechanism. It sends a combined string, which contains username and password encoded with base64 encoding, inside a special HTTP header. Password and username can be very easily discovered, if the HTTP request is intercepted by an attacker. On the other hand, if a request goes through using the HTTPS protocol, then header discovery is less likely to happen. The combination of HTTPS and basic authentication makes a rather popular choice as a starting security scheme for web services.

In this recipe, we will demonstrate how to use the HTTPBuilder library, which we already covered in previous recipes (for example, the *Issuing a SOAP request and parsing a response* recipe), to achieve the basic request authentication.

How to do it...

The following steps present how simple it is to inject basic authentication credentials into your requests:

1. First of all we need to create an instance of HTTPBuilder pointing to our service URL:

   ```
   def service = new HTTPBuilder('https://localhost:5000/')
   ```

2. Username (groovy) and password (cookbook) values can be set in the following way:

   ```
   service.auth.basic('groovy', 'cookbook')
   ```

3. At this point, you can construct HTTP requests to the secured web service as follows:

   ```
   def response = service.get(path: 'secret-service')
   ```

How it works...

Under the hood, the `HTTPBuilder` library just encodes username and password into the required HTTP header. All other HTTPBuilder's methods can be used in the same way they were used in other recipes.

See also

▶ http://groovy.codehaus.org/modules/http-builder/

▶ http://groovy.codehaus.org/modules/http-builder/doc/auth.html

Using OAuth for web service security

The `OAuth` protocol became one of the dominant ways to perform authorization in the emerging amount of web applications and services. The final draft of v1.0 was released in 2007. In 2009, v1.0a was published to fix a security flaw known as session fixation.

In October 2012, OAuth 2.0 was released. It is not backward compatible with OAuth 1.0a. OAuth 2.0 received a lot of negative criticism, even though some of the major providers (such as Google or Facebook) support OAuth 2.0 already. Furthermore, the new protocol specification leaves too many open points to the implementer, which makes it somewhat hard to apply a generic approach to.

In this recipe, we will cover the OAuth 1.0a protocol and how it can be used to authorize your access to the Twitter API.

Getting ready

The scenario that we will try to achieve is a standalone application that reads tweets on a user's behalf:

1. First of all, you need to register your application (script) with Twitter through this page https://dev.twitter.com/apps/new. Obviously, before you can do it, you should also sign up for a Twitter account. After you registered your application, you will get a unique consumer key and consumer secret values that you will need to identify your application.

2. That's only half of the story, because now you need to get an access token and a token secret from the user, on whose behalf you are going to access Twitter's API. In order to do that, we will use the `oauth-signpost` library (http://code.google.com/p/oauth-signpost/) that offers lightweight support for the OAuth 1.0a protocol.

3. The following script performs the application authorization flow, which involves interaction with a user who needs to open the authorization URL in his browser, accept the authorization request, and give a generated PIN code back to the script:

```
@Grab('oauth.signpost:si parentFilegnpost-core:1.2.1.2')
import oauth.signpost.basic.DefaultOAuthConsumer
import oauth.signpost.basic.DefaultOAuthProvider
import oauth.signpost.OAuth

def consumer = new DefaultOAuthConsumer('...', '...')

def provider = new DefaultOAuthProvider(
    'http://twitter.com/oauth/request_token',
    'http://twitter.com/oauth/access_token',
    'http://twitter.com/oauth/authorize')

String authUrl = provider.
                    retrieveRequestToken(
                        consumer,
                        OAuth.OUT_OF_BAND
                    )

println "Open this URL in the browser: ${authUrl}"
print 'Authorize application and enter pin code: '

def pinCode = null
System.in.withReader {
  pinCode = it.readLine()
  println()
}

provider.retrieveAccessToken(consumer, pinCode)

println "Access token: ${consumer.token}"
println "Token secret: ${consumer.tokenSecret}"
```

4. While executing, the script will print the authorization URL, which you should open in your browser.

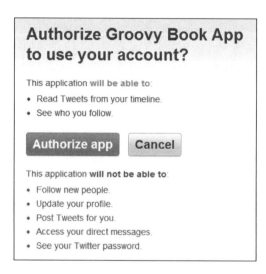

Authorize Groovy Book App to use your account?

This application will be able to:

- Read Tweets from your timeline.
- See who you follow.

[Authorize app] [Cancel]

This application **will not be able to**:

- Follow new people.
- Update your profile.
- Post Tweets for you.
- Access your direct messages.
- See your Twitter password.

5. After you pressed the **Authorize app** button, you are supplied with a PIN code that you should submit back to the running script console, which is waiting for user input.

You've granted access to Groovy Book App!

Next, return to Groovy Book App and enter this PIN to complete the authorization process:

7200710

6. Eventually the script will print the access token and token secret that can be used to call Twitter's API in the script described in the next section.

How to do it...

Now, we are ready to send authorized requests to twitter through our script:

1. First of all we need to import the RESTClient class, which is part of the HTTPBuilder library:

```
@Grapes([
  @Grab(
    group='org.codehaus.groovy.modules.http-builder',
```

```
    module='http-builder',
    version='0.6'
  ),
  @Grab('oauth.signpost:signpost-commonshttp4:1.2.1.2'),
  @Grab('oauth.signpost:signpost-core:1.2.1.2')
])
import groovyx.net.http.RESTClient
```

2. Then we need to define the variables that hold our security keys, tokens, and secrets:

```
def consumerKey = '...'
def consumerSecret = '...'
def accessToken = '...'
def tokenSecret = '...'
```

For obvious reasons, you need to add your own values.

3. After that, we can create a RESTClient instance:

```
def url = 'https://api.twitter.com/1.1/statuses/'
def twitter = new RESTClient(url)
```

4. Then we need to set OAuth details in the following way:

```
twitter.auth.oauth(consumerKey,
                   consumerSecret,
                   accessToken,
                   tokenSecret)
```

5. Now, we are ready to use the Twitter's API and call operations to retrieve JSON data with tweet information:

```
println twitter.get(path : 'mentions_timeline.json').data
```

How it works...

Under the hood, HTTPBuilder uses the oauth-signpost library to sign HTTP requests with OAuth-specific headers. This gives the ability to access the public APIs on behalf of a user. It is important to understand that, for each new application (consumer) and for each different Twitter user you need a separate set of keys, tokens, and secrets. If your script needs to access different user data on their behalf, then you need to generate a new access token and a token secret, which requires the active involvement of the user.

See also

▶ http://groovy.codehaus.org/modules/http-builder/

▶ http://groovy.codehaus.org/modules/http-builder/doc/auth.html

▶ http://code.google.com/p/oauth-signpost/

9
Metaprogramming and DSLs in Groovy

In this chapter, we will cover:

- ▸ Querying methods and properties
- ▸ Dynamically extending classes with new methods
- ▸ Overriding methods dynamically
- ▸ Adding performance logging to methods
- ▸ Adding a caching functionality around methods
- ▸ Adding transparent imports to a script
- ▸ DSL for executing commands over SSH
- ▸ DSL for generating reports from logfiles

Introduction

The recipes presented in this chapter will cover a number of advanced metaprogramming concepts in Groovy in detail. Metaprogramming is the characteristic of a programming language to modify the aspect of a class at runtime or compile time, that is, adding and intercepting methods, implementing new interfaces, and so on.

Groovy, thanks to its dynamic nature, makes metaprogramming extremely easy. This capability is considered by many to be one of the most helpful features of the language.

Taking an advantage of Groovy's metaprogramming capabilities bring great new possibilities that would be very difficult or just plain impossible to write with Java alone. The first recipes of this chapter cover several interesting solutions such as dynamically adding methods to classes, intercepting methods, and exploring **Abstract Syntax Tree** (**AST**) capabilities.

Metaprogramming is especially important for the creation of **DSLs** (**Domain Specific Language**), small domain-specific languages dedicated to a particular domain problem. In this chapter, we will also dedicate two recipes to different aspects of how to write a DSL with Groovy.

Querying methods and properties

In this first recipe about metaprogramming, we begin by looking at the introspection capabilities of Groovy. Introspection is a major feature of the Java language and, by extension, of the Groovy language. Using introspection, we can get the internal information of a class at runtime, including fields, methods, constructors, and so on.

Getting ready

To test out the introspection feature, let's create a couple of Groovy classes:

```groovy
package org.groovy.cookbook

class Book {

    String title
    Author author
    Long year
    Long pages

    Long getAmazonSalesPosition() {
        new Random().nextInt(1) + 1
    }

    void attachReview(String review) { }

}

class Author {
    String name
    String lastName
}
```

How to do it...

The following steps offer an example of the introspection capabilities of the language:

1. To check the type of a class, you can just execute the following code snippet:

```
assert 'java.lang.String' == String.name
assert 'org.groovy.cookbook.Author' == Author.name
```

2. To list all the properties of the object:

```
Author a = new Author(name: 'Ernest',
                      lastName: 'Hemingway')
Book book = new Book()
book.with {
   title = 'The Old Man and the Sea'
   year = 1952
   pages = 200
   author = a
}
book.properties.each { println it }
```

The output of looping on the instance's properties is as follows:

```
title=The Old Man and the Sea
class=class org.groovy.cookbook.Book
amazonSalesPosition=1
year=1952
pages=200
metaClass=
   org.codehaus.groovy.runtime.HandleMetaClass
      @41ce774e[groovy.lang.MetaClassImpl@41ce774e[
         class org.groovy.cookbook.Book]]
author=org.groovy.cookbook.Author@59fac3a2
```

3. One of the properties returned from the query is `metaClass`. Through this property, we can access quite many interesting methods to figure out what our class can do. For instance, to check the existence of a property, we can use the following code snippet:

```
assert book.metaClass.hasProperty(book, 'pages')
```

4. Or list all the methods and properties:

```
println '#### METHODS ####'
book.metaClass.methods.each { println it }

println '#### PROPERTIES ####'
book.metaClass.properties.each { println it.name }
```

Note how the methods' property prints all the methods inherited from Java (such as equals and hashCode) as well as the local methods of the class:

```
### METHODS ####
public boolean java.lang.Object.equals(java.lang.Object)
public final native java.lang.Class java.lang.Object.getClass()
public native int java.lang.Object.hashCode()
...
public void Book.attachReview(java.lang.String)
public java.lang.Long Book.getAmazonSalesPosition()
public Author Book.getAuthor()
public groovy.lang.MetaClass Book.getMetaClass()
public java.lang.Long Book.getPages()
...
### PROPERTIES ###
title
class
amazonSalesPosition
year
pages
author
```

5. Finally, the `metaClass` gives access to the `respondsTo` method, to directly interrogate an instance about the presence of a method:

```
assert book.metaClass.respondsTo(book, 'getAmazonSalesPosition')
assert book.metaClass.respondsTo(book, 'attachReview', String)
```

The `respondsTo` method can be directly invoked on any object, as it is also exposed on the Groovy enhanced `java.lang.Object` class:

```
assert book.respondsTo('attachReview', String)
```

How it works...

Every class in the class loader has a reference to an object of type `metaClass`. This `metaClass` maintains the list of all methods and properties of a given class, starting with the bytecode information and adding the additional methods that Groovy knows about by default (`DefaultGroovyMethods`). Normally, all instances of a class share the same `metaClass`. However, Groovy allows per instance metaclasses, that is, different instances of a class that may refer to different metaclasses.

The first example in Step 1 is nothing more than calling `getClass().getName()` on a Java class; therefore, piggybacking on the Java reflection capabilities. The remaining examples are more interesting because they leverage the dynamic properties of the Groovy language through the `metaClass` attribute. The `respondsTo` method, in particular, is useful when writing a dynamic code; for example, populating an arbitrary object from some data on a file.

See also

▶ http://groovy.codehaus.org/api/groovy/lang/MetaClass.html

▶ http://groovy.codehaus.org/api/org/codehaus/groovy/runtime/DefaultGroovyMethods.html

Dynamically extending classes with new methods

One of the exciting characteristics of Groovy is **Meta Object Protocol** (**MOP**). In a nutshell, the term metaprogramming refers to writing code that can dynamically change its behavior at runtime. A Meta Object Protocol refers to the capabilities of a dynamic language that enable metaprogramming. In this recipe, we are going to look at one of the capabilities of the MOP, which is `ExpandoMetaClass`.

Groovy's `ExpandoMetaClass` lets you assign behavior and state to classes at runtime without editing the original source code; it is essentially a layer above the original class. In the next section of the recipe, we will show you how to achieve such a result.

How to do it...

Adding a new method to a Groovy (or Java) class is straightforward. We are going to perform the following given steps to add a `getInEuros` method to the `BigDecimal` Java class in order to convert US dollars to euros:

1. In a new Groovy script, type the following code:

```
import java.text.NumberFormat

BigDecimal.metaClass.getInEuros = { ->
    def exchangeRate = 0.763461
    def nf = NumberFormat.getCurrencyInstance(Locale.US)
    nf.setCurrency(Currency.getInstance('EUR'))
    nf.format(delegate * exchangeRate)
}
```

2. Now, we are ready to test the conversion rate:

```
assert 1500.00.inEuros == 'EUR1,145.19'
```

How it works...

Each Groovy object has an accompanying instance of a class named `ExpandoMetaClass` (reachable through the `metaClass` property) that holds a reference to the methods that can be called on an object, including:

▶ The base methods that the type allows

▶ More methods added for that type by Groovy (such as, `find` on collections)

▶ Methods added at runtime, using `metaClass`

Every time a method on an object is invoked, a dynamic dispatcher mechanism is used to delegate to the companion `ExpandoMetaClass`.

The `getInEuros` closure, which we have added to the `BigDecimal` class, contains only the US dollar/euro conversion code. The only aspect worth mentioning is the delegate variable, which refers to the object on which we call the method.

It is important to note that a method added to a class using `ExpandoMetaClass` will effectively modify the class across all the threads of the application; therefore, it is not a local modification. If you need to modify only a single instance of a class, you can access the `metaClass` property on an instance, as in the following code snippet:

```
class Customer {
    Long id
    String name
```

```
    String lastName
}

def c = new Customer()
c.metaClass.fullName { "$name $lastName" }
c.name = 'John'
c.lastName = 'Ross'

assert c.fullName() == 'John Ross'
```

There's more...

`ExpandoMetaClass` can also be used to add:

- Constructors to a class:

```
// defines a new constructor
Customer.metaClass.constructor << {
  String name -> new Customer(name: name)
}
def c = new Customer('John')
assert 'John' == c.name
```

In this example, we use the left shift operator to append a new constructor. The `<<` operator can be used for chaining constructors or methods, like in this example:

```
Customer.metaClass.constructor << { String name ->
  new Customer(name: name)
} << { Long id, String fullName ->
  new Customer(
    id: id,
    name: fullName.split(',')[0],
    lastName: fullName.split(',')[1]
  )
}

def c0 = new Customer('Mike')
c0.name = 'Mike'
def c1 = new Customer(1000, 'Mike,Whitall')
assert c1.name == 'Mike'
assert c1.lastName == 'Whitall'
```

The `Customer` class has been enhanced with two concatenated constructors: the first accepting a string and the second accepting a `Long` and a string. The second constructor uses the `split` function to assign the name and last name of the customer.

▶ Static methods:

```
Customer.metaClass.'static'.sayHello = {   ->
  "hello! I'm your customer"
}
assert  "hello! I'm your customer" == Customer.sayHello()
```

▶ Properties:

```
Customer.metaClass.gsm = null
def c = new Customer()
c.gsm = '123456'
assert '123456' == c.gsm
```

See also

▶ http://groovy.codehaus.org/ExpandoMetaClass

▶ http://groovy.codehaus.org/api/groovy/lang/MetaClass.html

▶ http://groovy.codehaus.org/api/groovy/lang/ExpandoMetaClass.html

Overriding methods dynamically

In the previous recipe, *Dynamically extending classes with new methods*, we learned how to dynamically add a method to a class through one of the metaprogramming features of Groovy, named `ExpandoMetaClass`.

In this recipe, we will see how to intercept and replace a call to an existing method of a class. This technique can be very handy when writing unit tests for classes that have dependencies to other classes.

Getting ready

Let's introduce three classes for which we want to write a unit test:

▶ `Customer.groovy`:

```
package org.groovy.cookbook
class Customer {
  String name
}
```

- CustomerDao.groovy:

```
package org.groovy.cookbook
class CustomerDao {
  Customer getCustomerById(Long id) {
    // DO SOME DATABASE RELATED QUERY
    ...
  }
}
```

- CustomerService.groovy:

```
package org.groovy.cookbook
class CustomerService {
  CustomerDao dao
  void setCustomerDao(CustomerDao dao) {
    this.dao = dao
  }
  Customer getCustomer(Long id) {
    dao.getCustomerById(id)
  }
}
```

The fictional `CustomerService` class has a dependency towards `CustomerDao` that is somehow injected at runtime (dependency injection is a well-known pattern made famous by the ubiquitous Spring framework). The `CustomerDao` is a class that would normally access some kind of data store to retrieve the customer data. We are not interested in the details of how the DAO accesses the database. What we know is that unit testing the `CustomerService` class would be very difficult without satisfying the hard dependency of the DAO and the database. In other words, the `CustomerService` class can be only tested if the database required by the DAO is actually running.

In the context of this recipe, the DAO's method `getCustomerById` does nothing; but in real life, it would contain code to query the database.

How to do it...

A unit test is all we need to put this simple mocking technique into practice:

1. Let's write a unit test for `CustomerService`, as follows:

```
package org.groovy.cookbook

import static org.junit.Assert.*
import org.junit.*
```

```
class TestCustomerService  {
  @Test
  void testGetCustomer() {
    boolean daoCalled = false
    CustomerDao.metaClass.getCustomerById = { Long id ->
      daoCalled = true
      new Customer(name:'Yoda')
    }
    def cs = new CustomerService()
    def cDao = new CustomerDao()
    cs.setCustomerDao(cDao)
    def customer = cs.getCustomer(100L)
    assertTrue(daoCalled)
    assertEquals(customer.name,  'Yoda')
  }
}
```

How it works...

The unit test has the usual plumbing code to instantiate the class under test (CustomerService), and injects the CustomerDao into the service. Before that part, we override the getCustomerById method by overwriting the method with our own closure. The intercept and replace mechanism is again based on the ExpandoMetaClass class and the metaprogramming features of Groovy. When the mocked method is invoked, the closure is triggered, and the local daoCalled variable gets updated.

A small detail that you should remember is you need to qualify the first argument with the type if the method has a typed parameter; otherwise Groovy won't override the behavior. These two examples would not work:

```
CustomerDao.metaClass.getCustomerById = { ->
  ...
}


CustomerDao.metaClass.getCustomerById = { id ->
  ...
}
```

Adding performance logging to methods

In this recipe, we will learn how to add the logging of execution time metrics to any method of a class, without littering the actual method with logging code. Java has used **Aspect Oriented Programming** (**AOP**) for many years now to add aspects (or common features) to functions, without having the functions to know that the code was there. It is behavior that looks and smells like it should have a structure, but you can't find a way to express this structure in code with traditional object-oriented techniques.

Metrics is one common aspect that is often added to the code to figure out where the bottleneck is that is keeping you awake at night. Let's look at a typical example:

```
def createCustomer() {
    long start = System.currentTimeMillis()

    ... // Slow operation

    long spentTime = System.currentTimeMillis() - start
    log.debug("Execution time: ${spentTime}ms.")
}
```

Imagine repeating such code in hundreds or thousands of methods and you will quickly realize that there should be something better than copy/paste.

It turns out that there is, and it's called `invokeMethod`. The `invokeMethod` is one of the little things that make Groovy the favorite programming language among magicians.

Consider the following Groovy code:

```
class Test {
    def invokeMethod(String name, args) {
        println "called invokeMethod $name $args"
    }

    def test() {
        println 'in test'
    }
}

def t = new Test()
t.test()
t.bogus('testing!', 1, 2, 3)
```

This code prints out the following text when run in `groovyConsole`:

in test

called invokeMethod bogus [testing!, 1, 2, 3]

The first call goes to the test method, as expected. The second call, instead of resulting in a `MissingMethodException`, as the `bogus` method is not declared on the class, gets routed through the `invokeMethod` method. `invokeMethod` is a method of the `GroovyObject` class.

We will use `invokeMethod` along with a marker interface to intercept the calls to the methods of a class and dynamically add logging to each method.

Getting ready

This recipe requires a Gradle build script to compile and execute the code. We have already met Gradle in the *Integrating Groovy into the build process using Gradle* recipe in *Chapter 2, Using Groovy Ecosystem*. So, hopefully, you should be comfortable with this build tool.

In a new folder, add a file named `build.gradle` with the following code content:

```
apply plugin: 'groovy'

repositories {
  mavenCentral()
}

dependencies {
  compile localGroovy()
  compile 'ch.qos.logback:logback-classic:1.0.11'
  compile 'org.slf4j:slf4j-api:1.7.4'
}
```

The build script references the `Logback` library, a very popular Java logging framework.

To complete the build setup, create the following folder structure in the same folder where the build file is:

`src/main/groovy/org/groovy/cookbook/intercept`

`src/test/groovy/org/groovy/cookbook/intercept`

How to do it...

Let's start by writing a superclass, which hold our logging code:

1. Create a new Groovy class named `PerformanceLogger` and place it in the `src/main/groovy/org/groovy/cookbook/intercept` folder:

```groovy
package org.groovy.cookbook.intercept

import groovy.util.logging.Slf4j
import org.codehaus.groovy.runtime.InvokerHelper

@Slf4j
class PerformanceLogger implements GroovyInterceptable {
  def invokeMethod(String name, Object args) {

    long start = System.currentTimeMillis()

    def metaClass = InvokerHelper.getMetaClass(this)
    def result = metaClass.invokeMethod(this, name, args)

    long spentTime = System.currentTimeMillis() - start
    log.debug("Execution time for method ${name}: " +
            "${spentTime}ms.")

    result
  }
}
```

2. Now that our intercepting code is ready, we simply need to extend the `PerformanceLogger` class to apply the performance logging to each method of a class. Create a new `SlowClass` class having the following code:

```groovy
package org.groovy.cookbook.intercept

class SlowClass extends PerformanceLogger {

  void test(String a) {
    Thread.sleep(rnd())
  }

  /* return a value between 1000 and 5000 */
  static rnd() {
    Math.abs(new Random().nextInt() % 5000 + 1000)
  }

}
```

3. Create a unit test in the `src/test/groovy/org/groovy/cookbook/intercept` folder named `TestIntercept`:

```
package org.groovy.cookbook.intercept

import org.junit.*

class TestIntercept {
  @Test
  void methodIsIntercepted() {
    SlowClass sc = new SlowClass()
    (1..3).each {
      sc.test('hello')
    }
  }
}
```

4. Executing the unit test by typing `gradle -i test` yields the following output:

```
...
12:58:22.199 [Test worker]
   DEBUG o.g.c.intercept.PerformanceLogger
      - Execution time for method test: 2130 ms.
12:58:23.995 [Test worker]
   DEBUG o.g.c.intercept.PerformanceLogger
      - Execution time for method test: 1790 ms.
12:58:26.644 [Test worker]
   DEBUG o.g.c.intercept.PerformanceLogger
      - Execution time for method test: 2648 ms.
...
```

The test method sleeps for a random amount of milliseconds, and the execution time is clearly visible in the log.

How it works...

In order for the `PerformanceLogger` class to intercept calls, it has to implement `GroovyInterceptable` and override the `invokeMethod` method. `GroovyInterceptable` is an interface that signals to the runtime that all the methods of a class extending the interface should be intercepted by `invokeMethod`. The code should be easy to follow; we simply wrap the actual method call with an unsophisticated calculation of time spent executing the method. The dynamic invocation takes places in these two code lines:

```
def metaClass = InvokerHelper.getMetaClass(this)
def result = metaClass.invokeMethod(this, name, args)
```

The `InvokerHelper` class is a static helper resembling a Swiss Army knife for metaprogramming. It exposes numerous methods for working dynamically with a class. In this case, we use it to access the `metaClass` class of the intercepted object and subsequently call the original method on the wrapped class.

Note how the logging aspect is applied by using the `@Slf4j` annotation, which essentially removes a lot of boilerplate code (see the *Adding automatic logging to Groovy classes* recipe in *Chapter 3, Using Groovy Language Features*). The annotation requires some dependencies that can be added via `@Grab`, or better by a build script (such as Gradle or Maven).

Using `GroovyInterceptable` is a very simple way to decorate any method with code that is executed before and after the actual method execution, but it has some limitations. If a class already extends another class, we can't have the same class extending our `GroovyInterceptable` class. Furthermore, the solution only works on Groovy objects and not on arbitrary Java objects.

There's more...

A more sophisticated and flexible way to apply an interceptor to any class (Groovy or Java) is by using the `groovy.lang.ProxyMetaClass` class. The class name may sound a bit threatening, but it's not very complicated to use.

Let's start from our original `SlowClass` and remove the extends `PerformanceLogger` bit so that the class is now free from any link to the original interceptor.

Add a new interceptor class:

```
package org.groovy.cookbook.intercept

import groovy.util.logging.Slf4j

@Slf4j
class PerformanceInterceptor implements Interceptor {

  private Long start = 0

  Object beforeInvoke(Object object,
                      String methodName,
                      Object[] arguments) {
    start = System.currentTimeMillis()
    null
  }

  boolean doInvoke() { true }
```

```
Object afterInvoke(Object object,
                   String methodName,
                   Object[] arguments,
                   Object result) {
    long spentTime = System.currentTimeMillis() - start
    log.debug("Execution time for method ${methodName}: " +
            "${spentTime}ms. ")
    result
}

}
```

The new interceptor's code is quite similar to the old one. The difference is that the class now implements the groovy.lang.Interceptor interface, which adds three methods that have to be supplied. The interception is now split in two separate methods: beforeInvoke and afterInvoke. The logic behind the performance logging stays the same.

Finally, we write a unit test that uses the proxy to invoke the class:

```
@Test
void methodIsInterceptedByUsingProxy() {

    useInterceptor(InterceptedClass,
                   PerformanceInterceptor) {
        def ic = new InterceptedClass()
        ic.test('a')
        ic.test('b')
        ic.test('c')
    }

}

def useInterceptor = { Class theClass,
                       Class theInterceptor,
                       Closure theCode ->

    def proxy = ProxyMetaClass.getInstance(theClass)
    def interceptor = theInterceptor.newInstance()
    proxy.interceptor = interceptor
    proxy.use(theCode)

}
```

The test method uses a useInterceptor closure that puts together all the pieces. The closure creates a proxy out of the original intercepted class and assigns the interceptor to the proxy.

Running the test yields the following output:

```
...
13:45:18.857 [Test worker]
  DEBUG o.g.c.i.PerformanceInterceptor
    - Execution time for method test: 5521 ms.
13:45:23.265 [Test worker]
  DEBUG o.g.c.i.PerformanceInterceptor
    - Execution time for method test: 4408 ms.
13:45:24.717 [Test worker]
  DEBUG o.g.c.i.PerformanceInterceptor
    - Execution time for method test: 1451 ms.
...
```

As mentioned before, the proxy-based interceptor can also be applied to the Java classes.

See also

▶ The *Adding automatic logging to Groovy classes* recipe in *Chapter 3, Using Groovy Language Features*

▶ `http://groovy.codehaus.org/api/groovy/lang/GroovyInterceptable.html`

▶ `http://groovy.codehaus.org/api/groovy/lang/Interceptor.html`

▶ `http://groovy.codehaus.org/gapi/groovy/util/logging/Slf4j.html`

▶ `http://logback.qos.ch/`

Adding a caching functionality around methods

We have already encountered AST transformations in *Chapter 3, Using Groovy Language Features*, in the form of out-of-the-box annotations available in Groovy. In this recipe, we will show how to create a brand-new AST transformation to apply to your code.

But first, we'll see some theory as this is required before you dive into AST transformations. An AST transformation is a clever mechanism to modify the bytecode generation at compile time, hence the association with the broader term compile-time metaprogramming.

By modifying the bytecode, we can augment our code with additional features that are added transparently during compilation time; for example, adding getters and setters to a class.

In Java and other languages, it is relatively easy to generate source code, think of domain entity classes generated out of database tables.

But, compile-time metaprogramming goes to the next level and directly generates bytecode that is loaded directly into the JVM. Let me tell you that the last sentence is not completely correct; through AST transformation we don't generate bytecode, but the abstract syntax tree, which is turned into bytecode by the Groovy compiler.

So, what is AST exactly? AST is a tree-based representation of the code that will be eventually compiled into bytecode. Each node of the tree contains an instruction from the source code. The AST is abstract because it doesn't contain all the information of the program such as spaces, parenthesis, comments, and brackets. The AST transformations essentially provide a means of extending the Groovy language without requiring language grammar changes, by introducing a mechanism to manipulate the AST during compilation prior to bytecode generation.

In some ways, the AST is comparable to the DOM tree model of an XML file.

Here are some examples of ASTs. Each image contains an instruction and the AST representation of it:

Here's the first example:

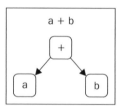

Here's the second example:

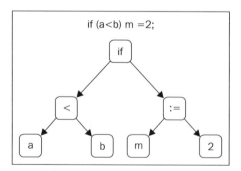

In Groovy, there are two types of AST transformations: local and global.

A local transformation uses annotations to generate the code, and it's the easiest to write and debug.

Global transformations are applied to every compilation unit; so, no annotation is used to enforce the transformation.

Enough with the theory; let's get our hands dirty with an actual implementation of a local AST transformation. In this recipe, we will implement a caching annotation.

Getting ready

A cache is often used to store the results of an expensive operation. Typically, a somewhat simple (and unsafe code) would look like the following code snippet:

```
def cacheMap = [:]
def expensiveMethod(Long a) {
  def cached = cacheMap.get(a)
  if (!cached) {

    // Very expensive operation
    Long res = service.veryLongCall(a)

    cacheMap.put(a, res)
    cached = res

  }
  cached
}
```

The code simply checks if the argument of the function is a key of the Map, and it executes the expensive code if the key is missing. Otherwise, it returns the value associated to the key.

A more elegant and more idiomatic variation of the previous code can be expressed by using a closure:

```
def cacheMap = [:]
Long expensiveMethod( Long a ) {
  withCache (a) {
    // Very expensive operation
    ...
  }
}

def withCache = { key, Closure operation ->
  if (!cacheMap.containsKey(key)) {
    cacheMap[key] = operation()
  }
  cacheMap.get(key)
}
```

The caching AST transformation will be based on the less elegant code, except that it will be implemented as an annotation. Furthermore, in this recipe, we show different ways to manipulate the AST.

 Groovy also offers the `memoize` method to force a closure to cache the result of the computation. It's a powerful performance optimization feature that can only be applied to closures for which a set of inputs will always result in the same output.

Before we begin, we will create a simple Gradle build (see the *Integrating Groovy into the build process using Gradle* recipe in *Chapter 2, Using Groovy Ecosystem*) to hold our code together and help with the test. In a new folder, touch a `build.gradle` file and add the following content:

```
apply plugin: 'groovy'

repositories { mavenCentral() }

dependencies {
  compile localGroovy()
  testCompile 'junit:junit:4.+'
}
```

Create the following folder structure in the same folder where the build file resides:

```
src/main/groovy/org/groovy/cookbook/
src/test/groovy/org/groovy/cookbook/
```

How to do it...

Groovy local AST transformations are based on Java annotations. The first step is to write the code for an annotation that we will use on any method for which the return value is cached:

1. Create a new interface in the `src/main/groovy/org/groovy/cookbook` folder:

```
package org.groovy.cookbook

import org.codehaus.groovy.
            transform.GroovyASTTransformationClass

import java.lang.annotation.*

@Retention (RetentionPolicy.SOURCE)
@Target ([ElementType.METHOD])
@GroovyASTTransformationClass (
   ['org.groovy.cookbook.CacheableTransformation']
)
@interface Cacheable {

}
```

2. Next, we create the actual transformation:

```
package org.groovy.cookbook

import org.codehaus.groovy.ast.*
import org.codehaus.groovy.ast.builder.AstBuilder
import org.codehaus.groovy.ast.expr.ArgumentListExpression
import org.codehaus.groovy.ast.expr.ConstructorCallExpression
import org.codehaus.groovy.ast.stmt.BlockStatement
import org.codehaus.groovy.ast.stmt.Statement
import org.codehaus.groovy.control.CompilePhase
import org.codehaus.groovy.control.SourceUnit
import org.codehaus.groovy.transform.ASTTransformation
import org.codehaus.groovy.transform.GroovyASTTransformation

import java.lang.reflect.Modifier

@GroovyASTTransformation(phase = CompilePhase.SEMANTIC_ANALYSIS)
class CacheableTransformation implements ASTTransformation {

  @Override
  void visit(ASTNode[] astNodes, SourceUnit sourceUnit) {
    if (doTransform(astNodes)) {

      MethodNode annotatedMethod = astNodes[1]
      BlockStatement methodCode = annotatedMethod.code

      def methodStatements =
          annotatedMethod.code.statements
      def parameterName =
          annotatedMethod.parameters[0].name
      def cachedFieldName = annotatedMethod.name
      def declaringClass = annotatedMethod.declaringClass

      FieldNode cachedField =
        new FieldNode(
          "cache_${cachedFieldName}",
          Modifier.PRIVATE,
          new ClassNode(Map),
          new ClassNode(declaringClass.getClass()),
          new ConstructorCallExpression(
            new ClassNode(HashMap),
            new ArgumentListExpression()
          )
        )
```

```
declaringClass.addField(cachedField)

Statement oldReturnStatement =
            methodCode.statements.last()

def ex = oldReturnStatement.expression

def stats = """
  def cached = cache_${cachedFieldName}.
                  get(${parameterName})
  if (cached) {
    return cached
  }
"""

List<ASTNode> checkMap = new AstBuilder().
  buildFromString(
    CompilePhase.SEMANTIC_ANALYSIS,
    true,
    stats
  )

def putInMap = new AstBuilder().buildFromSpec {
  expression {
    declaration {
      variable "localCalculated_${cachedFieldName}"
      token '='
      { -> delegate.expression << ex }()
    }
  }
  expression {
    methodCall {
      variable "cache_$cachedFieldName"
      constant 'put'
      argumentList {
        variable parameterName
        variable "localCalculated_${cachedFieldName}"
      }
    }
  }
  returnStatement {
    variable "localCalculated_${cachedFieldName}"
  }
}
```

```
      methodStatements.remove(oldReturnStatement)
      methodStatements.add(0, checkMap[0])
      methodStatements.add(putInMap[0])
      methodStatements.add(putInMap[1])
      methodStatements.add(putInMap[2])
    }
  }

  boolean doTransform(ASTNode[] astNodes) {
    astNodes && astNodes[0] && astNodes[1] &&
    (astNodes[0] instanceof AnnotationNode) &&
    (astNodes[1] instanceof MethodNode) &&
    (astNodes[1].parameters.length == 1) &&
    (astNodes[1].returnType.name == 'void')
  }

}
```

3. In order to try the transformation on a method, create a class named `MyTestClass` in the usual `src/main/groovy/org/groovy/cookbook/` folder:

```
package org.groovy.cookbook

class MyTestClass {

  def cacheMap1 = [:]

  @Cacheable
  Long veryExpensive(Long a) {
    sleep(rnd())
    a * 20
  }

  static rnd() {
    Math.abs(new Random().nextInt() % 5000 + 1000)
  }
}
```

This class has only one `veryExpensive` method that does nothing but sleep for a random amount of milliseconds. The method is annotated with the `@Cacheable` annotation so that the result is cached after the first invocation. Note how the method always return the same result.

4. In the `src/test/groovy/org/groovy/cookbook/` folder, create a simple unit test to verify that our transformation works:

```groovy
package org.groovy.cookbook

import org.junit.*

class TestAst  {

  @Test
  void checkCacheWorks() {
    def myTest = new MyTestClass()

    (1..3).each {
      withTime { println myTest.veryExpensive(10) }
    }

  }

  def withTime = {Closure operation ->
    def start = System.currentTimeMillis()
    operation()
    def timeSpent = System.currentTimeMillis() - start
    println "TIME IS > ${timeSpent}ms"
  }
}
```

The test doesn't really assert anything; but we can still use it to print out the timing of the method invocation.

5. From the root of the project, type `gradle -i clean test` from the command line. The output should look as follows:

```
...
Gradle Worker 2 finished executing
  tests.org.groovy.cookbook.TestCacheableAST
    > testInvokeUnitTest STANDARD_OUT
    50
    TIME IS > 3642ms
    50
    TIME IS > 0ms
    50
    TIME IS > 0ms
...
```

From the output, it is clearly visible how the first method took almost four seconds to execute, while the second and third invocations executed instantaneously thanks to the caching annotation.

How it works...

Let's start by taking a look at the annotation declared in step 1. The `RetentionPolicy` is set to `SOURCE`, which means that the compiler will discard the annotation; after all it is not needed at runtime. This annotation can be only used at the `METHOD` level because we want only certain methods to cache the result and not the whole class.

The last annotation's attribute is `@GroovyASTTransformationClass`. The value is set to the actual source code of the transformation we wish to implement.

The code for the AST transformation in step 2 is not very easy to follow, and we are going to analyze it step-by-step. The `CacheableTransformation` class used in this recipe uses two different styles of abstract syntax tree modification:

▶ The old Groovy 1.6 `ASTNode` subclasses approach
▶ The newer `ASTBuilder`-based approach, which is easier to read and maintain

An AST transformation class must implement `ASTTransformation`. The class itself must also be annotated with the `@GroovyASTTransformation`.

Following the class declaration, we find some sanity checks, which will exit the transformation if some conditions are true. This should never happen, but it is better to exercise some defensive programming style with AST transformations. The expression assigned to a `cacheField` variable does create a private `Map` variable named after the annotated method. For example, consider the following snippet:

```
@Cacheable
Long veryExpensive(Long a) { ... }
```

The `cacheField` variable will be named `cache_veryExpensive`, as the annotated method is named `veryExpensive`.

As you can notice, the AST API expression, which is required to create a statement as simple as `private Map cache_veryExpensive = [:]`, is indeed quite complex, and it requires a deep knowledge of the `org.codehaus.groovy.ast` package. Imagine what the statement would look like for something more complex. There is no abstraction over the AST, and the code to create the AST doesn't remotely resemble the Groovy code we are trying to execute.

In order to facilitate manually writing AST code, we can take a little shortcut in the shape of `groovyConsole`. Let's fire up `groovyConsole` and type into the main window:

```
class MyClass {
  private final Map m = [:]
}
```

Select the **Script** menu and click on **Inspect AST**. A new window should pop-up. Then select **Semantic Analysis phase** in the drop-down list and expand the **Fields** node and its sub-elements to show the classes required to define the Map variable using AST.

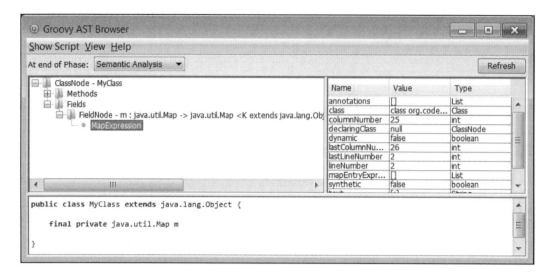

The AST inspector can be used as a guide to instantiate the right classes. Even with the help of the AST inspector, building AST code by hand is not trivial, and the resulting code is not easy to maintain.

Let's move on to the next statements:

```
Statement oldReturnStatement = methodCode.statements.last()
def ex = oldReturnStatement.expression
```

These two lines are required to extract the return statement in the annotated function. We are going to need it later.

```
def stats = """
    def cached = cache_${cachedFieldName}.get(${parameterName})
    if (cached) {
        return cached
    }
"""
List<ASTNode> checkMap = new AstBuilder().
                    buildFromString(
                        CompilePhase.SEMANTIC_ANALYSIS,
                        true,
                        stats
                    )
```

The second style of AST manipulation uses the `org.code.codehaus.groovy.ast.builder.AstBuilder` class, written by *Hamlet D'Arcy*, to ease the pain of creating an AST. The class provides three ways of building an AST. The three methodologies allow you to create Groovy code:

- From an AST DSL via the `buildFromSpec` method
- From a string via the `buildFromString` method
- From Groovy code via the `buildFromCode` method

In the previous code snippet, the `buildFromString` method is used. With this approach, you can use any string containing valid Groovy code to build an AST. Alternatively, with `buildFromCode`, you can pass the Groovy source code directly, instead of a string. The `buildFromCode` method approach has some strengths and weaknesses. The code is automatically validated by the compiler when it is passed as a closure.

On the other hand, certain operations that are available by using `buildFromString` are not possible with `buildFromCode`; for example, creating a new class or binding data from the enclosing context. The `stats` variable contains the first part of the code that we want to add to an annotated method before the method body is invoked. The `buildFromString` method takes three arguments:

- The first argument from the left indicates the phase in which the AST will be generated. Local AST transformations can only be applied at semantic analysis or later phases. For a list of compilation phases and their meaning, please refer to the Groovy documentation.
- The second argument, a `boolean` type named `statementsOnly`, indicates that when true, only the script statements are returned. When false, a `Script` class is returned.
- The third argument is obviously a string containing the code to generate.

The second part of our caching transformation uses the `buildFromSpec` method approach to finalize the caching behavior. The `buildFromSpec` method uses a thin DSL on top of the ASTNode API. The reason we switched from `buildFromString` to `buildFromSpec` is the following code statement:

```
expression {
  declaration {
    variable "localCalculated_$cachedFieldName"
    token '='
    { -> delegate.expression << ex }()
  }
}
```

This DSL entry assigns the body of the return statement (the ex variable declared earlier) to a local variable named localCalculated_$cachedFieldName. This would be impossible to achieve using buildFromString because the ex variable would not be accessible from within the string.

The last lines of the transformation are used to assign the newly created statements to the function's body.

The statements in the last part of the visit function are used to:

▶ Remove the original return statement

▶ Add the AST rendering of the buildFromString method in which we create the call to the Map used for caching

▶ Add the AST rendering of the buildFromSpec method

Let's look at how a function annotated with the @Cacheable annotation gets modified. Here, is the original function:

```
@Cacheable
Long veryExpensive(Long a) {
    callVerySlowMethod(a)
}
```

Here is the modified one:

```
private Map cache = [:]
Long veryExpensive(Long a) {
    def cached = cache.get(a)
    if (cached) {
        return cached
    }
    localCalculated = callVerySlowMethod(a)
    localCalculated.put(localCalculated)
    localCalculated
}
```

The caching done by the transformation is not very sophisticated, but for the sake of brevity and to alleviate an already intricate topic, we have simplified the code a bit.

See also

▶ For more information about AST transformations in Groovy, please refer to the official documentation available at http://groovy.codehaus.org/Compile-time+Metaprogramming+-+AST+Transformations

Adding transparent imports to a script

In this recipe, we will learn how to transparently add one or more import statements to a Groovy script.

Why is this feature significant? For a start, it reduces the amount of code required to use a library. But above all, it may be the first step in building your own DSL as it helps to remove friction. This is because your DSL users don't have to write any import statements. The `ImportCustomizer` class allows the following import variants:

- Class imports, optionally aliased
- Star imports
- Static imports, optionally aliased
- Static star imports

Getting ready

For the sake of demonstration, we will create a script that requires some classes from the amazing Google Guava library. Additionally, we will also need to statically import a `groovy.json.JsonOutput` utility class, which is indisputably a very fine collection of the utility methods for JSON printing. A script that wishes to use the classes mentioned previously would start with the following import statements:

```
import static groovy.json.JsonOutput.*
import com.google.common.hash.*
```

In order for the script to run, you will need to download the Google Guava library from `https://code.google.com/p/guava-libraries/` and place it in the `lib` folder.

How to do it...

Let's see how to put `ImportCustomizer` to use to avoid importing the classes explicitly:

1. We need to create a configuration script holding the customization code. Let's create a new file named `config.groovy` containing the following code:

```
import org.codehaus.groovy.
                    control.customizers.ImportCustomizer

def imports = new ImportCustomizer()
imports.addStarImports('com.google.common.hash')
imports.addStaticStars('groovy.json.JsonOutput')
configuration.addCompilationCustomizers(imports)
```

2. The fictional script (for example, `script.groovy`) that needs the imported classes looks like the following code snippet:

```
// from groovy.json.JsonOutput
def jsonString = toJson([a: 123, b: 'John', c: true])

// from com.google.common.hash
HashFunction hf = Hashing.md5()
HashCode hc = hf.newHasher()
                .putLong(123)
                .putString('John')
                .putBoolean(true)
                .hash()
```

3. Let's run the script, assuming that the JAR files containing the classes which we need to import are located in a `lib` folder.

```
groovy -cp ./lib/guava-14.0.1.jar script.groovy
```

The command should fail with an exception:

```
org.codehaus
    .groovy.control.MultipleCompilationErrorsException: ...
```

4. Add `--configscript` flag to the groovy command and pass the name of the `config.groovy` location:

```
groovy -cp ./lib/guava-14.0.1.jar --configscript config.groovy
script.groovy
```

This time the code gets executed without errors.

How it works...

Step 1 shows a configuration script where a couple of methods of the `ImportCustomizer` class are invoked to set the packages to import. The `addStarImports('a.b.c')` statement produces the same effect as `import a.b.c.*`; whereas the `addStaticStars('a.b.c.MyClass')` statement adds the static keyword to the `import` statement such as `import static a.b.c.MyClass.*`.

In step 2, the Groovy compiler dutifully complains and throws an unable to resolve class `HashFunction` error. The reason is that we are not passing the configuration file to the compiler. When, in step 3, we pass the `--configscript` option, the script executes without errors. This configuration option is only available from Groovy 2.1.

You may have noticed that the configuration variable appearing in the script in step 1 is not declared anywhere. The variable is passed to the script automatically by the Groovy runtime. The variable's type is `CompilerConfiguration`. It's used to hold information including the encoding or the classpath and configure certain aspects of the compilation stage (such as applying/removing AST transformations).

There's more...

The `ImportCustomizer` class has a number of additional methods which are useful for different types of import. We have already encountered `addStarImports` and `addStaticStar`. Other methods are as follows:

▶ `addImport`: to add a single aliased import statement. For instance:

```
imports.
   addImport('AInteger',
              'java.util.concurrent.atomic.AtomicInteger')
```

▶ `addImports`: to add multiple import entries. For instance:

```
imports.
    addImports('java.util.concurrent.atomic.AtomicInteger',
               'java.util.concurrent.atomic.AtomicLong')
```

▶ `addStaticImport`: to add a static method from a package. For instance:

```
imports.addStaticImport('java.lang.Math', 'PI')
imports.addStaticImport('Euler', 'java.lang.Math', 'E')
```

See also

▶ http://groovy.codehaus.org/api/org/codehaus/groovy/control/customizers/ImportCustomizer.html

▶ http://groovy.codehaus.org/api/org/codehaus/groovy/control/CompilerConfiguration.html

DSL for executing commands over SSH

DSL is quite a popular technique to help a developer to define program or business logic in a more readable and concise way compared to using the general-purpose language features. There are two types of DSLs: internal and external. Internal (or embedded) DSLs exploit host language features to build a fluent library API that makes certain concepts more readable in the host language itself. External DSLs call for a specifically designed language that is not bound to host language and usually requires a separately developed DSL parser.

With the help of Groovy, you can create both DSL types with ease. In this recipe, we will define an internal DSL for executing remote SSH commands.

Getting ready

We are going to use the `JSch` library (`http://www.jcraft.com/jsch/`), which is used by many other Java libraries that require SSH connectivity.

The following Gradle script (see the *Integrating Groovy into the build process using Gradle* recipe in *Chapter 2, Using Groovy Ecosystem*) will help us to build the source code of this recipe:

```
apply plugin: 'groovy'

repositories {
  mavenCentral()
}

dependencies {
  compile localGroovy()
  compile 'ch.qos.logback:logback-classic:1.+'
  compile 'org.slf4j:slf4j-api:1.7.4'
  compile 'commons-io:commons-io:1.4'
  compile 'com.jcraft:jsch:0.1.49'
  testCompile 'junit:junit:4.+'
}
```

For more information on Gradle, you can take a look into the *Integrating Groovy into the build process using Gradle* recipe in *Chapter 2, Using Groovy Ecosystem*.

How to do it...

Let's start by creating Groovy classes needed to define elements of our DSL:

1. First of all, we will define a data structure to hold remote command result details such as exit codes, standard output data, and if any, exceptions thrown by the processing code:

    ```
    class CommandOutput {

      int exitStatus
      String output
      Throwable exception

      CommandOutput(int exitStatus, String output) {
        this.exitStatus = exitStatus
        this.output = output
    ```

```
    }

    CommandOutput(int exitStatus,
                  String output,
                  Throwable exception) {
      this.exitStatus = exitStatus
      this.output = output
      this.exception = exception
    }
}
```

2. We define another structure for holding SSH connectivity details:

```
import java.util.regex.Pattern

class RemoteSessionData {

  static final int DEFAULT_SSH_PORT = 22

  static final Pattern SSH_URL =
      ~/^(([^:\@]+)(:([^\@]+))?\@)?([^:]+)(:(\d+))?$/

  String    host      = null
  int       port      = DEFAULT_SSH_PORT
  String    username  = null
  String    password  = null

  def setUrl(String url) {
    def matcher = SSH_URL.matcher(url)
    if (matcher.matches()) {
      host = matcher.group(5)
      port = matcher.group(7).toInteger()
      username = matcher.group(2)
      password = matcher.group(4)
    } else {
      throw new RuntimeException("Unknown URL format: $url")
    }
  }
}
```

3. The next step defines the core of our DSL: a remote SSH session implementation that will hold our DSL verbs implemented as methods such as `connect`, `disconnect`, `reconnect`, and `exec`:

```
import org.apache.commons.io.output.CloseShieldOutputStream
import org.apache.commons.io.output.TeeOutputStream
```

```
import com.jcraft.jsch.Channel
import com.jcraft.jsch.ChannelExec
import com.jcraft.jsch.JSch
import com.jcraft.jsch.JSchException
import com.jcraft.jsch.Session

class RemoteSession extends RemoteSessionData {

  private Session        session  = null
  private final JSch     jsch     = null

  RemoteSession(JSch jsch) {
    this.jsch = jsch
  }

  def connect() {
    if (session == null || !session.connected) {
      disconnect()
      if (host == null) {
        throw new RuntimeException('Host is required.')
      }
      if (username == null) {
        throw new RuntimeException('Username is required.')
      }
      if (password == null) {
        throw new RuntimeException('Password is required.')
      }
      session = jsch.getSession(username, host, port)
      session.password = password
      println ">>> Connecting to $host"
      session.connect()
    }
  }

  def disconnect() {
    if (session?.connected) {
      try {
        session.disconnect()
      } catch (Exception e) {
      } finally {
        println "<<< Disconnected from $host"
      }
    }
  }
}
```

```
def reconnect() {
  disconnect()
  connect()
}

CommandOutput exec(String cmd) {
  connect()
  catchExceptions {
    awaitTermination(executeCommand(cmd))
  }
}

private ChannelData executeCommand(String cmd) {
  println "> $cmd"
  def channel = session.openChannel('exec')
  def savedOutput = new ByteArrayOutputStream()
  def systemOutput =
    new CloseShieldOutputStream(System.out)
  def output =
    new TeeOutputStream(savedOutput, systemOutput)
  channel.command = cmd
  channel.outputStream = output
  channel.extOutputStream = output
  channel.setPty(true)
  channel.connect()
  new ChannelData(channel: channel,
                  output: savedOutput)
}

class ChannelData {
  ByteArrayOutputStream output
  Channel channel
}

private CommandOutput awaitTermination(
                      ChannelData channelData) {
  Channel channel = channelData.channel
  try {
    def thread = null
    thread =
        new Thread() {
          void run() {
            while (!channel.isClosed()) {
              if (thread == null) {
```

```
                return
              }
              try {
                sleep(1000)
              } catch (Exception e) {
                // ignored
              }
            }
          }
        }
      thread.start()
      thread.join(0)
      if (thread.isAlive()) {
        thread = null
        return failWithTimeout()
      } else {
        int ec = channel.exitStatus
        return new CommandOutput(
                ec,
                channelData.output.toString()
              )
      }
    } finally {
      channel.disconnect()
    }
  }

  private CommandOutput catchExceptions(Closure cl) {
    try {
      return cl()
    } catch (JSchException e) {
      return failWithException(e)
    }
  }

  private CommandOutput failWithTimeout() {
    println 'Session timeout!'
    new CommandOutput(-1, 'Session timeout!')
  }

  private CommandOutput failWithException(Throwable e) {
    println "Caught exception: ${e.message}"
    new CommandOutput(-1, e.message, e)
  }
}
```

4. Now, we are ready to create an entry point to our DSL in the form of an `engine` class:

```
import com.jcraft.jsch.JSch

class SshDslEngine {

  private final JSch jsch
  private RemoteSession delegate

  SshDslEngine()  {
    JSch.setConfig('HashKnownHosts',  'yes')
    JSch.setConfig('StrictHostKeyChecking', 'no')
    this.jsch = new JSch()
  }

  def remoteSession(Closure cl) {
    if (cl != null) {
      delegate = new RemoteSession(jsch)
      cl.delegate = delegate
      cl.resolveStrategy = Closure.DELEGATE_FIRST
      cl()
      if (delegate?.session?.connected) {
        try {
          delegate.session.disconnect()
        } catch (Exception e) {
        }
      }
    }
  }
}
```

5. Now, it is time to try the DSL out:

```
new SshDslEngine().remoteSession {

  url = 'root:secret123@localhost:3223'

  exec 'yum --assumeyes install groovy'
  exec 'groovy -e "println \'Hello, Remote!\'"'

}
```

How it works...

In the previous code example, we construct a DSL engine object and call the
`remoteSession` method to which we pass a closure with our DSL code. The snippet,
after connecting to a remote server, installs Groovy through the Yum package manager
and runs a simple Groovy script through the command line, which just prints the message:
`Hello, Remote!`.

The principal stratagems employed by Groovy for the definition of a DSL are the closure
delegates. A closure delegate is basically an object that is dynamically queried for methods/
fields from within the closure's code. By default, delegate equals to the object that contains
the closure; for example, enclosing a class or surrounding a closure.

As you can notice in the `remoteSession` method, the closure input parameter is given
a delegate object (`cl.delegate = delegate`) that represents the `RemoteSession`
implementation. Also, the closure's `resolveStrategy` is set to `DELEGATE_FIRST`; this
means the closure's code will first call a method from the given `RemoteSession` instance,
and only after that will it call methods from other available contexts. This is the reason why, in
the DSL usage example, the closure that we pass to the `remoteSession` method has access
to `setUrl` and `exec` methods.

The remote connection is automatically started upon the first command execution; but the
connection logic can be controlled explicitly since it is defined by our DSL. Additionally, normal
Groovy code can be added around methods of the `RemoteSession` class, like the following
code snippet:

```groovy
new SshDslEngine().remoteSession {

  url = 'root:secret123@localhost:3223'

  connect()
  if (exec('rpm -qa | grep groovy').exitStatus != 0) {
    exec 'yum --assumeyes install groovy'
  }
  disconnect()

  connect()
  def result = exec 'groovy -e "println \'Hello, Remote!\'"'
  if (!result.contains('Hello')) {
    throw new RuntimeException('Command failed!')
  }
  disconnect()

}
```

See also

▶ A more sophisticated implementation of the previous DSL is put into practice by the Groovy SSH DSL project available at `https://github.com/aestasit/groovy-ssh-dsl`. It supports SCP operations, tunneling, key-based authentication, and many other useful features.

▶ Specifics of the SSH implementation are not covered in this recipe since most of the functionality is delegated to the `JSch` library, which can be found at `http://www.jcraft.com/jsch/`.

DSL for generating reports from logfiles

In this recipe, we will give another DSL example for constructing a simple configuration language for the analysis of logfiles, and the generation of reports based on the content of such logfiles. The technique used in this recipe is similar to the one used in the recipe *DSL for executing commands over SSH*.

Getting ready

Let's consider having the following performance log data:

```
execution of getCustomerName took 244ms
execution of getCustomerName took 144ms
execution of getAccountNumber took 44ms
execution of getCustomerName took 244ms
execution of getCustomerName took 24ms
execution of getAccountNumber took 112ms
execution of getCustomerName took 200ms
execution of getCustomerName took 22ms
...
```

The goal is to calculate the average and total times spent on each method. Of course, we could have written a very simple script to reach the same result, but our purpose is to create a DSL that will allow parsing any arbitrary logfile format and extract both grouped and aggregated numeric information from it. A reasonable DSL may look like the following code snippet:

```
format '^execution of (\\w+) took (\\d+)ms$'
column 1, 'methodName'
column 2, 'duration'

source('PerformanceData2012') {
  localFile 'log1.log'
  localFile 'log2.log'
}
```

```
report('Duration') {
  avg 'duration'
  sum 'duration'
  groupBy 'methodName'
}
```

We will try to define the language exactly like this example.

The first expression defines a log line format; then we define a regular expression group mapping to column names, which are used later to refer to log data inside the report definition. The report definition contains a list of calculated values (average of duration and sum of duration) and a column to group report data by. Another important component of the DSL is the definition of the data source.

How to do it...

To define our internal DSL, we first need to define its building blocks, that is, the data structures that compose our mini language:

1. The first step is to define the report data structure:

```
class Report {

  def name

  def sumColumns = [] as Set
  def avgColumns = [] as Set
  def groupByColumns = [] as Set

  Report(String name) {
    this.name = name
  }

  void sum(String columnName) {
    sumColumns << columnName
  }

  void avg(String columnName) {
    avgColumns << columnName
  }

  void groupBy(String columnName) {
    groupByColumns << columnName
  }
}
```

2. We also define the data source structure:

```
class Source {

  def name
  def files = [] as Set

  Source(String name) {
    this.name = name
  }

  void localFile(File file) {
    if (file) {
      files << file.absoluteFile.canonicalFile
    }
  }

  void localFile(String file) {
    localFile(new File(file))
  }
}
```

3. Then we compose a common configuration object, which hold sources, reports, format, and column mapping data:

```
class Configuration {

  def format

  private final columnNames = [:]
  private final columnIndexes = [:]
  private final sources = [:]
  private final reports = [:]

  private static int sourceCounter = 0
  private static int reportCounter = 0

  void format(String format) {
    this.format = format
  }

  void column(int group, String name) {
    columnNames[group] = name
    columnIndexes[name] = group
  }
```

```groovy
  void source(Closure cl) {
    def generatedName = "source${sourceCounter++}"
    source(generatedName, cl)
  }

  void source(String name, Closure cl) {
    Source source = new Source(name)
    cl.delegate = source
    cl.resolveStrategy = Closure.DELEGATE_FIRST
    cl()
    sources[name] = source
  }

  void report(Closure cl) {
    def generatedName = "report${reportCounter++}"
    report(generatedName, cl)
  }

  void report(String name, Closure cl) {
    Report report = new Report(name)
    cl.delegate = report
    cl.resolveStrategy = Closure.DELEGATE_FIRST
    cl()
    reports[name] = report
  }
}
```

4. The final step is to define the `engine` class that will glue together the configuration creation and actual report generation:

```groovy
class LogReportDslEngine {

  void process(Closure cl) {

    Configuration config = new Configuration()
    cl.delegate = config
    cl.resolveStrategy = Closure.DELEGATE_FIRST
    cl()

    config.sources.values().each { Source source ->
      config.reports.values().each { Report report ->

        // Collect report data.
        def reportData = [:]
        source.files.each { File sourceFile ->
```

```
sourceFile.eachLine { String line ->

  // Match the data line.
  if (line =~ config.format) {
    def fields = (line =~ config.format)[0]

    // Map column names
    def fieldMap = fields.collect {}

    // Generate group key, for which
    // to aggregate the data.
    def group = report.groupByColumns
        .collect {
          fields[config.columnIndexes[it]]
        }.join(', ')

    // Create empty group record
    // if it does not exist.
    reportData[group] =
      reportData[group] ?: emptyRecord

    // Calculate report values for given key.
    def g = reportData[group]
    report.avgColumns.each { String column ->
      def fieldIndex =
        config.columnIndexes[column]
      g['avg'][column] = g['avg'][column] ?: 0
      g['avg'][column] +=
        fields[fieldIndex].toDouble()
    }
    report.sumColumns.each { String column ->
      def fieldIndex =
        config.columnIndexes[column]
      g['sum'][column] = g['sum'][column] ?: 0
      g['sum'][column] +=
        fields[fieldIndex].toDouble()
    }
    g['count'] += 1

  }
}
}
```

```
        // Produce report output.
        def reportName = "${source.name}_${report.name}"
        def reportFile = new File("${reportName}.report")
        reportFile.text = ''
        reportData.each { key, data ->
          reportFile <<
            "Report for $key\n"
          reportFile <<
            "  Total records: ${data['count']}\n"
          data['avg'].each { column, value ->
            reportFile <<
              "  Average of ${column} is " +
              "${value / data['count']}\n"
          }
          data['sum'].each { column, value ->
            reportFile <<
              "  Sum of ${column} is ${value}\n"
          }
        }

      }
    }
  }

  def getEmptyRecord() {
    [count: 0, avg: [:], sum: [:]]
  }
}
```

5. At this point, you are ready to use the DSL internally from your Groovy code:

```
def engine = new LogReportDslEngine()

engine.process {

  format '^execution of (\\w+) took (\\d+)ms$'

  column 1, 'methodName'
  column 2, 'duration'

  source('PerformanceData2012') {
    localFile 'log1.log'
```

```
      localFile 'log2.log'
    }
    source('PerformanceData2013') {
      localFile 'log3.log'
      localFile 'log4.log'
    }

    report('Duration') {
      avg 'duration'
      sum 'duration'
      groupBy 'methodName'
    }

  }
```

6. The previous script will produce two report files (one for each data source), named
   `PerformanceData2012_Duration.report` and `PerformanceData2013_Duration.report`. The report will look approximately like the following example:

```
Report for getCustomerName
  Total records: 12
  Average of duration is 179.0
  Sum of duration is 2148.0
Report for getAccountNumber
  Total records: 4
  Average of duration is 64.0
  Sum of duration is 256.0
```

How it works...

The `Source` and `Report` classes defined previously are simple structures holding information needed to build the reports; therefore, we will not spend any time on them.

The `Configuration` class is a bit more involved because it makes use of closure delegates (similar to the *DSL for executing commands over SSH* recipe).

The `Configuration` object is also constructed through a closure delegate inside the process method of the `LogReportDslEngine` class. After the configuration closure is executed, we get back a fully constructed data structure, which we are ready to use for further processing.

The code executed after we have a configuration object does the following:

- ▶ Loops through all data sources, and for each of them
- ▶ Loops through all report definitions, and for each of them
- ▶ Goes through all source files and reads every line
- ▶ For each line, it tries to match it against configured format expression and then fills in internal report data array
- ▶ When the file processing is done, the collected data is printed into a report file

There's more...

Obviously, this DSL implementation is rather primitive and can be extended with many more features such as:

- ▶ DSL validation rules (for example, `groupBy` columns cannot appear in an aggregated function)
- ▶ More grouping functions (for example, min and max)
- ▶ More data source types (for example, URL, FTP, and JDBC)
- ▶ More column types (for example, date, time, Boolean, and IP address)

10
Concurrent Programming in Groovy

In this chapter, we will cover:

- ▶ Processing collections concurrently
- ▶ Downloading files concurrently
- ▶ Splitting a large task into smaller parallel jobs
- ▶ Running tasks in parallel and asynchronously
- ▶ Using actors to build message-based concurrency
- ▶ Using STM to atomically update fields
- ▶ Using dataflow variables for lazy evaluation

Introduction

The chapter you are about to read contains several recipes that deal with concurrent programming. We are going to examine a number of very efficient algorithm and paradigms to leverage the modern architecture of multi-core CPUs.

Most of the recipes in this chapter will use the awesome **GPars** (**Groovy Parallel System**) framework. GPars, which reached v1.0 at the end of 2012, is now a part of the Groovy distribution. Its main objective is to abstract away the complexity of parallel programming. GPars offers a number of parallel and concurrent programming tools that has almost no paragon in the JVM ecosystem. Most of the recipes will show how to execute tasks in parallel to save time and use resources at their best.

Processing collections concurrently

As mentioned in the introduction, this chapter's recipes will recourse to the spectacular features of the GPars framework.

In this recipe, we take a look at the `Parallelizer`, which is the common GPars term that refers to Parallel Collections. These are a number of additional methods added by GPars to the Groovy collection framework, which enable data parallelism techniques.

Getting ready

We will start with setting up the Gradle build (see the *Integrating Groovy into the build process using Gradle* recipe in *Chapter 2, Using Groovy Ecosystem*) and the folder structure that we will reuse across the recipes of this chapter. In a new folder aptly called `parallel`, create a `build.gradle` file having the following content:

```
apply plugin: 'groovy'

repositories {
  mavenCentral()
}

dependencies {
  compile 'org.codehaus.groovy:groovy-all:2.1.6'
  compile 'org.codehaus.gpars:gpars:1.0.0'
  compile 'com.google.guava:guava:14.0.1'
  compile group: 'org.codehaus.groovy.modules.http-builder',
    name: 'http-builder', version: '0.6'
  compile('org.multiverse:multiverse-beta:0.7-RC-1') {
    transitive = false
  }
  testCompile 'junit:junit:4.+'
    testCompile 'edu.stanford.nlp:stanford-corenlp:1.3.5'
}
```

Some dependencies may appear obscure, but they will be revealed and explained in every recipe. The GPars dependency is visible after the Groovy one (note that the Groovy distribution is already packaged with GPars 1.0.0, located in the `lib` folder of the Groovy's binary distribution).

Before delving into the code, we also need to create a folder structure to hold the classes and the tests. Create the following structure in the same folder where the build file resides:

`src/main/groovy/org/groovy/cookbook`

`src/test/groovy/org/groovy/cookbook`

How to do it...

In the following steps, we are going to fill our sample project structure with code.

1. Let's create a unit test, named `ParallelTest.groovy` in the new `src/test/groovy/org/groovy/cookbook` directory. The unit test class will contain tests in which we sample the various parallel methods available from the `Parallelizer` framework:

```groovy
package org.groovy.cookbook

import static groovyx.gpars.GParsPool.*

import org.junit.*

import edu.stanford.nlp.process.PTBTokenizer
import edu.stanford.nlp.process.CoreLabelTokenFactory
import edu.stanford.nlp.ling.CoreLabel

class ParallelizerTest {

  static words = []


  . . .


}
```

2. Now we add a couple of test setup methods that generate a large collection of test data:

```groovy
@BeforeClass
static void loadDict() {
  def libraryUrl = 'http://www.gutenberg.org/cache/epub/'
  def bookFile = '17405/pg17405.txt'
  def bigText = "${libraryUrl}${bookFile}".toURL()
  words = tokenize(bigText.text)
}

static tokenize(String txt) {
  List<String> words = []
  PTBTokenizer ptbt = new PTBTokenizer(
    new StringReader(txt),
    new CoreLabelTokenFactory(),
    ''
  )
```

```
      ptbt.each { entry ->
        words << entry.value()
      }
      words
    }
```

3. And finally, add some tests:

```
@Test
void testParallelEach() {
  withPool {
    words.eachParallel { token ->
      if (token.length() > 10 &&
      !token.startsWith('http')) {
        println token
      }
    }
  }
}


@Test
void testEveryParallel() {
  withPool {
    assert !(words.everyParallel { token ->
      token.length() > 20
    })
  }
}


@Test
void combinedParallel() {
  withPool {
    println words
    .findAllParallel { it.length() > 10 &&
      !it.startsWith('http') }
    .groupByParallel { it.length() }
    .collectParallel { "WORD LENGTH ${it.key}: " +
      it.value*.toLowerCase().unique() }
  }
}
```

How it works...

In this test, we sample some of the methods available through the `GParsPool` class. This class uses a "fork/join" based pool (see `http://en.wikipedia.org/wiki/Fork%E2%80%93join_queue`), to provide parallel variants of the common Groovy iteration methods such as `each`, `collect`, `findAll`, and others.

The `tokenize` method, in step 2, is used to split a large text downloaded from the Internet into a list of "tokens". To perform this operation, we use the excellent **NLP (Natural Language Processing)** library from Stanford University. This library allows fast and error-free tokenizing of any English text. What really counts here is that, we are able to quickly create a large `List` of values, on which we can test some parallel methods. The downloaded text comes from the Gutenberg project website, a large repository of literary works stored in plain text. We have already used files from the Gutenberg project in the *Defining data structures as code in Groovy* recipe in *Chapter 3, Using Groovy Language Features* and *Processing every word in a text file* recipe from *Chapter 4, Working with Files in Groovy*.

All the tests require the `GParsPool` class. The `withPool` method is statically imported for brevity.

The first test uses `eachParallel` to traverse the `List` and print the tokens if a certain condition is met. On an 8-core processor, this method is between 35 percent and 45 percent faster than the sequential equivalent.

The third test shows a slightly more complex usage of the Parallelizer API and demonstrates how to combine several methods to aggregate data. The list is first filtered out by word length, and then a grouping is executed on the token length itself, and finally, the `collectParallel` method is used to create a parallel array out of the supplied collection. The result of the previous test would print something as follows:

```
[WORD LENGTH 22: [-LRB-801-RRB- 596-1887],
 WORD LENGTH 20: [trademark\/copyright]
 WORD LENGTH 19: [straightforwardness],
 WORD LENGTH 18: [commander-in-chief,
                 business@pglaf.org],...
```

The original list of tokens is aggregated into a `Map`, where the key is the word length and the value is a `List` of words having that length found in the text.

There's more...

In this short recipe, we only tried out few of the many "parallel" methods. In the following recipes, we will see more examples of the `Parallelizer` in action. For a complete list of parallel operations, refer to the `Javadoc` page of `GParsUtil`: `http://gpars.org/1.0.0/javadoc/groovyx/gpars/GParsPoolUtil.html`.

See also

  ▸ *Downloading files concurrently*

  ▸ `http://gpars.codehaus.org/`

  ▸ `http://www.gpars.org/guide/`

  ▸ `http://gpars.org/1.0.0/javadoc/groovyx/gpars/GParsPoolUtil.html`

  ▸ `http://nlp.stanford.edu/nlp`

  ▸ `http://nlp.stanford.edu/nlp/javadoc/javanlp/edu/stanford/nlp/process/PTBTokenizer.html`

Downloading files concurrently

This recipe is about downloading files concurrently from the network. As for most recipes in this chapter, we will use the GPars framework to leverage the concurrent features required by the parallel downloading.

Getting ready

This recipe reuses the same build infrastructure created in the *Processing collections concurrently* recipe.

How to do it...

The download logic is completely encapsulated in a Groovy class.

  1. Add a new `FileDownloader` class to the `src/main/groovy/org/groovy/cookbook` folder:

```
package org.groovy.cookbook

import static groovyx.gpars.GParsPool.*
import static com.google.common.collect.Lists.*

class FileDownloader {
```

```
    static final int POOL_SIZE = 25
    static pool

    FileDownloader() {
      pool = createPool(POOL_SIZE)
    }

    private void downloadFile(String remoteUrl,
      String localUrl) {
      new File("$localUrl").withOutputStream { out ->
      new URL(remoteUrl).withInputStream { from ->
      out << from
    }
      }
    }

    private void parallelDownload(Map fromTo) {
      withExistingPool(pool) {
        fromTo.eachParallel { from, to ->
          downloadFile(from, to)
        }
      }
    }

    void download(Map fromTo, int maxConcurrent) {
      if (maxConcurrent > 0) {
        use(MapPartition) {
          List maps = fromTo.partition(maxConcurrent)
          maps.each { downloadMap ->
            parallelDownload(downloadMap)
          }
        }
      } else {
        parallelDownload(fromTo)
      }
    }
}

class MapPartition {
  static List partition(Map delegate, int size) {
    def rslt = delegate.inject( [ [:] ] ) { ret, elem ->
      (ret.last() << elem).size() >= size ?
        ret << [:] : ret
    }
    rslt.last() ? rslt : rslt[0..-2]
  }
}
```

2. Let's write a unit test, to test our newly created class. Don't forget to place the test in the `src/main/groovy/org/groovy/cookbook` folder:

```groovy
package org.groovy.cookbook

import org.junit.*

class FileDownloaderTest2 {

  static final DOWNLOAD_BASE_DIR = '/tmp'
  static final TEST_SERVICE =
    'https://androidnetworktester.googlecode.com'
  static final TEST_URL =
    "${TEST_SERVICE}/files/1mb.txt?cache="

  def downloader = new FileDownloader()
  Map files

  @Before
  void before() {
    files = [:]
    (1..5).each {
      files.put(
        "${TEST_URL}1.${it}",
        "${DOWNLOAD_BASE_DIR}/${it}MyFile.txt"
      )
    }
  }

  @Test
  void testSerialDownload() {
    long start = System.currentTimeMillis()
    files.each{ k,v ->
      new File(v) << k.toURL().text
    }
    long timeSpent = System.currentTimeMillis() - start
    println "TIME NOPAR: ${timeSpent}"
  }\
  @Test
  void testParallelDownload() {
    long start = System.currentTimeMillis()
    downloader.download(files, 0)
    long timeSpent = System.currentTimeMillis() - start
```

```
        println "TIMEPAR: ${timeSpent}"
    }

    @Test
    void testParallelDownloadWithMaxConcurrent() {
        long start = System.currentTimeMillis()
        downloader.download(files, 3)
        long timeSpent = System.currentTimeMillis() - start
        println "TIMEPAR MAX 3: ${timeSpent}"
    }

}
```

3. As usual, execute the test by issuing the following command in your shell:

    `groovy -i clean test`

4. The results are highly dependent on your network latency, but you should see an output as follows:

    TIME NOPAR: 635

    TIMEPAR: 391

    TIMEPAR MAX 3: 586

How it works...

The `FileDownloader` class uses the Parallel Arrays implementation offered by GPars. This implementation provides parallel variants of the common Groovy iteration methods such as `each`, `collect`, and `findAll`. Every time you come across a collection that is slow to process, consider using parallel collection methods. Although enabling collections for parallel processing imposes a certain overhead (mostly because of the cost of initializing a thread pool), it frequently outweighs the ineffectiveness of processing a collection in a sequential fashion. GPars gives you two options here:

►   GParsPool, which uses the "fork/join" algorithm, using a "fork/join" based thread pool;

►   GParsExecutorsPool, which uses the Java 5 executors.

In the majority of cases, the first option is more efficient, but it is always worth trying both thread pools, to verify which one performs better for a specific case.

The `FileDownloader` class resorts to `GParsPool`, which gets initialized in the class constructor. The pool creation operation is an expensive one and adds the higher overhead on the parallel framework.

The class entry point is the download method, which takes a Map and the number of parallel downloads to run. The actual parallel downloading process is carried out by the private function parallelDownload that accepts a Map containing the URL from where to download a file as a key, and the destination file as a value. The method uses the eachParallel method to concurrently execute the download operation on each entry of Map.

One interesting feature of this class is the use of the MapPartition category. Categories in Groovy are a very elegant way to add a method to a class not under your control. The MapPartition category allows us to "split" a Map into smaller maps in order to enable the "concurrency" feature of the FileDownloader class.

See also

> http://gpars.org/guide/guide/single.html#dataParallelism_
> parallelCollections

> http://gpars.org/1.0.0/groovydoc/groovyx/gpars/GParsPool.html

Splitting a large task into smaller parallel jobs

CPUs are not getting any faster, so manufacturers are adding more cores to the processors. That means that single-threaded applications are not able to leverage the "parallelization" offered by a multi-core processor. But how to put those cores to work?

The concept of parallelization is based on the assumption that often large problems can be divided into smaller ones, which are solved "in parallel". The smaller task execution can be spread through several cores to complete the main task faster.

Concurrent programming is not easy, mostly because of synchronization issues and the pitfalls of shared data. Historically Java has offered excellent support for multi-threaded programming, partially shielding the developer from the complexity of writing code that runs many tasks in parallel.

One of the most useful algorithms to successfully leverage multiple cores is "fork/join". The "fork/join" algorithms essentially divide a problem into many smaller subproblems and apply the same algorithm to each of the subproblems recursively. Once the subproblem becomes small enough it is resolved directly.

Hierarchical problems such as sort algorithms or file system/tree navigation greatly benefit from "fork/join" (also known as divide and conquer).

This recipe will show how to use the "fork/join" implementation of GPars to calculate the frequency of words in a large text.

How to do it...

Let's add a class that contains the logic to execute the frequency counting algorithm using "fork/join".

1. Create a new class in the `src/main/groovy/org/groovy/cookbook` directory created in the *Processing collections concurrently* recipe.

```groovy
package org.groovy.cookbook

import static groovyx.gpars.GParsPool.runForkJoin
import static groovyx.gpars.GParsPool.withPool
import static com.google.common.collect.Lists.*

class WordAnalyzer {

  static final Integer THRESHOLD = 50000
  static final int MAX_THREAD = 8

  private Map calculateFrequency(List<String> words) {
    def frequencies = [:]
    words.each {
      Integer num = frequencies.get(it)
      frequencies.put(it, num ? num + 1 : 1)
    }
    frequencies
  }

  Map frequency(List<String> tokens) {
    def frequencyMap = [:]
    def maps

    withPool(MAX_THREAD) {
      maps = runForkJoin(tokens) {  words ->
        if (words.size() <= THRESHOLD) {
          // No parallelism
          return calculateFrequency(words)
        } else {
          partition(words, THRESHOLD).each { sublist ->
            forkOffChild(sublist)
          }
          // Collect all results.
          return childrenResults
        }
      }
    }
```

```
      }
      maps.each {
        frequencyMap.putAll(it)
      }

      // Reverse sort.
      frequencyMap.sort { a,b -> b.value <=> a.value }

    }
  }
```

2. In order to test the previous code, we can use the following unit test, placed in the src/main/groovy/org/groovy/cookbook folder:

```
package org.groovy.cookbook
import org.junit.*
import edu.stanford.nlp.process.PTBTokenizer
import edu.stanford.nlp.process.CoreLabelTokenFactory
import edu.stanford.nlp.ling.CoreLabel

class WordAnalyzerTest {

  @Test
  void testFrequency() {
    def bigText = 'http://norvig.com/big.txt'.toURL()
    def wa = new WordAnalyzer3()
    def tokens = tokenize(bigText.text)
    long start = System.currentTimeMillis()
    def m = wa.frequency(tokens)
    def timeSpent = (System.currentTimeMillis() - start)
    println "Execution time: ${timeSpent}ms"
    println 'For calculating frequency over: '
    println "${tokens.size()} tokens"
    m.sort{ -it.value }.each {
      if (it.value > 50) {
        println it
      }
    }
  }

  def tokenize(String txt) {
    List<String> words = []
    PTBTokenizer ptbt = new PTBTokenizer(
      new StringReader(txt),
      new CoreLabelTokenFactory(),
```

```
        ' '
      )
      ptbt.each { entry ->
        words << entry.value()
      }
      words
    }
  }
```

3. The output of the unit test is as follows:

```
Execution time: 1007ms
For calculating frequency over:
1297801 tokens
the=1799
,=1720
of=1301
.=967
and=907
to=745
that=505
a=456
in=443
is=436
it=266
not=234
as=231
or=204
...
```

How it works...

The code in step 1 requires a bit of explanation. The core function is `calculateFrequency`. The function creates a `Map` containing the frequency of the words found in the `List` passed as an argument.

Once the `Map` is constructed from the frequency calculation, it looks as follows:

```
John      |    10
Michael   |    8
Jeff      |    4
```

The first column contains the words found in the analyzed document and the right column contains the number of times the word is found.

The algorithm is not very sophisticated and can probably be improved, but this is not the focus of the recipe.

The `frequency` function contains the call to the "fork/join" API. The code follows a simple pattern. If the job is small enough, then execute it directly. Otherwise, split the job and apply the `calculateFrequency` algorithm to the smaller chunks (in this case, sublists of words).

The smaller jobs are executed by concurrent threads. The number of these threads can be tuned by modifying the value passed to the `withPool` method.

Things get interesting in the `else` branch of the condition that determines if the job has to be divided into chunks.

The `partition` function is statically imported from the `com.google.common.collect.Lists` class, which belongs to the amazing Guava library. It slices up a list and returns consecutive sublists of the list, each of the same size (the last sublist may be smaller).

For each sublist, the `forkOffChild` method is invoked. This method returns immediately and schedules a task for execution (the task in this case is the `calculateFrequency` function).

When all the tasks are eventually executed, we can collect and return them by calling `childrenResults`, which contains a list of whatever is returned by `runForkJoin`. The `runForkJoin` factory method will execute the provided recursive code along with the supplied values and build a hierarchical "fork/join" calculation. The number of values passed to the `runForkJoin` method has to match the number of the closure's expected parameters, as well as the number of arguments passed into the `forkOffChild` method.

The last segment of the `frequency` function iterates on the `Maps` returned by the parallel computation and adds them to a master `Map`, which contains the full list of words, ordered by frequency.

The test executes the following steps:

1. Download a rather large chunk of text (over 1 million tokens).
2. Split it into tokens using the PTBTokenizer from the NLP library (better than using split(' ')) developed by the Stanford University.
3. Call the `frequency` method and compute the time it took to run the frequency operation;
4. Sort the map by frequency and print out the frequency values for words appearing more than 50 times.

The divide and conquer algorithm is approximately 25 percent to 50 percent faster than the same single threaded algorithm. It is necessary to fiddle around with the maximum number of threads and the optimal threshold (the size of each chunk) to achieve the best throughput. Results may vary depending on the hardware and the size of the token list.

This recipe should serve as a basis for better understanding when this algorithm can be put into practice.

See also

- ▸ `http://en.wikipedia.org/wiki/Divide_and_conquer_algorithm`
- ▸ `http://gpars.codehaus.org/ForkJoin`
- ▸ `http://gpars.org/guide/guide/dataParallelism.html#dataParallelism_fork-join`
- ▸ `https://code.google.com/p/guava-libraries/`

Running tasks in parallel and asynchronously

One of the recurring problems that a developer has to face when working on integrating with external systems, is how to deal with sluggish response time.

Very often, a slow response time from a system, out of our control, ends up negatively affecting the user experience of a web application that feeds on the data coming from the slow system.

The first line of defense against such services is adding a caching layer. A cache helps to mitigate the effects of unreliable external systems, but it is not always the definitive cure. Depending on the business domain, a cache may have a large ratio of cache miss (occurs when a specific data is not found in the cache). Furthermore, on large systems caches can take time to warm up.

So, the second weapon in a developer arsenal against sleepy services, is using asynchronous calls. An asynchronous call is a non-blocking call to a method. A separate thread runs the method and returns the result whenever it is ready. In the meanwhile, the caller of the method receives a **future** (see `http://en.wikipedia.org/wiki/Futures_and_promises`), from which it will be able to retrieve the results. A future is an object that is returned immediately after calling an asynchronous method to escape blocking. Once the caller gets hold of a future, it can continue executing other code until the results from the original call are available.

For this recipe, let's imagine that we are building a super-secret international criminal database. Our system is able to fetch the criminal records of citizens of any country. In order to do so, it must be able to interface with the criminal database of each and every country it needs data from.

The system is used by the cops to track international criminals who are active in more than one nation.

From a design point of view, our system would look as follows:

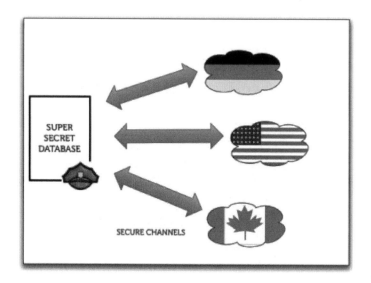

Fancy! Each country exposes a **REST** based interface to access the criminal records. Unfortunately, some countries such as the United States, have a very large amount of criminal data and each request takes up to 10 seconds to complete. Some other countries didn't invest much in the system, and they deployed their service on very slow and old hardware, causing the response times to be erratic and inconstant.

One fundamental functionality of this system is being able to collect data from multiple countries and present the user with a unified view of the data coming from each nation. Implementing an asynchronous call pattern allows for retrieving and showing data as soon as they are ready, without blocking and waiting for the slowest invocation to return.

Getting ready

Before we begin to write the asynchronous call framework, we need to create three REST-based web services to simulate a latency in the response. A quick way to create the REST service in Groovy (or Java) is to use the **Ratpack** framework. Ratpack is a mini framework inspired by Ruby's **Sinatra**. It will allow us to quickly start a web service with three endpoints. Each endpoint will reply with a random response time.

Create a new folder named `ratpack` and add two Groovy scripts to it. The `app.groovy` file will contain the minimal Ratpack application:

```
@GrabResolver(
  name = 'Sonatype OSS Snapshots',
  root =
    'https://oss.sonatype.org/content/repositories/snapshots',
      m2Compatible = true
)
@Grab('org.ratpack-framework:ratpack-groovy:0.7.0-SNAPSHOT')
import static org.ratpackframework.groovy.Ratpack.ratpack
ratpack {
}
```

And the `ratpack.groovy` file will contain configuration for different endpoints we are going to serve:

```
get('/') {
  text 'Welcome to the world criminal database'
}

get('/us') {
  Thread.sleep(rnd(10000L))
  render 'us.json'
}

get('/canada') {
  Thread.sleep(rnd(5000L))
  render 'can.json'
}

get('/germany') {
  Thread.sleep(rnd(7000L))
  render 'de.json'
}

static rnd(long maxMilliseconds) {
  def rnd = new Random().nextInt()
  Math.abs(rnd % maxMilliseconds + 1000)
}
```

To complete the setup, create an additional folder named `templates` and add three files to it:

- Data for Germany in `de.json`:

  ```
  {
    "country": "germany"
  }
  ```

- Data for Canada in `can.json`:

  ```
  {
    "country": "canada"
  }
  ```

- And data for United States in `us.json`:

  ```
  {
    "country": "united states"
  }
  ```

Not very exciting JSON content, but we just need to simulate some request/response here.

Open a command prompt and launch the web service, typing `groovy app.groovy`. The Groovy process should reply with:

```
> groovy app.groovy
May 02, 2013 9:15:04 PM o.r.b.i.NettyRatpackServer startUp
INFO: Ratpack started for http://0:0:0:0:0:0:0:0:5050
```

In order to test the service, open a browser and navigate to `http://localhost:5050/de`. The content of the `de.json` file should appear on the page after some delay forced by the `sleep` function.

How to do it...

Now that our testing infrastructure is in place, we can write the code to invoke the three web services asynchronously.

1. In a new file, let's create a class named `CriminalDataService`:

    ```
    @Grab(
      group='org.codehaus.groovy.modules.http-builder',
      module='http-builder',
      version='0.6'
    )
    import static groovyx.net.http.Method.*
    import static groovyx.net.http.ContentType.*
    import groovyx.net.http.HTTPBuilder
    ```

```
import groovyx.gpars.GParsPool

class CriminalDataService {

  // Database logic.
  ...

}

// Client code.
...
```

2. Add one function and one closure to the class:

```
List getData(List countries) {
  def response = []
  GParsPool.withPool {
    countries.each { country ->
      response << this.&fetchData.callAsync(country)
    }
  }
  response
}

def fetchData(String country) {
  def http = new HTTPBuilder('http://localhost:5050')
  def jsonData
  def start = System.currentTimeMillis()
  http.request( GET, JSON ) {
    uri.path = "/${country}"
    response.success = { resp, json ->
      jsonData = json
    }
  }
  def timeSpent = System.currentTimeMillis() - start
  jsonData.put('fetch-time', timeSpent)
  jsonData
}
```

3. Finally, following is the "client" code, calling the class:

```
CriminalDataService cda = new CriminalDataService()

def data = cda.getData(['germany', 'us', 'canada'])
assert 3 == data.size()
```

```
data.each {
  println "data received: ${it.get()}"
}

def timeSpent = System.currentTimeMillis() - start
println "Total execution time: ${timeSpent}ms"
```

4. The script should show an output similar to the following:

   data received: [fetch-time:1750, country:germany]

   data received: [fetch-time:8775, country:united states]

   data received: [fetch-time:1562, country:canada]

   Total execution time: 8878ms

How it works...

The `getData` method displayed in step 2, accepts a `List` containing the country monikers we want to query for criminal records. For each element in the list, we execute a call to the `fetchData` closure. However, the call is not a standard one. You may have noticed that the method name (`fetchData`) is followed by `callAsync`. The `callAsync` method is automatically added to the closure by the `GPars.withPool` block. It calls the closure in a separate thread, immediately returning a `java.util.concurrent.Future`, which will be populated with the "real" result when the routine completes.

The `fetchData` method uses the `HTTPBuilder` to execute a REST request against the Ratpack REST endpoint. The entire recipe *Issuing a REST request and parsing a response in Chapter 8, Working with Web Services in Groovy* is dedicated to the REST operations.

The client code demonstrated in step 3, loops on the returned array. Each element of the array is a Future, to extract the actual result, the client calls the `get` method on the Future. Note that the `get` method blocks until the Future returns the result or an exception.

See also

- http://gpars.codehaus.org/
- https://github.com/ratpack/ratpack
- http://docs.oracle.com/javase/7/docs/api/java/util/concurrent/Future.html

Using actors to build message-based concurrency

The concept of **actors** as a strategy for running concurrent tasks has recently gained new popularity (thanks to Scala, Erlang, the Akka Framework, and other programming languages). Originally proposed by Carl Hewitt in 1973, actors offer a programming model that inherently guarantees concurrent code when compared with the traditional approach based on shared memory. Actors are similar to Object-Oriented objects (they follow the rule of encapsulation), but they can only communicate by sending immutable messages asynchronously to each other. The internal state of an actor is not exposed and can only be accessed from the outside by sending a message to the actor and receiving a reply.

Due to the asynchronous nature of the message passing pattern, an actor must be active in order to receive a message. One way to make an object active, is to allocate a system thread to it. Unfortunately, threads are a finite resource, and this is not good news for the scalable systems; actors often need to scale beyond the number of threads available on the system. To overcome this scarcity of resources, actor implementation resorts to sharing threads among actors, leading to a system where unused actors do not consume any thread.

Traditionally, programming languages utilize system threads for concurrency. In this model, the execution of an algorithm is divided into concurrently running tasks. It is as if the algorithm is being executed multiple times; the difference being that each of these copies operates on shared memory.

In an actor-based system, each message is processed by one thread and one thread only. This fundamental assumption makes the code implicitly thread-safe, removing the need for any other extra (synchronization or locking) effort.

In this recipe, we will demonstrate a simple actor-based implementation for concurrent calculation of word frequency in a large text.

How to do it...

As for other recipes in this chapter, we are going to use the GPars framework to implement an actor-based system. This recipe will reuse the code and the example from the *Splitting a large task into smaller parallel jobs* recipe, but instead of using the "fork/join" framework, this time, we will use actors to spread the tasks.

1. The first step is to create the actual messages that actors will use to communicate between each other. Create a new file named `ActorBasedFrequencyAnalyzer.groovy` and add the following classes:

```
final class CalculateFrequencyMessage {
  List<String> tokens
}

final class StartFrequency {

}

final class FrequencyMapMessage {
  Map frequencyMap
}
```

2. Now, we add one of the two actors of this recipe. This actor is responsible for analyzing chunks of words. It's a "worker" actor.

```
final class WordFrequencyActor extends DynamicDispatchActor {

  void onMessage(CalculateFrequencyMessage message) {
    reply new FrequencyMapMessage(
      frequencyMap: calculateFrequency(message.tokens)
    )
  }

  private Map calculateFrequency(List<String> words) {
    // The code for this function can be found in the
    // recipe Splitting a large task into smaller parallel jobs.
  }

}
```

3. The second actor is responsible for coordinating the work of the workers.

```
final class FrequencyMaster extends DynamicDispatchActor {

  static final Integer THRESHOLD = 2000
  Map totalFreqMap = [:]
  List<String> tokensList = []
  int numActors = 1

  private final CountDownLatch startupLatch =
    new CountDownLatch(1)
  private CountDownLatch doneLatch

  private List createWorkers() {
    (1..numActors).collect {
      new WordFrequencyActor().start()
    }
  }

  private void beginFrequency() {
    def slaves = createWorkers()
    int cnt = 0
    def partitioned = partition(tokensList, THRESHOLD)
    partitioned.each { sublist ->
      slaves[cnt % numActors] <<
        new CalculateFrequencyMessage(tokens: sublist)
      cntnt += 1
    }
    doneLatch = new CountDownLatch(partitioned.size())
  }

  Map waitUntilDone() {
    startupLatch.await()
    doneLatch.await()
    totalFreqMap
  }

  void onMessage(FrequencyMapMessage frequenceMapMessage) {
    if (frequenceMapMessage.frequencyMap) {
      println '::::::: got a frequency map. ' +
        'Content is ' +
        frequenceMapMessage.frequencyMap.size()
    }
```

```
        totalFreqMap.putAll(frequenceMapMessage.frequencyMap)
        doneLatch.countDown()
    }

    void onMessage(StartFrequency startFrequency) {
        beginFrequency()
        startupLatch.countDown()
        println ':::::: Start Frequency Operation'
    }

}
```

4. The last bit of code that we require to run our example is a simple class responsible for instantiating the `FrequencyMaster` actor.

```
class ActorBasedWordAnalyzer {
    Map frequency(List<String> tokens) {
        def master = new FrequencyMaster(
            tokensList: tokens,
            numActors: 5
        ).start()
        master << new StartFrequency()
        master.waitUntilDone()
    }
}
```

5. Let's write a simple test case to test the actor infrastructure:

```
package org.groovy.cookbook

import org.junit.*
import edu.stanford.nlp.process.PTBTokenizer
import edu.stanford.nlp.process.CoreLabelTokenFactory
import edu.stanford.nlp.ling.CoreLabel
class ActorBasedFrequencyTest {

    @Test
    void testFrequency() {
        def bigText = 'http://norvig.com/big.txt'.toURL()
        def analyzer = new ActorBasedWordAnalyzer()
        analyzer.frequency(tokenize(bigText.text))
        res.each {
            println "[ ${it.key} ${it.value} ]"
        }
    }
```

```
def tokenize(String txt) {
    List<String> words = []
    PTBTokenizer ptbt = new PTBTokenizer(
        new StringReader(txt),
        new CoreLabelTokenFactory(),
        ''
    )
    ptbt.each { entry ->
        words << entry.value()
    }
    words
}

}
```

How it works...

In step 1, three message types are defined. Messages are simple classes; they can even be String or Integer types. The most important aspect of a message in an actor based system is immutability. Immutability guarantees that an actor never has to lock to read a state, greatly simplifying the overall architecture of the message-passing semantic.

In step 2, we introduce the first actor. GPars actors can be divided into two subtypes, stateful and stateless.

Stateless actors keep no memory of processed messages; they simply handle messages as they arrive. A stateless actor extends `DynamicDispatchActor`. Stateful actors, on the contrary, are more sophisticated, because they need to maintain implicit state between subsequent message arrivals. Stateful actors extend `DefaultActor`. Stateless actors are obviously more efficient and highly performant than stateful ones. In this recipe, we use stateless actors, as the problem we need to solve doesn't require a complex logic based on continuations. A continuation is an abstract representation of a state; in the actor model, an actor processes the request in chunks, separated by idle periods during which it awaits a new message. Each message may determine a modification of the actor state. Stateful actors allow for encoding such state transitions directly in the structure of the message handling flow.

The `WordFrequencyActor` only handles one type of message, through the `onMessage` function. The message is expected to contain a sublist of tokens to analyze. The `calculateFrequency` function was already described in the *Splitting a large task into smaller parallel jobs* recipe from this chapter. Once the analysis is done, the actor replies with `FrequencyMapMessage` containing the frequency results for the batch that was passed to the worker actor.

The `FrequencyMaster` actor has a slightly more complex logic. For a start, it handles two types of messages, `StartFrequency` and `FrequencyMapMessage`. The `StartFrequency` message triggers the business logic required to split the list of tokens to analyze into smaller chunks. Each chunk is passed to one of the worker actors and processed asynchronously. The `onMessage` function that handles the `FrequencyMapMessage` is actually handling the reply from the worker actor and adding the result to the `Map` containing the result of the analysis.

Step 4 shows the class that has the responsibility for sending the `StartFrequency` message and initiating the process.

```
def master = new FrequencyMaster(
   tokensList: tokens,
   numActors: 5
   ).start()
master << new StartFrequency()
```

Messages can be sent to actors in three ways:

- Using the `send` method

- Using the `<<` operator, as in the example

- Using the implicit `call` method, such as `master new StartFrequency`

The `FrequencyMaster` actor is initialized with the list of tokens to analyze and the number of active actors, 5 in this example.

The actors collectively share a big thread pool, but any given actor at any given time has at most one active thread. In its thread, an actor takes messages from its incoming queue, processes them, and sends out responses. It never does anything aside from this message-processing loop.

Finally, the class calls the `waitUntilDone` method to retrieve the `Map` containing the result of the analysis. The function is based on two `CountDownLatch` classes that are initialized and used to keep track of the workers' tasks. `CountDownLatch` is often used to wait for several threads to complete, and this is how it has been used in the example. The `waitUntilDone` method blocks until all the actors have done processing.

See also

- `http://gpars.codehaus.org/Actor`

- `http://en.wikipedia.org/wiki/Actor_model`

- `http://en.wikipedia.org/wiki/Continuation`

- `http://gpars.org/0.12/groovydoc/groovyx/gpars/actor/DynamicDispatchActor.html`

- `http://docs.oracle.com/javase/7/docs/api/java/util/concurrent/CountDownLatch.html`

Using STM to atomically update fields

STM (**Software Transactional Memory**) is a concurrency control mechanism for managing access to shared memory. In the traditional threaded model of concurrent programming, when we share data among threads, we keep it consistent using locks. A lock is an object which signals ownership of some resource, and which has one really important property; it references at most one process, and when you want to look at it and update it, nothing can intervene between the read and write. On simple systems, reasoning in terms of threads and locks is relatively simple. But as soon as the system grows in complexity, it becomes really complicated to understand and debug hundreds of threads updating several shared variables. A typical issue is a **deadlock**; when two threads wait on each other to acquire a resource they are locking.

There are several methods that try to make it easier to do coordination between multiple tasks such as enforcing ordering, semaphores, and monitors.

STM tries to resolve the problem of accessing shared memory introducing a well-known semantic: transactions. In the same way as database engines protect their data, with STM we can protect data against concurrent access.

STM enforces the organization of code into transactions. A transaction makes the code run in atomic isolation. The data used by the transactional code remains consistent irrespective of whether the transaction finishes normally or abruptly. The transactional code modifies the data while other tasks do not see the modification until the transaction is committed.

Groovy has support for Software Transactional Memory through the GPars library. To enable the STM API it is necessary to add a dependency to the Multiverse library. Multiverse is a Java-based Software Transactional Memory implementation for the JVM.

This recipe will show how a number of threads can incorrectly update a global variable (a simple counter) and how to fix the problem using STM.

Getting ready

In order to use STM with GPars, we need to add a dependency to the Gradle build script shown in the introduction of this chapter.

```
compile('org.multiverse:multiverse-beta:0.7-RC-1') {
    transitive = false
}
```

At the time of writing, the GPars API 1.0 are still using a beta version of Multiverse.

How to do it...

The following steps will introduce us to the world of STM with the help of GPars and Multiverse.

1. Let's start with a simple class:

    ```
    package org.groovy.cookbook.stm

    import static org.multiverse.api.StmUtils.newIntRef

    import groovyx.gpars.actor.*
    import groovyx.gpars.stm.GParsStm

    import org.multiverse.api.references.IntRef

    class StmValueIncreaser {

      int value = 0
      IntRef stmValue = newIntRef(0)

      ...

    }
    ```

2. Let's throw an actor into the mix. Add the two classes inside the main `StmValueIncreaser` class:

    ```
    // Message
    final class Increase {
    }

    final class ValueAccessActor extends DynamicDispatchActor {
      void onMessage(Increase message) {
        value++ // unsafe increment
        GParsStm.atomic {
          stmValue.increment() // safe increment
        }
      }
    }
    ```

3. Finally, we add a start method to trigger the logic that will update the counters:

    ```
    def actors = [:]
    Random random = new Random()
    int max = 20

    Map start() {
    ```

```
// init actors
(1..20).each {
  actors.put(it,new ValueAccessActor().start())
}

// spawn actors and increase counter
(1..100).each {
  actors.get(rnd(1,20)) << new Increase()
}

( actors.values()*.stop() )*.join()
int stmProtected = 0
GParsStm.atomic {
  stmProtected  = stmValue.get()
}

['withStm': stmProtected, 'noStm': value]

}
```

4. The class also requires this little randomizing closure:

```
// return random number from range
def rnd = { from, to ->
  random.nextInt(to - from + 1) + from
}
```

5. As usual, we complete the recipe with a nifty unit test:

```
@Test
void testFrequency() {
  def stm = new StmValueIncreaser()
  def results = stm.start()
  assert results.get('withStm') == 100
  assert results.get('noStm') != 100
}
```

How it works...

So, what is happening in this class? The `start` method initializes twenty stateless `ValueAccessActor` actors and puts them into a `Map`. The key of the Map is the number of the actor (1, 2, 3,...20). These actors only accept one type of message, the very anemic `Increase`.

After the actor initialization, the code loops one hundred times, and for each iteration it sends a `Increase` message to one of the actors in the actor pool. Note that each message is sent to a randomly chosen actor:

```
actors.get(rnd(1,20))
```

The reason for the random message sending, is that we want to reproduce several threads accessing the same variable concurrently. Using a single actor would defy the purpose of this exercise, as actors process messages through a mailbox, sequentially, one after the other. Accessing the actor in a round-robin fashion would also decrease the chances of a race condition on the variable.

Upon message reception, the actor does two simple operations; it increases the two variables by one unit, defined in the body of the class.

The first variable is, well, just a variable which gets hammered by the actors. Each message increments the variable by one unit. The second variable is an STM variable. The variable can only be updated atomically, in the context of a globally defined STM transaction.

The actor increase the variables in two different ways:

```
value++

GParsStm.atomic {
    stmValue.increment()
}
```

The `value` variable gets incremented without any lock. Several actors running on different threads will read and write the variable at the same time.

The `GParsStm.atomic` static method runs the closure inside a transaction, and the value of `stmValue` gets updated atomically.

> If you want to alter the default transaction properties (for example, read-only transactions, locking strategy, isolation level), it is possible to do so using the `createAtomicBlock` method of `GParsStm`.

Each actor sees its "own copy" of the variable and the increase operation is executed and committed by each actor running on its own thread. This guarantees that, when we finally access the `stmValue` after the 100 messages have been fired, the value of the variable is actually 100. On the contrary, the `value` variable's value changes at every test run. It fluctuates between 14 and 35, depending on a number of factors, such as number of cores and speed of the hardware.

The unit test can be used to verify that the STM "protected" variable is always set to 100 while the other variable is always smaller than 100.

There's more...

STM is a very powerful tool in the hands of the "concurrent developer". It is important to understand that this power doesn't come cheap. A simple increment of an `Integer` variable does indeed provoke many more CPU cycles than the couples required to update a variable in Java. If we run `javap -c` over the Java bytecode produced by the compilation of the `StmValueIncreaser` class, we will see a very long Java bytecode list of instructions. Removing the STM references, the bytecode shrinks dramatically. This shows that the Multiverse STM implementation used by GPars is not lightweight. Nevertheless it's a very efficient paradigm to reason about and implement heavily concurrent systems. In this recipe, we addressed a relatively simple problem that could also have been solved using the JDK's `AtomicInteger`. However Multiverse supports many more data types and data structures: take a look at the documentation and Javadoc for a deeper understanding of what the framework has to offer.

See also

- `http://multiverse.codehaus.org`
- `http://gpars.codehaus.org/STM`
- `http://en.wikipedia.org/wiki/Software_transactional_memory`
- `http://gpars.org/0.12/javadoc/groovyx/gpars/stm/GParsStm.html`

Using dataflow variables for lazy evaluation

Dataflow concurrency is a concurrent programming paradigm that has been around for three decades now. What is so exciting about it?

The main idea behind Dataflow concurrency is to reduce the number of variable assignments to one. A variable can only be assigned a value once in its lifetime, while the number of reads is unlimited. If a variable value is not written by a write operation, all the read operations are blocked until the variable is actually written (bind). With this straightforward, single-assignment approach, it is impossible to access an inconsistent value or experience data race conflicts. The deterministic nature of Dataflow concurrency ensures that it will always behave the same. You can run the same operation 5 or 10 million times the result will always be the same. Conversely, if an operation enters into a deadlock the first time, it will do the same every other time you run it. These qualities make it very easy to reason about concurrency, but it comes at a price: code must be deterministic. Random, time, exceptions, and so on are not allowed. The section of code that employs Dataflow concurrency must act as a pure function, with input and output.

The Groovy's GPars framework exposes this alternative concurrency model, and in this recipe we are going to explore how to solve the problem of high latency when invoking external systems, exposed in the *Running tasks in parallel and asynchronously* recipe.

Getting ready

For setting up this recipe, please refer to the *Getting Ready* section of the *Running tasks in parallel and asynchronously* recipe.

Start the dummy web service using `groovy app.groovy`.

How to do it...

The following steps expose how to modify the `CriminalService` class to leverage Dataflow concurrency.

1. Create a new Groovy class named `CriminalServiceWithDataflow`.

```
package org.groovy.cookbook.dataflow

import static groovyx.gpars.dataflow.Dataflow.task
import groovyx.gpars.dataflow.DataflowVariable

class CriminalServiceWithDataflow {

  def baseUrl

  CriminalServiceWithDataflow(String url) {
    baseUrl = url
  }

}
```

2. Add a function to retrieve the JSON data for the specified country:

```
def fetchData(String country) {
  println "fetching data for ${country}"
  def jsonResponse = new DataflowVariable()
  task {

    try {
      "${baseUrl}/${country}".toURL().openConnection().with
        {
        if( responseCode == 200  ) {
          jsonResponse << inputStream.text
        } else {
          jsonResponse << new RuntimeException(
            'Invalid Response Code from HTTP GET:' +
            responseCode
          )
```

```
        }
        disconnect()
      }
    } catch( e ) { jsonResponse <<  e }
  }
  jsonResponse
}
```

3. Add the main function from which data aggregation is done:

```
List getData(List countries) {
  List aggregatedJson = []
  countries.each {
    aggregatedJson << fetchData(it)
  }
  aggregatedJson*.val
}
```

4. To test our new class, let's add a simple test case:

```
@Test
void testDataflow() {

  def serviceUrl = 'http://localhost:5050'
  def criminalService =
    new CriminalServiceWithDataflow(serviceUrl)

  def data = criminalService.
    getData(['germany', 'us', 'canada'])

  assert 3 == data.size()

  data.each {
    try {
      println it
    } catch (e) {
      e.printStackTrace()
    }
  }

}
```

How it works...

The `fetchData` function of the `CriminalServiceWithDataflow` class is where the power of Dataflow in action is really visible. The function contains a `DataflowVariable` named `jsonResponse` and a task that has the responsibility to populate the variable. This variable can be written only once, through the `<<` operator. The task contains the actual code to access the Criminal Service web service with some simplistic exception handling code. When the value of a `DataFlowVariable` is read, it will block until the value is set (using `<<`). In this way, the time required to collect the data for three countries will be equal to the longest response time.

The `getData` function spans the HTTP requests over 3 threads. Note that the `fetchData` method is not blocking. The blocking takes place only in the last line of the `getData` method, when the `val` method is invoked (and therefore the variable read) on each `DataflowVariable` containing the HTTP GET response.

It's also worth noting how the exception handling is organized. Let's zoom into the code:

```
def jsonResponse = new DataflowVariable()
try {
  ...
} catch( e ) {
  jsonResponse <<  e
}
```

When an exception occurs inside the task, we assign the Exception to the `jsonResponse` variable of type `DataflowVariable`. The `DataflowVariable` class has two methods to access the stored value:

- The `val` method that simply returns the Exception
- The `get` method that will rethrow the Exception, if any

Use `val` or `get` depending on your exception handling requirements. You can test how the exception handling works, by shutting down the Ratpack server or passing invalid countries that will yield a 404 response code.

There's more...

Dataflow concurrency is a very elegant paradigm, and there are more concepts in this model than the one expressed in this recipe. The best way to learn them is head to the official GPars Dataflow documentation located at the following link: `http://www.gpars.org/guide/guide/dataflow.html`

See also

- `http://en.wikipedia.org/wiki/Dataflow`
- `http://gpars.org/0.12/javadoc/groovyx/gpars/dataflow/DataflowVariable.html`

Index

Thank you for buying
Groovy 2 Cookbook

About Packt Publishing

Packt, pronounced 'packed', published its first book "*Mastering phpMyAdmin for Effective MySQL Management*" in April 2004 and subsequently continued to specialize in publishing highly focused books on specific technologies and solutions.

Our books and publications share the experiences of your fellow IT professionals in adapting and customizing today's systems, applications, and frameworks. Our solution based books give you the knowledge and power to customize the software and technologies you're using to get the job done. Packt books are more specific and less general than the IT books you have seen in the past. Our unique business model allows us to bring you more focused information, giving you more of what you need to know, and less of what you don't.

Packt is a modern, yet unique publishing company, which focuses on producing quality, cutting-edge books for communities of developers, administrators, and newbies alike. For more information, please visit our website: www.packtpub.com.

About Packt Open Source

In 2010, Packt launched two new brands, Packt Open Source and Packt Enterprise, in order to continue its focus on specialization. This book is part of the Packt Open Source brand, home to books published on software built around Open Source licences, and offering information to anybody from advanced developers to budding web designers. The Open Source brand also runs Packt's Open Source Royalty Scheme, by which Packt gives a royalty to each Open Source project about whose software a book is sold.

Writing for Packt

We welcome all inquiries from people who are interested in authoring. Book proposals should be sent to author@packtpub.com. If your book idea is still at an early stage and you would like to discuss it first before writing a formal book proposal, contact us; one of our commissioning editors will get in touch with you.

We're not just looking for published authors; if you have strong technical skills but no writing experience, our experienced editors can help you develop a writing career, or simply get some additional reward for your expertise.

Groovy for
Domain-Specific Languages

Extend and enhance your Java applications with Domain-Specific Languages in Groovy

Fergal Dearle

[PACKT] open source *

Groovy for Domain-Specific Languages

ISBN: 978-1-84719-690-3   Paperback: 312 pages

Extend and enhance your Java applications with Domain-Specific Languages in Groovy

1. Build your own Domain Specific Languages on top of Groovy Integrate your existing Java applications using Groovy-based Domain Specific Languages (DSLs) Develop a Groovy scripting interface to Twitter A step-by-step guide to building Groovy-based Domain Specific Languages that run seamlessly in the Java environment

Java 7 New Features
Cookbook

Over 100 comprehensive recipes to get you up-to-speed with all the exciting new features of Java 7

Richard M. Reese
Jennifer L. Reese

[PACKT] enterprise 88

Java 7 New Features Cookbook

ISBN: 978-1-84968-562-7   Paperback: 384 pages

Over 100 comprehensive recipes to get your up-to-speed with all the exciting new features of Java 7

1. Comprehensive coverage of the new features of Java 7 organized around easy-to-follow recipes

2. Covers exciting features such as the try-with-resources block, the monitoring of directory events, asynchronous IO and new GUI enhancements, and more

3. A learn-by-example based approach that focuses on key concepts to provide the foundation to solve real world problems

Please check **www.PacktPub.com** for information on our titles

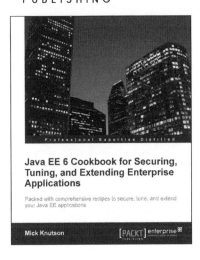

Printed in Great Britain
by Amazon.co.uk, Ltd.,
Marston Gate.